Rorke's Drift By Those Who Were There

'Those Zulus were an enemy that it was some credit to us to have defeated. Their bravery and courage could not have been excelled, and their military organisation and their discipline might have given a lesson to more civilised nations. Cruel and savage as they were, the Zulus were, however, a gallant enemy …'

Captain and Brevet Major John Rouse Merriott Chard, VC
Western Daily Mercury, 18 November 1879

Rorke's Drift By Those Who Were There

VOLUME 2

Lee Stevenson, Ian Knight
and
Alan Baynham-Jones

Greenhill Books

Rorke's Drift By Those Who Were There: Volume 2

Greenhill Books

First published by Greenhill Books, 2023
Greenhill Books, c/o Pen & Swords Books Limited, George House, Unit 12 & 13,
Beevor Street, Off Pontefract Road, Barnsley, South Yorkshire S71 1HN
For more information on our books, please visit
www.greenhillbooks.com, email contact@greenhillbooks.com
or write to us at the above address.

PUBLISHING HISTORY
Rorke's Drift By Those Who Were There was first published in 2003 by Lee Stevenson Publishing. This is volume 2 of an expanded edition, with new illustrations, maps and expanded and revised text.

CIP data records for this title are available from the British Library

ISBN 978-1-78438-842-3

Typeset by JCS Publishing Services Ltd
Typeset in 11.5/15pt Baskerville
Printed and bound in Great Britain by
CPI Group (UK) Ltd, Croydon, CRO 4YY

Contents

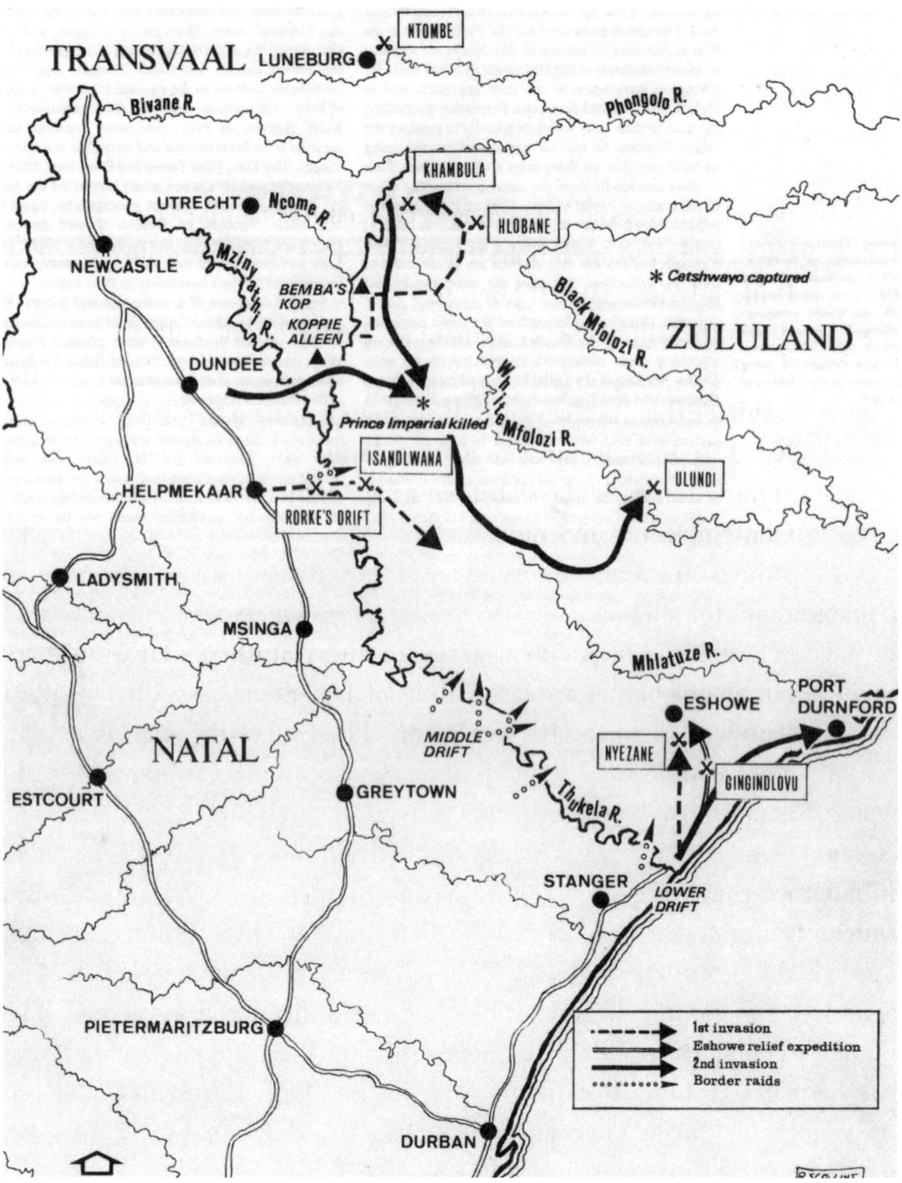

The invasion of Zululand, 1879

Introduction to Volume 2

This is the second volume of eyewitness accounts of participants in the battle of Rorke's Drift, in the Anglo-Zulu War of 1879, and, like our first volume, at its heart are the accounts by men who actually fought in the battle.

The battle of Rorke's Drift undeniably attracted the attention of the contemporary British press and public in a way which other conflicts of the time did not. It is perhaps not difficult to see why: coming immediately after the catastrophic defeat at iSandlwana on 22 January 1879 – the greatest British military defeat of the Victorian era – the story of a small garrison of men defending a frontier outpost against an overwhelming and determined military attack for ten hours seemed to characterise that spirit and courage in the face of adversity which the British public most admired in their ordinary soldiers. For a while the glow of both official and public appreciation shone on the defenders; the senior officers were showered with everything from presentation weapons to prestigious dinner invitations. B Company, 2/24th, who made up the bulk of the defenders, were cheered through the streets of colonial Natal on their way back from the front, indeed proposals for them to march through the streets of London at the head of the annual Lord Mayor's Parade were only thwarted when the War Office pointed out that most of the defenders were still stationed overseas. Gallantry medals were awarded, and commemorative Bibles and decorative scrolls presented. The battle was depicted in suitably heroic form in the illustrated newspapers and was recreated by both Alphonse de Neuville and Lady Elizabeth Butler – at the request of Queen Victoria herself, in the latter's case – two of the great military battle-painters of the day.

Yet underpinning the glamour which became attached to the name of Rorke's Drift was the harsh reality of a particularly intense colonial conflict, and its effects on those who took part would last long after the first flush of public glory faded. While some of the defenders continued to enjoy a degree of celebrity throughout their lives, others slid back into the obscurity which more often characterised the Victorian soldier's return to civilian life. Some were asked to tell their story many times; others never were. For some, the details of the fighting remained fixed and intense, even when they were interviewed years after the battle, but for others time pushed aspects of their experience to the background of their minds, and only specific incidents remained. Either way, few among them could count many material benefits to show for the brief fame accorded the defenders, and it is interesting to note the heavy thread of hardship that runs through the later lives of many of them. Service in the army provided a small pension after retirement but it was never sufficient to provide for a comfortable life, and most were forced back into the civilian employment they had pursued before enlisting.

Even for those whose gallantry had been rewarded by the Victoria Cross – which carried with it public respect and an annual gratuity – later life could be harsh: 'the lionhearted John Williams has to slave as best he can in an iron factory for just enough to keep his body and soul together. And he can count himself lucky too, for men quite as brave as he died from cold and starvation in the gutters of the capital city of the land for which they so nobly fought and fell,' wrote one newspaper commentator. Corporal Schiess of the Natal Native Contingent, the last of the defenders to be awarded the Victoria Cross, so celebrated by the Natal government at the time, later found it impossible to find work in the colony and died en route to England – his voyage paid for by charitable collection. The *Natal Witness*, on hearing in 1905 that 'Henry' Hook, VC, had been refused a pension increase, pithily noted, 'And when the fighting is over, and the fervent patriotism has died away, what does the paternal British government do for the men who sold their lives dearly for the honour of the nation? Too often it would seem, they shamefully neglect them.' Yet there was nothing to help with the psychological scars of combat either, as the sad fate of both Robert Jones and William Jones attests.

In truth many of the defenders ended up on decidedly hard times. Several found themselves up before a judge, or spent time in prison, the asylum or the workhouse. Heavy drinking was often cited as a factor in their decline – a reflection not only of the need to escape their memories, perhaps, but also of the extent to which heavy drinking was in any case a fact of military life. In this respect it should not be supposed that the survivors of Rorke's Drift were particularly blighted; in many ways, they were no more than a cross-section of the experience to be endured by ordinary Victorian soldiers as a whole.

In this volume we have also included accounts from men who were not present at the battle, but who were with Lord Chelmsford's force when it returned to Rorke's Drift on the morning of 23 January 1879. Their accounts reflect the widespread amazement that the garrison had survived, and an appreciation of the courage which had ensured that, as well as providing vivid descriptions of the aftermath of the battle, of the hospital building gutted by fire, and the post strewn with dead and dying Zulus, and littered with all the chaotic debris of war.

They reflect, too, another aspect which was left out of the heroic narrative portrayed at the time, but which is explored in depth here: the treatment of the Zulu wounded left on the field after the battle. Whilst many of the wounded were able to make their way from the immediate area, either by their own means or with the help of others, many more – those too badly wounded or simply too close to the British defences – were abandoned where they fell. In the overwrought, vengeful and desperate atmosphere which prevailed after the two battles, and lacking in any case the facilities to treat and guard Zulu prisoners, the British killed them.

In reproducing accounts from a wide range of sources, including previously unpublished documents, we faced a number of practical challenges. Spelling is often inconsistent, and some of the more verbatim accounts pay little lip-service to grammar. Some accounts, moreover, reflect contemporary attitudes towards race which are not acceptable today, and which certainly do not reflect our views as editors; nevertheless, we felt that it was important to include these as they were expressed to give a true portrayal of the views of the time. Although the fierce defence of their country earned the Zulus, in the end, the long-standing respect of their enemies, this was not always reflected during the tensions which prevailed in the immediate aftermath of iSandlwana, when the use of racial slurs was commonplace.

In both volumes it will be clear that participants in these events sometimes, when they told the story more than once, and perhaps over a long time, contradicted themselves, stressed the importance in one version of an incident that they left out completely in another, or even told the story in a way their audience clearly wanted to hear it. This is a natural process of which any student of history will be aware; the mind generally forms impressions of traumatic events in a jumbled way, and with time it sorts them into more coherent memories which are both easier to live with and to communicate to others, whilst at the same time often allowing itself to be unconsciously influenced by the impressions and opinions gleaned from others. As Captain (later General) William Penn Symons – who served with the 24th during the war, was with Lord Chelmsford's force and interviewed some of the survivors of both iSandlwana and Rorke's Drift – noted, even at the time, 'It was most remarkable how their accounts afterwards varied. Men forgot what they, amidst great excitement, saw and did and mixed up what others told them with their own experiences and reminiscences.'*

Nevertheless, these accounts are the raw material of a history which continues to fascinate us nearly a century and a half later, and at the same time are a reminder that history is no less brutal, complicated, morally ambivalent and downright messy than current affairs, and that only in the cinema do staunch redcoats and heroic warriors battle without consequence – either to the countries for whom they fight, or to themselves.

Ian Knight and Lee Stevenson,
November 2022

* Penn Symons is credited with assisting both Chard and Bromhead with their official records of the battle. Extracts from his own detailed account of iSandlwana and Rorke's Drift are included in this volume.

Acknowledgements

This updated version of our original book represents over forty years of research into the defence of Rorke's Drift. So many people have helped and offered assistance over the years, and we are indebted to them for their time and generosity. In particular we would like to thank the following for their material assistance with the production of this work.

Major Martin Everett, former curator of the Royal Welsh Regimental Museum, Brecon, for granting us permission to reproduce numerous records from the vast regimental archives at Brecon, also a special thank you to Celia Green, for her kindness and assistance with our research; Lt. Col. Ian Bennett for his assistance with W.A. Dunne's account of the battle and for his help in tracing the letters of Francis Attwood; Pamela Clark, and the staff, past and present, at the Royal Archives. Helen Griffiths, from the Newport Reference Library, for successfully undertaking the long and seemingly impossible search through the *South Wales Argus* looking for a copy of the Bourne roll of defenders. Ron Sheeley, for the free use of his photographs.

In South Africa, remembering the help and friendship of the late Ron Lock; Mrs Pam Barnes for the excellent job of collating information from the numerous sources at her disposal in KwaZulu-Natal and elsewhere; the staffs of: the Killie Campbell Africana Library; the Brenthurst Library, Johannesburg; the Pietermaritzburg Archives Repository, Pietermaritzburg; the Natal Museum, Pietermaritzburg; and the South African Library, Cape Town.

In Sweden, Alfhild Oenema and Nils Högman, archivists of the Church of Sweden in Uppsala, for their considerable assistance, and patience, whilst locating and photographing numerous documents pertaining to

Pastor Otto Witt. Our special thanks must also go to Hans Rosenberg for all his kindness and willingness to translate so many of those original documents on our behalf.

Finally a special thank you to the descendants of the garrison of Rorke's Drift, who have been most courteous in allowing us to delve into their family histories over the years. Without their contributions and support many of these stories would be lost: Mrs Cecilia Cheetham, Mrs Kathleen Mysberg, Mrs Elizabeth Sutcliffe, Mrs Rose Morgan, Mrs Rena Mills, Nick Kennedy, Major James Lloyd, Roger Lane, Bill Jones, Edwin Ewart, the Prothero family and many, many more.

CHAPTER 1

'We've got bags of mealies and biscuits. We can build barricades and we'll hold this place': The Defenders of Rorke's Drift – Part 2: Jones to Wood

36. 25B/1428 Private Evan Jones (Evan Cosgrove), 'B' Company, 2/24th Foot

36a. *Montgomery County Times and Shropshire and Mid Wales Advertiser,* 27 February 1915

A Welshpool Veteran.
Over Forty years' service and still in the Army.
For long military service, Drummer Instructor Evan Jones, 18, Union street, Welshpool, now with 7th Batt. R.W.F. (Reserve) at Aberystwyth, has a remarkable record. He is probably the oldest drummer in the Army. He has over forty years' service to his credit, and now a veteran approaching 60, he is still in khaki, having even volunteered for Imperial service. The age limit, however, forbade it, although he looks hale and hearty, and to use his own words to a COUNTY TIMES representative as he recounted rather wistfully how he was not accepted for active service, he feels as fit as when he first enlisted. He served in two hard campaigns, including the heroic defence of Rorke's Drift, and is entitled to a high place in the Roll of Honour of Montgomeryshire men who have rendered worthy service to their country.

Drummer Jones entered on his military career in 1874, when he joined the Monmouth Militia, with whom he served for three years. In 1877 he enlisted in the famous 24th Foot Regiment (now the S.W.B.) and fought through the Kaffir War of 1877–78. He also served in the Zulu war of 1879 and as stated above, was one of the band of heroes who took part in the defence of Rorke's Drift, one of the most brilliant episodes in the history of British arms. The British numbered only 104, and for nearly two days kept an army of some thousands of Zulus at bay. Drummer Jones escaped unhurt, although the assault on the part of the defences where he was engaged became so hot that they all had to retire to another position. All the defenders were recommended for the V.C., but only about fourteen were granted, including seven to the men who rescued the patients from the hospital which the Zulus succeeded in firing.

From Africa, Drummer Jones accompanied his regiment to Gibraltar where they were stationed for about six months. They were then ordered out to India to take part in the Afghan war, but peace was declared before the 24th saw any more fighting. They did not enjoy barrack life for very long, however, for in 1887–89 Drummer Jones saw active service again in the Burma war.

In 1893, after 17 years' foreign service, he returned home, and six years later was discharged. Most men would then have considered that they deserved a rest. Not so Drummer Jones, however. In 1900 he joined the Royal Northern Reserve with whom he served twelve months followed by two annual trainings with the 3rd Monmouthshires. He then joined the Montgomeryshire Yeomanry, with whom he served until last May – a period of twelve years. Then when war was declared the veteran again responded to the call, and though denied leave to go abroad, engaged as Drummer-Instructor with the 7th R.W.F.

He is a complete master of both the big drum and the side drums, and when in India was accounted the best player among the troops in the country. He played for three years in the band of the Governor of Bombay, and, also in the bands of the 24th and the Montgomeryshire Yeomanry. Under his expert tuition the drummers of the 7th are making great progress and are rapidly becoming the pride of the battalion, and at the same time, the envy of the other regiments in the town.

Drummer Jones possesses the South African medal, 77–78–79, the Burma medal, 87–89, and the Territorial long service medal, and when discharged from the Regular Army he possessed five good conduct badges – the maximum possible.

36b. A private letter written by Evan Jones in 1925
[courtesy Bill Jones, grandson of Evan Jones]

18 Union St
Welshpool
16. Aug 1925

Dear Sir,

I received your most kind letter and enclosed cutting with photo and am most pleased to hear that there are still a few left in South Africa who can recall the part taken by my old Regt the 24th …

… Dear Sir talking now about Rourkes Drift all that now survive as far as I know are Col Bourne Williams V.C. myself and a man of the name of Tom Driscoll who I saw last year and who is living in Ebbw Vale, Mon.

As regards the defence of Rourkes Drift. I was the sentry on outpost who first saw the two survivors of the Isanduna disaster struggling in and reported to Lieut Bromhead and after their story we set too at once to put the place in a state of defence. After the Zulu war was over we went to Gibraltar and was sent to the Afghan Campaign but were too late as peace was proclaimed. Previous to the Zulu War I have been through the Kaffir war and East London was where we landed in serf boats a very nice doing. I also served in the Burmah campaign from 1887 to 1889.

Dear Sir I am sending you my photo hoping you will like to have it as a memento of the action. I am now 73 years old and have only this year missed the Annual Camp with the territorials owing to the long illness of my wife but am pleased to say I am fit as a fiddle myself.

Yours sincerely
Evan Jones

36c. *Merthyr Express*, 8 August 1931

Rorke's Drift Veteran.
Death of Sergt. Evan Jones, Ebbw Vale.

News reached Ebbw Vale at the weekend of the death at Welshpool, North Wales, of Sergeant Evan Jones, a Rorke's Drift veteran, a native of Ebbw Vale, who was known by the name of Sergeant Evan Cosgrove. He worked for many years in the town, and was a noted performer on the small drums, and engaged in the Palace Orchestra. He was 76 years of age, and had a dramatic career as a soldier. Joining the Army when quite a boy he saw service in many parts of the world and he was naturally very proud of his experiences at Rorke's Drift, and frequently described it in graphic terms.

The garrison of Rorke's Drift was B Company of the 2nd Battalion of the 24th (now the South Wales Borderers). It numbered 80 effectives, and 30 or 40 sick. This little body of men were attacked just after the disaster of Isandalwana by a Zulu impi of 4,000. They attacked just after mid-day on January 22nd, and the fight went on till 9 o'clock next morning. The Zulus reached the breastworks many times, but on each occasion they were beaten off with bayonets.

The dead lay in heaps before the breastwork, and were found for miles around after the beaten impi retired. Their losses were estimated at 350, and the loss of the British was 17 killed and ten wounded.

Sergeant Jones, who was on sentry duty at the time of the attack, said he would never forget the sight of the Zulus charging to the attack in the well-known crescent formation, the young, fleet runners on the wings closing round until the garrison was surrounded by attackers – a fearful spectacle in their savage panoply of war – black ostrich plumes, cow-tails, bull-hide shields – with their assegais gleaming in the sun. Sergeant Jones was a well-known and very popular figure at Welshpool, where he lived for 40 years. He was a member of the St. John Ambulance Band at the time of his death, and a member of the local branch of the British Legion.

Sergt. Jones first enlisted in the Monmouth Militia in 1874, and was transferred to the South Wales Borderers on July 20th, 1877. Within two years – on January 22nd, 1879 – he took part in the famous fight of Rorke's Drift, and afterwards completed 21 years service with the South

Wales Borderers, spending 16 years and 291 days in India. While in India he was a member of the Governor's band in Bombay. He also served in Burmah and Gibraltar, and after leaving the South Wales Borderers served with the Royal Reserves until 1900, when he came home and joined the Montgomeryshire Militia, to which he belonged until it became defunct. During the Great War he served at home with the 7th Battalion R.W.F., and although in his sixties he added to his long record of service by joining the Northumberland Fusiliers and serving in France. Sergeant Jones had a full collection of medals, including the South African medal, Burmah medal 1887–9, two clasps for 1877–9, and a Territorial efficiency medal.

36d. *Montgomery County Times and Shropshire and Mid Wales Advertiser*, c. July 1931

The survivors of the fight, in addition to Sergt. Jones, known to be alive at the 50th anniversary of the fight in 1929 were: – Lt. Col. F. Bourne, O.B.E., D.C.M., Beckenham, Kent (24th Regiment); Sergt. H.E. Gallagher, Drayton, Hants (24th Regiment); Sergt. A. Saxty (24th Regiment); Pte. T. Driscoll, Ebbw Vale (24th Regiment); Pte. J.S. Jobbins, Pontnewydd; Pte. Will Osborne, Blaenavon; Pte. J. Williams, V.C., Cwmbran (24th Regiment); Acting-Commist. Officer Dalton …

36e. Extract from an unidentified Welsh newspaper, c. July 1931

… On the morning of January 22nd, 1879, Drummer Jones was on sentry duty at the outpost of Rorke's Drift, with some ninety rank and file of the 24th Regiment, under Lieutenants Bromhead and Chard, when he heard the firing of guns, and drew the attention of Sergeant Lyons, who was in charge of the guard, to the sound. Not long afterwards he saw some horsemen coming over the brow of the hill, who reported there was a battle raging at Isandlwana some miles away, between the Zulus and a small British force …

37. 25B/970 Private John Jones, 'B' Company, 2/24th Foot

25B/970 Private John Jones is named in all of the contemporary rolls of defenders of Rorke's Drift. However, it should be noted that in this account he states that he was saved from iSandlwana as he was "out with the column".

37a. *Carmarthen Journal*, 28 March 1879

Letters from Welsh soldiers in Zululand.
Private John Jones, whose mother lives at Caedraw, has sent the following interesting letter home: –

Rorke's Drift, Natal.
January 28, 1879.

My dear Mother,

I now take my pen in hand to write you a few lines, as I daresay you will be anxious to hear from me before you receive this, as you will hear of the disastrous battle which we had on the 22nd of this month with the enemy.

But, dear mother, I am happy to inform you that I came through it all right without being touched. The enemy came down on our camp, 20 men to one of us, as the most of our column had gone out 15 miles further up the country, expecting to have an engagement, but they outflanked us and came down on the camp, which was defended by 1,000 men only and two guns, and the enemy's force being over 20,000 strong warriors. They came so numerous that every man in camp was slaughtered, but happily to me I was out with the column, so I was saved, but Billy Terrett, Hughey Perkins, Jamey Cantlon, commonly called "Jimmy knocked the house down", were all killed on the field, as five companies of the 1st Battalion and one company of ours, besides 100 artillerymen, and a great number of mounted volunteers of the colony, in all nearly 1,000, perished at the mercy of the enemy, but we took back our camp by 10 o'clock at night, after marching about 35 miles that day, but mostly everything in camp was lost – lost to us, as the enemy had our valises, blankets, big coats, tents, and, in fact, everything excepting what we stood in. There is no one that knows where James Terrett is. He is supposed to be up in the Diamond Fields with the mounted troops, but they will be called down here now as reinforcements, so I don't know how things will turn out as yet, and no one knows what number of lives will be lost by the time it is finished; but I trust in God to return home safe some day.

But this is a fearful war, and the havoc will be great among our troops, as it is such a fearful hilly country for marching; and now, since we lost our camp, we are obliged to sleep on the ground in the best way we can, without anything to cover us, and its very cold and wet here now the rainy season is on, but the heat of the sun is so scorchingly hot in the day that it has already caused a great deal of sickness amongst our troops; but in a few days, as soon as we get reinforcements, we will make a further advance into the country towards the King's kraals where he is supposed to have about from 40,000 to 58,000 troops, and we expect to have a great engagement when we get there, as no mercy is to be shown them any more, owing to the manner they cut and mutilated our dead bodies. The enemy has already lost nearly 20,000, and before we finished with them we hope to kill them to the last man. Our loss up to the present is about 1,000.

So now I beg to conclude. I shall write again soon with more particulars. Hoping I shall hear from you soon, and hoping also that you are all at home enjoying the best of health, give my best respects to all inquiring friends, and accept my kindest love to all at home. – Believe me to remain your very affectionate son, John.

Please address – No. 970. Private John Jones.

B. Company, 2-24th Regiment, Rorke's Drift, near Helpmakaar, Natal, South Africa.

37b. *Western Mail,* 18 May 1914 [believed to refer to 25B 970 Private John Jones]

Rorke's Drift Hero.
South Wales Veteran's Reminiscences.
British pluck against Zulu cunning.

One of the heroes who took part on the gallant defence of Rorke's drift and in the repulse of the Zulus lives at the Riverside, Merthyr. He is John

Jones, a broken-visaged man of 60 summers, who bears all the appearance of an old warrior, and one who has been kept aloof from pauperism by the charity of a few altruistic friends.

Many sanguine skirmishes he has survived, thrilling in character are his episodes of war, and when a *Western Mail* representative called upon him Jack, for that is the familiar designation by which he is called, related in a faltering voice the tragedy of Rorke's Drift. His physical infirmity will not permit of heavy toil, for the hand of Time has been unkind to him.

"Rorke's Drift!" he gazed wistfully at the drab-coloured walls as he abandoned himself to reflection. "Well do I remember it," he added; "the massacre and the cries of the mad-stricken Zulus will not easily be forgotten. I have a vivid impression of the scene, because, apart from some invalids, we were not a hundred strong.

No Trenches!

"It was about four o'clock on an afternoon in January, in 1879, when we were informed of the advance of the Zulus by an aide-de-camp from Isandhula, where the company had proceeded on a detour in pursuit of the main column, who, unhappily, had missed the course of the enemy. Time was short and we had no trenches.

"Necessity compelled us to move, and move rapidly. Taking a different course from that of our main column, the enemy had attacked the advance party, and slaughter followed in ruthless fashion. A large number of men were massacred, but some escaped and made a desperate rush to the camp. We were practically ready to meet the on-coming enemy, but we had to fight under difficulties.

"With no fortifications, save a hospital and a storage room, and hopelessly outnumbered, we erected a defence of biscuit boxes and mealies. It was an anxious time. What were we to do? We were all possessed of the pluck of the Britisher, and observing the advance of the Zulus, who flitted from the hillside in all directions, we set ourselves ready to the task. The air was soon red with bullets, the Zulus fell in hopeless numbers, but dexterous as we proved to be the cunning Zulus protected themselves in many ways. They concealed themselves in the ravines, some lay prostrate, others of the more reckless type rushed towards us indiscriminately. One of them even advanced towards the hospital and set fire to it, but the blaze only helped us to detect the enemy.

A Mere Handful.

"Night had fallen when they came into close touch with us," continued the old soldier, and here he paused to correct an account given by another survivor. "True they were upon us," he went on, "but they did not grip our bayonets. We were a mere handful in comparison to their numbers and had they been so near we would not have lived to tell the tale. We kept them away by a ceaseless fire, and, in spite of their wily methods, the dead being held up as objects of attack, with an endless repetition of their hideous yells – cries which meant to inform us of their advance when they were concealed in the crevices of the hill, the object being to reduce our ammunition – we succeeded in ploughing them down. We lost but a few comrades, and when our column returned they had to take their rest amongst the dead and dying. The enemy had by now retreated, and we waited for the dawn. Daylight revealed to us the tragedy of the night, the dead were huddled on the ground, the number being close upon a thousand. Some of the column returned in the morning, and thinking they were Zulus, we were ready for another shot, but we soon found that they were our own chaps. Those were the trials of Rorke's Drift!"

And, like many another old soldier, John Jones, lives a life of poverty, without reward from his country. He has served in three campaigns, and took part in the South African War. He enlisted in the Warwickshires, at Merthyr, in 1876, and saw active service in the Kaffir War, served a considerable period in India, and for sixteen years was associated with the Brecon Militia. For his conduct in the Zulu War, he obtained a medal and clasp, and received two bars after service in South Africa. What he once prized as valuable possessions have been lost to him – they were exchanged for coins of the realm, so as to keep away from the taint of pauperism.

38. 25B/716 Private Robert Jones, 'B' Company, 2/24th Foot

38a. *Strand Magazine,* Vol 1, January to June 1891

Stories of the Victoria Cross: Told by Those who have Won it. Private Robert Jones.

At the gallant defence of the fort at Rorke's Drift, every man fought like a hero, but some were fortunate enough to attract the particular attention of their superiors. Among these was a private of the 24th Regiment, named Robert Jones, who obtained the Victoria Cross for his conduct on the occasion. His story is as follows: –

"On the 22nd January, 1879, the Zulus attacked us, we being only a small band of English soldiers and they in very strong and overwhelming numbers. On commencing fighting, I was one of the soldiers who were in the hospital to protect it. I and another soldier of the name of William Jones were on duty at the back of the hospital, trying to defeat and drive back the rebels, and doing our endeavours to convey the wounded and sick soldiers out through a hole in the wall, so that they might reach in safety the small band of men in the square. On retiring from one room into another, after taking a wounded man by the name of Mayer, belonging to the volunteers, to join William Jones, I found a crowd in front of the hospital and coming into the doorway. I said to my companion, 'They are on top of us,' and sprang to one side of the doorway. There we crossed our bayonets, and as fast as they came up to the doorway we bayoneted them, until the doorway was nearly filled with dead and wounded Zulus. In the meanwhile, I had three assegai wounds, two in the right side and one in the left of my body. We did not know of anyone being in the hospital, only the Zulus, and then after a long time of fighting at the door, we made the enemy retire, and then we made our escape out of the building. Just as I got outside, the roof fell in – a complete mass of flames and fire. I had to cross a space of about twenty or thirty yards from the ruins of the hospital to the leagued company where they were keeping the enemy at bay. While I was crossing the front of the square, bullets were whishing past me from every direction. When I got in, the enemy came on closer and closer, until they were close to the outer side of our laager, which was made up of boxes of biscuits on sacks of Indian corn. The fighting lasted about thirteen hours, or better. As to my feelings at the time, they were that I was certain that if we did not kill them they would kill us, and after a few minutes fighting I did not mind it more than at the present time; my thought was only to fight as an English soldier ought to for his most gracious Sovereign, Queen Victoria, and for the benefit of old England."

38b. *Radnor Express,* 15 September 1898

Death of a Rorke's Drift Hero.
Sad end of a Victoria Cross man who helped to make the 24th "Noble."

On Tuesday in last week some sensation was caused in the Peterchurch district by the suicide of Robert Jones, a farm labourer, in the employ of Major Delahay. It seems that the deceased had not been well lately. On Tuesday morning he asked for a gun to scare some birds – a practice he often followed – in the garden. He went out, and directly afterwards the gun was discharged. No notice was taken at the time, but one of the maids shortly afterwards made a shocking discovery. Jones was then found to be dead. He had evidently placed the muzzle in his mouth, inflicting terrible injuries, which, according to the medical evidence, must have proved fatal instantaneously.

An inquest was held at the Broughton Arms, Peterchurch, by the Deputy-Coroner, Mr T. Hutchinson, on Wednesday in last week, touching the death of Robert Jones, Rose Cottage, Peterchurch.

Elizabeth Jones, said she lived at Rose Cottage, Peterchurch, and was the wife of the deceased. He was a farm labourer in the employ of Mr Delahay, and was 40 years old. She last saw her husband alive on Tuesday morning about quarter past seven. He was then in the middle of the orchard going towards the Crossways. He had had two cups of tea, but no food. The last words he said to her were, "The other sheep is at the Castle." After that he left her and went off in the direction of his work. About eight o'clock she had a message brought to her that her husband was very ill. Ada Morgan brought the message, and she asked if "he was dead," and she said "No, he is not dead." Witness asked "Are you sure?" and she made no answer, but said witness was to prepare a place for him. She asked Mrs Edwards if she would go down and see what was the matter, and she went and said he was dead. Deceased left in his usual health. She knew of nothing the matter with him. She had no reason for asking Ada Morgan if he was dead, only that she could not believe he was ill. She had never heard him threaten to take his life.

On Monday last he was the worse for drink, and she got him home by the policeman's wish. He sold a sheep on Monday unknown to her, and when he came to the house to fetch the sheep he gave her £2 5s. She asked him what it was for, and he said he had sold a sheep. Witness said that it was the same money that he gave for it twelve months ago. She saw he was the worse for drink and asked him to leave the sheep and take the money back to the man, but he went for a halter and put it on the sheep and took it to the fair. She followed him down and gave the money back to the man and had the sheep. She then sold it to Mr Price for 49s. She waited at the public for the deceased until he came home with her about six o'clock. They had no quarrel about the sheep. He had a good supper and went to bed about twelve o'clock. He was quite well and happy and seemed to be sober before he went to bed. He slept all night and got up about half-past six. He then said "Good morning," and that he was very hot. He was very wild, and said he was fit to do anything. She asked him to sit down and she would get him some tea. He insisted on going out, and to prevent him she fastened the front door, he went out at the back. she followed him some distance up the road, and pressed him to come back, and he said, "You had better go back yourself." The deceased came back in about half an hour's time. He then seemed all right and said "Good morning" to Mrs Edwards. He changed his trousers, shoes and shirt, and drank two cups of tea and then left home. He put his best shoes on. She wondered why he did so, but she did not ask him. He had never done such a thing before. He had been a soldier and served in South Africa. He was at Rorke's Drift, where

HE WAS WOUNDED IN FIVE PLACES,

and he obtained the Victoria Cross. At times he complained of his head. He was wounded close to the eye. He had complained of his head very much this summer. He had also suffered from lumbago and sciatica lately. About three weeks last Saturday he was found in a fit in Major De-la-Hay's garden, and since then he had been different to what he usually was. He went round the grounds when he first started out yesterday. He was a good husband and a kind father.

Louisa Wills said she lived at the Crossway House, and she was a laundrymaid in the employ of Major De-la-Hay. On Tuesday morning about half-past seven Robert Jones came to the Crossway House. She was having her breakfast. He said "Good morning" to her and said he wanted the gun. She fetched it, and as he came back he said he was going to shoot a quist in the celery bed. The conversation took place in the kitchen. They were all having their breakfast. Directly after he went out they heard the gun go off. After finishing breakfast she went out to get some wood. Going from the orchard to the kitchen garden, she opened the door and saw a hat. She went a few steps further and saw a lot of blood, and then she ran away. (The witness fainted and was carried out.)

William Henry De la Hay said he lived at the Crossway House and was a retired major. On Tuesday morning he was summoned by the last witness's screams. He had heard the report of the gun about a quarter of an hour before, and knew by the sound it came from the garden. The deceased was in the habit of using the gun to shoot birds about the garden. He heard from his wife that the servants said Jones had shot himself. Witness dressed himself, and went into the garden and found deceased. His hat was in the middle of the path near the garden door and full of brains; his body was lying face downwards and about two feet from the hat on the path. The gun was underneath him. He did not touch the body, but at once sent for the police, and in the meantime his wife had sent the grooms for the doctor. They both arrived and went into the garden together. The last time witness saw deceased alive was on Monday morning, and he thought his manner was peculiar then. As a rule he was a sober man: a small quantity of drink, however affected him.

P.C. Bowen deposed to finding the body.

Dr. McMichael said on Tuesday morning he was called to Crossways, and got there about nine o'clock. He went in the garden, found the body, turned it over, and examined it. There was a large hole in the back of the roof of the mouth, and the top of the head was blown out. There was no mark of powder on the face, and from the position of the wound the muzzle of the gun must have been put in his mouth and then discharged. The deceased was a big man with long arms, and would have no difficulty in holding the gun in such a position and firing it with his right hand. That was what, in his opinion, took place. He attended the deceased about three weeks ago. It was drink that was the matter with him then. The deceased had a sore throat. He had recently had scarlet fever in the house. He had doctored him at intervals for four years; he had never complained to him about his wounds. Death must have been instantaneous.

The jury returned a verdict of "Suicide whilst of unsound mind."

A truly painfully sad termination to a life which had almost been given away 19 years ago in his endeavour to save others. Pte Robert Jones' deed which won him the coveted piece of gun metal, which made the army proud of his valour and the 24th Regiment proud of his name, will always bear retelling so long as the English flag flies, and so long as English blood runs through the veins of our English youth. Of course it was at Rorke's Drift, along with his pal William Jones, in a ward facing the hill, that Robert Jones defended the door of the hospital until six out of the seven patients it contained had been removed. There stood Jones erect, steady, and cool with rifle in hand stemming the strong, ferocious swarthy ride of Zulu horde, and Canute-like forbade the human billow to enter his charge. One by one the black savages fell as Jones unflinchingly picked them off. When the barrel of his weapon became almost red-hot, we are told, he picked up another which was near by and for hour after hour throughout that frightful night – a night which would strain and almost destroy the nerves of the strongest – Jones used both rifles alternatively until the sick was safely removed, with the exception of poor Sergt. Maxfield, who, in a state of delirium, could not be induced to leave his bed. Jones, however, not to be outdone, endeavoured to snatch him away from his assailants but the Zulus stabbed poor Maxfield before the noble Jones could perform his task. Such was the deed, and never had the cross been more deservingly won, although on that historical night we must: –

"Let no name of any be set above the rest,
Where all were braver than the brave, and better than the best."

We are told that deceased was wounded five times in his heroic act, and it was more than probable that the wound which he received on the head accounted for the painfully sad end of such a noble fellow. It will be remembered that Jones was one of the seven heroes who took part in the dedication of the memorial tablet in the Priory Church in January last, when he appeared to be much affected, especially when Dean Howell so eloquently referred to the brilliant fight at Rorke's Drift. And again on the following day when a friend met Jones coming from the church after having viewed the memorial for the last time, wiping the tears from his eyes, and upon asking him what was the matter, he said – "Oh, man, it was terrible! terrible!!"

The deceased was laid to rest in the peaceful pretty little churchyard at Peterchurch last Thursday amidst many a mark of respect. A few friends went down from the Depot to pay their last tribute to one whom the regiment thought so much of. They were Qrt.-Mstr.-Sergt. Rozier, Col.-Sergt. Johnson, Col.-Sergt Cobner, and Sergt. Williams, who took down with them a magnificent wreath from the soldiers of the Depot to place on his grave. The officiating clergyman was the Vicar of Peterchurch. The deceased leaves a wife and five children, which are the recipients of much heartfelt sympathy, and for whom may friends be found in their sad bereavement. And so in this peaceful spot sleeps, restfully, one of England's heroes, and we sincerely hope that when a visit is paid to the little churchyard neath the tall stately spire, one may be able to recognise the spot; even if we find no monument marks the spot, may the mound never be obliterated for his name is writ in fire on the nation's long beadroll.

38c. *Bristol Times*, 18 February 1911

Two Jones V.C.'s
Comrades in heroism at Rorke's Drift.
Bristol Story.

Apropos of the sad account of the misfortune that had befallen a V.C. hero named Jones, a Bristol born man, who was found wandering in a Northern town in a starving condition, Mrs. Haskins, 49, Redcliff Street, has written us a letter casting doubt on the old man's story. Inquiries by a "Bristol Evening Times and Echo" representative have thrown an interesting light on the matter. Mrs. Haskins, it appears, is the sister of one Robert Jones, who was born at Tynewydd Farm, Clyther, South Wales. He enlisted in the Second Batt. of the 24th Regiment (the Borderers); and for conspicuous bravery at Rorke's Drift in the Zulu campaign was awarded the V.C. He died tragically 12 years ago, committing suicide through domestic trouble. When, therefore, Mrs. Haskins read of 'Jones, V.C.' having been admitted to a workhouse in the North of England destitute she thought he must be an imposter.

But through the kindness of Mr. W.S. Paul, the hon. secretary of the Bristol Crimea and Indian Mutiny Veterans Association, we were able to look up a most interesting book at their club and find an explanation of the case. It was a simple one – there were two Jones, V.C.'s who won the coveted decoration fighting as comrades hand to hand.

How they won their V.C.'s

The following notes quoted from the book record the parts the two men played in that terrible episode in British warfare: –

ROBERT JONES – Private 2nd Batt. 24th Regt.

Decorated for conspicuous bravery and devotion to the wounded at Rorke's Drift, Jan 22nd, 1879. Privates Robert and William Jones placed in a room of the hospital facing the hill kept up a steady fire against enormous odds, and while one worked to cut a hole through the partition to the next room the other shot Zulu after Zulu through the loopholed walls, using his own and his comrade's rifle alternatively when the barrel became too hot to hold owing to the incessant fire. By their united heroic efforts six out of seven patients were saved by being carried through the broken partition. The seventh Sergt. Maxwell, being delirious, refused to be helped, and on Robert Jones returning to take him by force he found him being stabbed by the Zulus on his bed.

WILLIAM JONES – Private, 2nd Batt. 24th Regt.

To the heroic efforts of this man and his namesake, Robert Jones, six out of seven patients were saved from the burning hospital at Rorke's Drift on January 22nd, 1879. The fate of the seventh, together with the courageous defence of both these men in a room of the building against tremendous odds, is described in the record of Robert Jones.

It appears that Robert Jones was one of a family of eighteen, and he, with six brothers, entered the Army, whilst another brother entered the police force. Two sisters of the family are now living in Bristol, and the oldest son, George, is still surviving, and lives at Livingstone Place, Maindee, Newport. It was only natural that Mrs. Haskins should be anxious to vindicate her family's honour.

"My brother," she said, "would never have been allowed to want while we had anything, and had we not had means to help him, hundreds of people who knew him in South Wales would have subscribed to aid him."

39. 2-24/593 Private William Jones, 'B' Company, 2/24th Foot

39a. *Natal Mercury* (South Africa), 18 June 1879

... When he (Wm. Jones) came here with his Regiment his wife came with him, but after he had been at the front some time she became dangerously ill, and he obtained leave of absence to come down to attend to her. Jones took a room in a house facing the St. George's Hotel Tap, and there, by working night and day repairing boots and shoes, he managed to earn many comforts for his then dying wife. He was a steady, plodding fellow, but his wife was beyond recovery, and he remained with her until she died. The next day he buried her remains and at once started off to join his Regiment ...

39b. *The Era*, 6 February 1886

Mr. W. Jones, V.C. (Victoria Cross)

Having completed his engagement with H.H. Hamilton, is open to an Engagement with any Entertainment showing the South African Scenes, specially those of Rorke's Drift.

Address, Mr. W. Jones, No. 111, Water-street, Manchester.

39c. *Army and Navy Gazette*, 21 January 1888

South Wales Borderers (24th)

A correspondent writes: – "As an instance of the difficulty discharged soldiers of good character have in finding employment of any kind, the case of William Jones, V.C., late of the 'old 24th,' and one of the heroes of Rorke's Drift, fought January, 1879, may be quoted. Pte. Jones was in possession of four good-conduct badges, receives a pension of 1s. 3d. per diem, and £10 per annum for the Victoria Cross. He is intelligent, honest, and industrious. Failing to obtain a situation of any sort, he has had the incidents of Rorke's Drift represented on canvas, in a crude fashion, which he exhibits, accompanied by his description of the whole affair, from the news of the disaster to Lord Chelmsford's column, the oft-repeated assaults of the Zulus, and the arrival of the relieving force early next morning, and mentioning the part he himself took in the struggle. The lecturer was much applauded when describing the rescue of the sick men from the burning Mission House in the face of the Zulus, in which Jones was prominent. This exhibition is available for bazaars and similar gatherings, and worthy of notice, especially in military circles."

39d. *Strand Magazine*, Vol. 1, January to June 1891

Stories of the Victoria Cross: Told by Those who have Won it. Private W. Jones.

No action in recent warfare is better known than that of the heroic defence of Rorke's Drift. We are here able to give the narratives of two soldiers who gained their Cross for bravery in that day's gallant struggle. Here, first, is Private Jones's account of the affair: –

"About half-past three o'clock on the afternoon of the 22nd January, 1879, a mounted man came galloping into our little encampment and told us that the Zulus had taken the camp at Isandlwana, and were making their way towards us at Rorke's Drift. We at once set to work, and with such material as we had at hand formed a slight barricade around us; this was formed of sacks of mealies (Indian corn), boxes of sea biscuits, &c., of which we had a good supply. We also loopholed the walls of the two buildings. We had scarcely completed our work when the Zulus were down upon us.

The hospital being the first building in their line of attack, they surrounded it. Having twenty-three sick men in the rooms, our officer, Lieutenant Bromhead, ordered six men into the hospital, myself being one of the number, to defend and rescue the sick from it. We had scarcely taken our post in the hospital when two out of our number were killed in the front or verandah, leaving four of us to hold the place and get out the sick. This was done by two (viz., Privates Hook and Williams) carrying the sick and passing them into the barricade through a small window, while myself (William Jones) and my comrade (Robert Jones) contended each door at the point of the bayonet, our ammunition being expended. The Zulus, finding they could not force us from the doors, now set fire to the thatched roof. This was the most horrifying time. What with the blood-thirsty yells of the Zulus, the cries of the sick that remained, and the burning thatch falling about our heads, it was sickening. Still we kept them at bay until twenty out of the twenty-three sick men were passed into the barricade under the fire of our own men; the other three sick I have every reason to believe must have wandered back into one of the rooms we had cleared, as they were men suffering from fever at the time. By this time the whole of the hospital was in flames, and we could not stay in it any longer, we had to make our own escape into the barricade, by the window through which the sick had been passed. This we did, thank God, with our lives."

39e. *Manchester Evening Chronicle*, 9 February 1911

Rorke's Drift.
Survivor's Story of the Fight.
A Manchester V.C.
Discovered Wandering in the City.
Graphic Narrative.
Heroic Defence by a Handful of Soldiers.

Some twenty years ago Private William Jones, V.C., one of the heroes of Rorke's Drift, was well-known to the public of Manchester and many other big centres in England.

Engaged by the proprietor of Hamilton's Panorama, he appeared nightly, for weeks at a time, at the Free Trade Hall, and thrilled thousands of people with the story of how he won the most-coveted honour that can be gained by a British soldier.

When that employment ceased he vanished from the public eye, and it was only through the announcement in the "Evening Chronicle" yesterday that Manchester people realised they had still living amongst them a hero of that famous fight. The old man is getting very feeble now, and, wandering away from home yesterday, he was unable to give any account of himself, except that he was "William Jones, V.C." A friendly policeman took charge of him, but he was soon traced again by his family, and when an "Evening Chronicle" representative called upon him this morning at his home in Rutland-street, Chorlton-on-Medlock, the war worn veteran was seated comfortably by the fireside.

In conversation with the hero and members of his family, assisted by records carefully preserved, our representative was able to gather up the main threads of the old man's history, and some details of the events which led him to appear before Queen Victoria on January 13, 1880, to have the Victoria Cross pinned on his breast by her Majesty.

Early Years in the Army.

Born in 1840, Private William Jones joined the 24th Regiment in 1858, and served in the Mauritius from 1860 to 1865. Four years' service in Burmah followed, and then the 24th were ordered to Madras, where they remained until 1873. After a period at home, Private Jones accompanied his regiment to Cape Colony and was there in 1879, when the memorable campaign against Cetewayo, the Zulu chief, began. His account of the battle of Rorke's Drift is as follows: –

"About half-past three in the afternoon of January 22, 1879, a mounted man galloped into our little encampment at Rorke's Drift, and told us the Zulus had taken the camp at Isandlhwana and were making for us at Rorke's Drift. We at once set to work and barricaded ourselves in with mealie bags, of which we had a good supply, making the barricade flush with the walls of two buildings, which we loopholed. We had scarcely completed our work when the Zulus were upon us, the hospital being the first place they reached.

There were 23 sick men in the hospital, and Lieutenant Broomhead, who was in charge of our small force, ordered six men to be sent into the hospital to defend it.

"I was one of the number, and in addition to defending the building, our duty was to rescue the sick. We had scarcely taken our place in the hospital before two of the six men were killed in front of the building, leaving only four of us to hold the building and get the sick men out. This was done by two men carrying out the sick while my comrade, R. Jones, and I kept the doors with our bayonets, all our ammunition being expended.

The Hospital on Fire.

"The Zulus, finding they could not force the doors, now set fire to the thatched roof. This was our worst time, for not only had we the enemy to fight, but the fire as well.

"Still we kept them at bay until 20 out of the 23 sick were passed safely out into the barricade. By this time the whole hospital was in flames, and as we could not render any more assistance inside, the three other poor fellows having fallen victims to the Zulus, we had now to make good our own escape. This we were fortunate in being able to do.

"Once inside the barricade we had to assist our comrades in defending it. The Zulus charged us from all quarters through the night, the burning hospital affording us great assistance in tracing them.

"We kept them off until daybreak, when we saw what appeared to us to be a black line winding down the Bashee on the other side of the Buffalo river. For some time we could not tell whether this meant friends or reinforcements for the enemy, but later we could bring the field-glasses and the telegraph flags to bear and we discovered it was a British force. We found it was General Lord Chelmsford returning with a portion of the column which he had taken out from the camp at Isandlhwana the day before. The Zulus seem to have known him as soon as we did, for as the troops advanced in one direction they retreated in the opposite, leaving over 500 dead behind them; our total loss being 14 after thirteen hours' fighting.

Figures of the Fight.

"The other three men who defended the doors of the hospital with me were Privates Williams, Hook and R. Jones. Only two of the Zulus succeeded in climbing the barricade, which soon became stained with their blood, many of them receiving the fire of the rifles while attempting to wrest them from the hands of the defenders. Our soldiers had fired almost straight downwards, as the Zulus were massed close under the mealie bags.

"I remember seeing between the party bearing the wounded from the hospital and the defenders at the mealie bags, the central group, consisting of Sergeant Reynolds, his bull-terrier, and a wounded man, the gallant Dalton, who played a prominent part in the defence. Dalton was a man of towering stature, and he had been foremost in the defence, exposing himself fearlessly above the low barricade, and using his rifle with deadly aim, and his bayonet with herculean strength. He was shot down while in the act of taking aim, and he passed his rifle to another commissariat officer, Mr. Byrne, who was himself shot almost immediately through the head, as he was bringing water to a wounded man of the Natal contingent.

"Dalton's rifle was passed to Lieutenant Chard at the barricade, and a wounded man handed him cartridges. Surgeon Reynolds applied a hasty bandage to Dalton's wound, and he remained to cheer on the defenders.

"Another notable figure I remember seeing there was the Rev. George Smith, the chaplain, who spent his time handing out cartridges to the defenders as well as administering spiritual consolation to the wounded.

"Lieutenant Chard took as active a part in the defence as any of the men, and Lieutenant Bromhead kept an eye on the removal of the sick as well as directing the defenders of the barricade.

"Between the hospital and the commissariat store there was a second line of mealie bags, defended not with the bayonet, but by marksmen, who had the hard task of keeping down the plunging fire of the enemy concealed among the stones, bush, and caves of the Oscarsberg. This was the most dangerous part of the defence, as the loss of life showed, though, thanks to the ravines just below, no hand to hand fighting took place here.

"The fire from the mealie bag redoubt, and the biscuit-box rampart was very fatal, and the enemy presented a fair mark, thanks to the burning hospital. After midnight the attack of the enemy slackened, but it was a quarter-past five the next morning before the last shot was fired. This was at a Zulu who was trying to fire the thatch of the store. It was not until dawn that the Zulus disappeared over the hill.

"I was mentioned in the dispatches sent home by Lieutenant Chard, and after the battle of Ulundi I came back to England, having completed 21 years' service."

Private Jones received his V.C. for his gallant defence of the hospital doors, one of the most notable things ever done by two British soldiers. It was hard hand-to-hand fighting for longer than he likes to think of now.

39f. *Haslingden Gazette,* 14 October 1911

V.C. Hero's Plight.

An elderly man named William Jones, an ex-soldier who was awarded the Victoria Cross in 1879 for bravery at Rorke's Drift, was charged at the Manchester City Police Court on Wednesday with wandering in Deansgate. Constable Edwards said he stopped the man on Tuesday night but could obtain no information as to his identity.

It was stated that Jones had recently been before the court on a similar charge and had been handed over to his friends. The stipendiary again discharged him, suggesting that he should be watched more carefully.

39g. *Haslingden Gazette,* 19 April 1913

Rorke's Drift Hero Dead.
Zula War Episode.
How two men guarded a burning hospital.

One of the heroes of the immortal episode of Rorke's Drift passed away on Tuesday night in the person of William Jones, V.C., who lived with his eldest daughter at 6, Brampton-street, Ardwick, Manchester. He had been ailing for about nine months, and was 73 years of age.

The deed of valour for which he received the Victoria Cross was the defence of the hospital at the Drift against the attacks of an overwhelming horde of Zulus. It was on January 22, 1879, when a mere handful of British soldiers, under Lieutenants Chard and Bromhead, successfully resisted the Zulu Army.

Private William Jones's account of the fight is as follows: – "About half-past three in the afternoon of January 22, 1879, a mounted man galloped into our little encampment at Rorke's Drift, and told us that the Zulus had taken the camp at Isandhlwana, and were making for us. We barricaded ourselves with mealie bags, and had scarcely completed the work, when the Zulus were upon us, the hospital being the first place they reached.

"There were 23 sick men in the hospital, and Lieutenant Bromhead ordered six men to be sent to the hospital to defend it. I was one of the number. In addition to defending the building our duty was to rescue the sick.

"We had scarcely taken our places before two of the six men were killed in front of the hospital leaving only four of us to hold the building, and get the sick men out. This was done by two men carrying our sick, while my comrade, R. Jones, and I kept the doors with our bayonets, all our ammunition being expended.

"The Zulus, finding they could not force the doors, now set fire to the thatched roof. This was our worst time, for not only had we to fight the enemy, but the fire as well. Still we kept them at bay until 20 of the 23 sick were passed safely out into the barricade. By this time the whole hospital was in flames, and those three poor fellows inside having fallen victims to the Zulus, we had now to make good our own escape. This we were fortunate in being able to do."

From inside the barricade the British troops kept off the Zulus until reinforcements arrived. The enemy left 500 dead behind them and the total British loss, after 15 hours' fighting, was 14.

40. 2-24/2437 Private Peter Judge, 'B' Company, 2/24th Foot

40a. *Roscommon and Leitrim Gazette* (Ireland), 5 April 1879

The Zulu War.

To the Editor of the Roscommon and Leitrim Gazette,

Sir, – The following letter to his parents from a young townsman, who has also two brothers in the 88th, now at the seat of war, may not add much to the information already received regarding the melancholy and now memorable disaster at Rorke's Drift, yet from the simple, circumstantial, and intellible way in which the sad event is here referred to, as well as from the fact, that it is an account of the matter written by a young native of Boyle, and well known to many in it. I am confident his letter will not fail to interest your readers if you are able to find a place for it in your journal

Yours F.B.

Boyle, March 31st 1879

Rorke's Drift, February 10th 1879.

Dear Father and Mother,

– I now take the pleasure of writing these few lines to you, hoping to find you in good health, as I am, thank God for it. On the 22nd of last month the general took out half of our division about 14 miles from camp, and he left over 1,000 men in camp and two big guns. The Zulus outflanked him and attacked the camp about 12 o'clock the same day and over-powered our men by their numbers, and killed and slaughtered every one of the 1,000 men in camp. I think there were not 20 men who made their escape. Our men fought well and killed over 7,000 of the Zulus, but there were 20,000 of them altogether, so our men could do no more. They took all our stores, kits, greycoats, ammunition, colours, and tents. There were 5 companies of the 1-24th regiment, and 1 company of the 2-24th cut up. There were 196 men of the 2-24th regiment killed and 5 officers.

About 7 miles in rere of the camp my company lay, and I as well, in charge of a commissary. There were 2 men who escaped from the camp, and told us there were Zulus coming in, in great numbers. There were only 120 men of us in the place, and a good many of them were sick. We had a half hour's warning, so we packed all the commissary stores around us, and about half-past 2 o'clock about 4000 Zulus attacked us. We fought all day and night and kept back the Zulus until 9 o'clock the next morning, when the general with the remainder of the division which he had all relieved us. There were 16 killed and 10 wounded of our men, and we killed 9 or 10 hundred of the Zulus.

We got great praise for fighting so well. They say we saved part of the Colony, and the part of the division which the general had out with him. Only for us keeping the Zulus back they would have gone down the country and killed and routed all in front of them, and attacked the division in front and rear and killed most of them, for they had not much ammunition. We have made a fort here now, and are waiting for more troops. Before we get them we cannot do any more. The general has sent home for some more troops, and when we get them we will make the Zulus pay for what they have done. I heard the 88th regiment is coming up from King Williams Town.

I have not heard from John or Charley since I wrote last, so I now conclude hoping to see you all in ten or twelve months' time. I remain your affectionate son,

Peter Judge.

41. 25B/1309 Private Joshua Lodge, 'B' Company, 2/24th Foot

41a. *Manchester Evening News*, 27 July 1906

A Drunkard's Death.

During an inquiry at the City Coroner's court, to-day, concerning the death of Joshua Lodge, aged 50, of Broughton-street, Ancoats, who died suddenly the previous day, it was stated that he had been subject to excessive drinking for many years. He drank whenever he could get it, and had pawned his clogs and some clothing in order to get money for drinking purposes. He had been dismissed from employment because of his drinking habits. Fits always followed a heavy drinking bout.

The Coroner having remarked on the fact that the man had pawned nearly everything he could lay his hands on, even some of his clothing, for purposes of drinking, the jury returned a verdict of death from natural causes, accelerated by excessive drinking.

42. Trooper Henry Lugg, Natal Mounted Police

42a. *Bristol Mercury and Daily Post,* 5 April 1879

A Young Bristolian at Rorke's Drift.
We have received from a young Bristolian, Harry Lugg, who left home in March, last year, the subjoined interesting account of the gallant affair at Rorke's Drift, in which he took part as a volunteer. He has also sent a pen and ink sketch of the Mealie Fort, which conveys a good idea of the situation: –

"I know you were surprised to hear from Fred that I had been at Rorke's Drift. I should have written you the same morning I wrote to Fred, but I could only find an old envelope and a small piece of paper, and then only a piece of pencil to write with. I shall not profess to give you an exact account of the fight, but will give you just the heads. It must have been about 2.40 p.m. when a carabineer rode into the little yard, without boots, tunic, or arms, and leading a spare horse. All we could glean from his excited remarks was, "Everyone killed in camp, and 4,000 Kafirs on their way to take the mission station," (or rather hospital) – not pleasant tidings for 100 men, you may be sure. When he came to himself a bit he said, "You will all be murdered and cut to pieces," and the only answer he received was – "We will fight for it, and if we have to die we will die like Britishers."

All who were able began to throw up sacks and knock loopholes out with pickaxes, and otherwise make preparations to receive them. We had some 2000 native contingent there on a mountain, and occupying the krantzes and caves. Noble savages! As soon as they heard the Zulus were to attack us they made a great noise, had a big dance, clashing their assegais against their shields, and otherwise showed their warlike spirit. Now I must describe the fort. The said fort consisted of two small houses, one used as a store and the other as a hospital and mission station. These houses were about forty yards apart, and our ramparts were composed of mealies three sacks high, and running from the corners of one house to the corners of the others, but the one great danger being thatch roofs to both. There were two missionaries (Swiss) living in the hospital. They were absent for some twenty minutes – out for a ride – and no one could help laughing at their gesticulations when they came back on seeing the best parlour paper being pulled down and loopholes being knocked out, while splendid furniture was scattered about the rooms. His first question was, in broken English, 'Vot is dish?' Someone replied, 'The Zulus are almost on us,' upon which he bolted, saying, "Mein Got! mein Got! Mein vife and mein childrens at ze Umsinga! Oh, mein Got! mein Got!"

In the meantime a mounted infantryman and two of our men – Shannon and Doig – came in, excited and breathless. Upon my asking, 'What is it? Is it true?' and so on, Doig replied, 'You will all be murdered,' and rode off with his comrade. Consolatory, certainly; but nothing remains but to fight, and that we will do to the bitter end. A man named Hall, of R.M.B., rode out to see if he could see anything of them, and on going about 1000 yards he could see them just a mile off, as he described it, 'as black as hell and as thick as grass.' 'Stay operations and fall in.' My carbine was broken, or rather the stock bent. I found a piece of rein, tied it up, and fell in with the soldiers. I thought – if I can get somewhere where I can sit down and pop away I shall be all right, because my knees were much swollen. I was told off in my turn to take a loophole, and defend the roof from fire. At about 3.30 they came on, first in sections of fours, then opened out in skirmishing order. Up came their reserve, then they were on us. The place seemed alive with them. No orders were given – every man to act as he thought proper. I had the satisfaction of seeing the first I fired at roll over, at 350, and then my nerves were as steady as a rock. I made sure almost before I pulled the trigger. There was some of the best shooting at 450 yards that I have ever seen.

Just before dark we had beaten them off with great losses, and only a few casualties on our side – two killed and one wounded. One of our fellows, named Hunter, also ill with rheumatism, was assegaied in the kidneys and five wounds in the chest. Before it got really dark the fiends lit the hospital thatch, which being very closely packed did not burn well. At about ten they came on in tremendous force, sweeping the fellows before them and causing them to retreat to the store. But Providence favoured us. The thatch roof burst out flames, and made it as light as day, and before they had time to retreat we were pouring bullets into them like hail. We could see them falling in scores. Then you could hear suppressed British cheers. They kept up the attack all night with no better luck. We knocked them down as fast as they came. At five a.m., 23rd, the last shot was fired, and the last nigger killed; he had a torch tied on his assegai, and was in the act of throwing it into the thatch, but he was "sold." The column came to our relief about 5.30, and real British cheers went up, I can tell you. When the major saw me he said, 'I never thought of seeing you alive again, my boy.' The tears were standing in his eyes. He said, 'We saw the fire last night, and thought you were all murdered.' Thank God, it is not so. I have sustained no damage beyond the loss of everything (except letters) and a little weakness of the eyes, I suppose from peering out of the loophole all night, the constant straining of the eyesight."

42b. *Western Times,* 23 April 1879

Okehampton.
Rorke's Drift: A letter from an Oktonian.

We have been favoured with the perusal of another letter from Mr. Harry Lugg, the native of this town, and whose family reside here. He now gives a very graphic narrative of the attack upon and heroic defence of the station, but as the events of that eventful occasion have been more than once described in our columns we must content ourselves with a few extracts. Mr. Lugg first refers to the terrible slaughter at Isandula, with reference to which he says: –

"One of the natives told me the name meant 'little hand.' Another told me it meant a little house, but there is little resemblance to either, being more like the 'Lion's Rump' at Cape Town. The Dutch Boers have named it 'Lion's Kopje,' or 'Lion Hill,' and during the war of some years back, between the Boers and the Zulus, the Boers were attacked in almost the same place, and so literally cut to pieces by the Zulus that out of some hundreds of Dutchmen about three escaped to tell the tale. While we were scouting on horseback in that direction one day, to the westward of the Lion's Kopje, we found a lot of bleached bones and skeletons still lying among the short grass.

We crossed Rorke's Drift into Zululand on the 11th, everyone in excellent spirits, and anxious to meet the valiant Zulus face to face. My first experience of hard fighting was at Sirayos Kraal (pronounced Sikayo). We could see niggers running along the top and edges of the table mountain, carrying guns and assegais. The mountain is one of Cetywayo's fastnesses, but it was not fast enough for us. Col. Russell was in command of the mounted men, and that gentleman quietly marched us along under their very noses, and we received the order, 'No one fire until ordered.' Stupid, I thought, and at the same time our arms were slung on our backs.

We rode up to within a hundred yards of them, the Mounted Infantry being in advance, when all at once we received a volley straight into us. The bullets and pot legs – legs of the iron crocks and pots put in the guns – whizzed about our ears like hail, and not a nigger to be seen. Rather an unenviable position – we on a flat, and the niggers nicely ensconced behind rocks, trees, &c. Almost before you could say 'Jack Robinson' we were off our horses, sent them back under cover in a deep ravine, and were lying down having a shot wherever a black head, and rifle-barrels showed itself. After firing for about ten minutes the order was given 'Fix knives, draw revolvers, and scale the krantz' (precipice). Up, with a shout; away rushed the niggers, and those who escaped the revolver and bayonet by rushing away were shot by some of our men, who were firing over us, covering us, in fact. We killed altogether some two or three hundred of them, and amongst them Sirayo's (one of Cetewayo's head chiefs) son; took his wife and daughters prisoners, along with lots of old women (about 150 years old, I should say). They had as much as they could eat, and were sent away by General Thisiger."

Mr. Lugg then describes his being ordered to Rorke's Drift, and describes with much minuteness the attack on that place, and ultimate routing of the Zulus. In describing the firing of the hospital, he says: – "Let anyone picture to himself fire, no ammunition, darkness, and 5,000 savage Zulus waiting to turn you out and disembowel you! I do not boast, neither am I a coward, but I hope I shall never again be in a similar situation. About ten o'clock there had been a lull in the firing for about ten minutes, when all at once the war call of the rattle snake, a ball frog, a bird, a slight clatter of shields, and on they came with a same cry, 'Usuta.' Bang, bang, bang. We stuck to it, and could defy them as long as we kept them off the roof. Attack after attack we repulsed until two o'clock in the morning (23rd), when they made one desperate assault, and with more success, they drove us out of our frail barricade, and even pushed the muzzles of their guns between the sacks and fired at our men; but the bayonet went to work, and soon shifted them from their positions – we drove them back once more. One poor fellow was shot in defending the next loophole to mine. Another was shot on the roof directly over my head (he was keeping a look-out on the roof); the bullet entered below the shoulder blade, and lodged the other side in the breast. There was an instance of true British pluck. His name was Brickey, and someone helping him off the roof, said, 'Poor old Brickey,' to which he replied, 'Never mind, my lads; better to be shot than assegaied; give it to the fiends.' Thanks to a good constitution, the bullet has been extracted, and he is getting on as well as can be expected. The other man, named Desmond, was shot through his hand. I tore up an old haversack and bound up his wound, after which he stood at his loophole, and fought through the night, and never a groan or word escaped him all that time …

… The last Zulu shot was trying to light the thatch by means of a torch tied on the handle of an assegai, and was in the act of throwing it to make it stick into the thatch, when a bullet pierced his brain, and the fire did no more damage than singe the grass …

… At 5.30 the niggers again formed into the same manner as when they came down the afternoon before, and, 'Stand to your arms,' was the order. No hurry, no confusion; and, while we were silently awaiting another attack, we were informed that four boxes of ammunition only remained; and, said a sergeant of the staff, 'Don't fire a shot at random; make every shot tell, and don't fire until they come within 50 yards.' They were then about 1,000 yards off, and in great force, having received reinforcements during the night. Silently we waited, and resolved to sell our lives dearly, a proof of which lay in the heaps around us; but they made no movement whatever. In a moment our thoughts were occupied in another direction. The look-out from the roof shouted, 'There are thousands of niggers coming in direction of the Drift.' (Buffalo Drift). About 20,000 cut the camp at Isandula to pieces, and, of course, it was quite likely they had come from the camp (eight miles as the crow flies). Bad news, our holding the place against such odds for twelve hours. Fifteen minutes' awful suspense, and then went up real British cheers – 'Hurrah! hurrah! for the column!' Away cleared the niggers over the hills, in the same way they came – the cowardly hounds. Up came the N.M.P., M.

Infantry, and Carabineers as hard as they could gallop. Hurrah! again and again. Our little garrison stood on the barricade of mealie sacks, and cheers were going up for some minutes. Then we felt more comfortable, for if ever red or any other coats were welcome they were that morning. I shook hands with our fellows, and there were congratulations from all of them. When the Major came up to me with tears in his eyes, and told men 'he was afraid to think what had become of our little garrison; all through the night they had seen the glare of the burning hospital, and, of course, thought it was all up with us, and that they would only find mutilated remains instead of live men.' But it was not to be. They paid dearly enough; we lost a fourth of our number, but theirs was 950."

42c. *Western Times,* 1 September 1899

Okehampton will be proud of the well-deserved honour and distinction conferred upon a native of the borough of Okehampton – Captain Lugg, transport officer, who was a member of the old force, known as the Natal Mounted Police, and served during the Zulu war, having been promoted to the rank of Major. He is a brother of Mr. Lugg, photographer, of Okehampton, and in his younger days served his apprenticeship with Mr. Jessop, ironmonger, of Fore-street. He left Okehampton about twenty years since and went out to Natal. He was present at the fight at Sirayo's kraal and took part in the celebrated defence of Rorke's Drift, where, with five others, he defended the north-east end of the roof of the small building throughout the night. He is a thorough linguist, and was the means of running several murderers to earth a few years ago, receiving the thanks of the authorities. In conjunction with Major Bru de Wold he raised the Umzimkulu Mounted Rifles in 1884, and was Captain and Adjutant of that regiment until his appointment to the staff in 1895. He was also then presented with a rifle by the Mayor of Durban.

43. 25B/1112 Corporal John Jeremiah Lyons, 'B' Company, 2/24th Foot

43a. *Pontypool Free Press*, 8 March 1879

The following letters are from Corporal John Lyons, 2nd Battalion, 24th Regiment, a native of Pontypool, who enlisted in that Regiment some years ago, having previously been in the Marines. From the envelope containing the letter of the 16th January having been "franked" by Lieut. G. Bromhead, of the 2-24th Regiment, and the letter being dated from the Camp at Rorke's Drift, as well as the name of "Corporal J. Lyons, 2nd Battalion, 24th foot" appearing among those of the wounded at Rorke's Drift on the 23rd January, we feel justified in concluding that our townsman took part in the gallant action at that place when Lieutenants Bromhead and Chard, with a mere handful of soldiers, successfully withstood the attack of about 3000 Zulus, and so saved the English Forces from a calamity greater still than that which had befallen them at Isandula on the previous day.

Camp Helpmakaar, 8th January, 1879.

My Dear Mother,

I received your kind letter; I was sorry to find that my silence caused you so much uneasiness, but you will please excuse me. It is only now that I can see how neglectful I have been; I would not have been so long silent, but the war being over in Cape Colony, and the troops being called in from the field, a few months soon passed over in seeking some amusement. Dear Mother, I will write as often as possible, but I cannot help it if you do not hear from me very regularly. I think we are about to commence a harder war than the one just concluded. I told you in my last that we were very close to the enemy's country. We have moved since then, and are now within a musket-shot of his land. The Buffalo River divides us; we are putting a pontoon bridge across it now, and I think we shall cross over on the 12th inst. We have only seen a few of them moving about on the other side of the river; but I dare say that the day we cross the river, or the day after, we shall be likely to meet some opposition, as they are very numerous. I will now conclude, hoping you are quite well, as this leaves me at present. Please give my love to Tom and all inquiring friends. Give my love to Tom Brown and cousin Kate. Accept the same yourself from your affectionate son,

J. Lyons.

43b. *Pontypool Free Press*, 5 April 1879

The following is from Corporal John Lyons, 2-24th Regiment: –

Helpmakaar, February 7th, 1879.

Dear Mother,

I now take the pleasure of writing these few lines, to let you know that I happened to be one of the unlucky ones that got wounded on the 22nd of last month; but thank God that I am getting round favourably again. Dear Mother, the Zulus attacked the camp of the 1-24th on the 22nd and slaughtered five companies of them, and slaughtered one company and a half of the 2-24th. They also attacked the company I belong to on the same day, at half past 3 in the afternoon. We were stationed at Rorke's Drift, guarding the commissariat and hospital. We were warned that they were going to attack us about one hour before they came. We all did the best in our power to make a laager to defend ourselves. There were about eighty of us, all told, and we fought like men and kept four thousand of them at bay until morning. Dear Mother, I do not know who all the boys are that got killed from Pontypool, but I know that Farr, the butcher, and young Harry Smith were killed. Dear Mother, I will be able to let you know more in my next letter. I am getting around alright at present. I suppose that I shall be on the road home soon. Give my best respects to Thomas and all my enquiring friends, and you must accept the same yourself,

I remain, your dear son,

John Lyons

ps. Write soon.

43c. *Pontypool Free Press,* 19 April 1879

The following letter is from Corporal Lyons, who was wounded at Rorke's Drift, and whose letter, dated from Helpmakaar on February 7th was published in our issue of April 5th: –

Ladysmith, Feb. 23rd, 1879.

My dear Mother,

You will be glad to hear that I am still in the land of the living, and in every way likely to get over my wound, which is much to be thankful to God for; and before long, if all goes well, I shall be on my road home. Since I wrote to you we have shifted sixty miles further down country. We came in waggons called ambulances, and I bore the journey surprisingly well. The people here are very good, and such little delicacies as rice puddings, sago, fruit, and other things are sent in every day to the sick and wounded. The ladies of the town also come in and visit us pretty often, and are always ready to send us anything we like to ask for. My dear Mother, you would think this a strange town if you were to see it; there are not two houses standing together; they are all what is called self-contained, and most of them stand in their own gardens. The inhabitants are mostly English and Dutch. We expect to move further down the country in a few days. And now, my dear mother, give my kind regards to all enquiring friends, and no more at present from your ever-loving and affectionate son,

John Lyons.

43d. *Pontypool Free Press,* 14 June 1879

The Zulu War.
Return of Wounded Men to England.
Statement of Corporal Lyons, of Pontypool.

The three wounded men, Corporal J. Lyons, Private Hitch, and Private Waters, who arrived in the *Tamar* from the Cape, were sent on Monday from Portsmouth to Netley Hospital, Hampshire. Hitch was wounded in the shoulder, Waters in the shoulder and knee, and Lyons in the neck. All three took part in the splendid defence of Rorke's Drift, under Chard and Bromhead, which, it is now confessed, was the saving of the colony from the Zulus. Since his return to England, Private Hitch has been made aware of his having been awarded the Victoria Cross for his bravery, and he was much overcome on the intelligence being communicated to him. We have before us a short letter to his mother from Corporal John Lyons, a Pontypool hero, some of whose letters from the seat of war have previously appeared in our columns. In his present communication, written from the ship *Tamar* immediately after his arrival at Portsmouth on Monday, he informs his anxious mother that he is (with the exception of his wounds) in good health, and is going into Netley Hospital; he promises all particulars in his next. Since his arrival at Netley, Corporal Lyons has given the following very interesting description of his experiences during the repulse of the Zulus at Rorke's Drift: –

"I belong to the B Company of the 2-24th, under Lieutenant Bromhead. I went up to Greytown with Private Hitch, who was one of the same company. We arrived at Rorke's Drift about Jan. 5. I saw Private Evans, of the Mounted Infantry, riding up at full gallop, without either coat or cap on, and I, of course, thought something was up. I was corporal in charge of the camp guard at the time outside the building. Shortly after Evans's arrival, Lieutenant Bromhead gave the order to strike tents, which was done immediately, as I had the guard tent pulled down and by Mr Bromhead's order extended my sixteen in skirmishing order along the left front to check the advance of the Zulus, who by this time, I had heard, were coming upon us. Corporal Allen was sent to the other flank on similar duty, and the rest of the company at once began to make preparations for the fight. Lieutenant Bromhead, Lieutenant Chard, Mr Dalton, and Dr. Reynolds being very busy in helping and encouraging the men in the work. Captain Stevenson's Native Contingent also lent a hand.

While this was going on Sergt. Williams (who was killed in the night), brought his guard up from the pontoon at the Blood River. He had only six men with him.

The Zulus were approaching the other bank of the river. When he left he joined Corporal Allen. I remained with my guard till I heard firing, and then both flanking parties retired within the fort, and lent a hand to finish the preparations, which was the only work for a few minutes.

Hitch had by this time reported that the Zulus were in sight, and we had scarcely finished before they were on us.

We were told not to fire without orders. This, I suppose was to make sure that the advancing force was really Zulus. Only a few seconds elapsed before the real character of it was made known to us.

The Zulus did not shout, as they generally do; but, after extending and forming a half-moon, they steadily advanced and kept up a tremendous fire. I took up a position to check the fire from the enemy's right flank, as it was thought the crack shots would go up there.

Corporal Allen, and several men were with me, and we all consider we did good service. Lieutenant Bromhead was on the right face, firing over the mealies with a Martini-Henry. Mr Chard was also very busy, I only turned round once to see this, and in that brief interval I saw Private Cole shot, and he fell dead.

Seeing this I kept myself more up over the bags, knowing that the shot which hit him had come over our heads, and I was determined to check this flank firing as much as possible. I became thus more exposed, and so did Corporal Allen. We fired many shots, and I said to my comrades, 'They (the Zulus) are falling fast over there;' and he replied, 'Yes, we're giving it to them.'

I saw many Zulus killed on the hill.

About half-past seven, as near as I can tell, after we had been fighting between two and three hours, I received a shot through the right side of the neck. The ball lodged in the back, striking the spine, and was not extracted till five weeks afterwards. My right arm was partially disabled. I said, 'Give it to them, Allen. I am done; I am dying,' and he replied, 'All right, Jack;' and while I was speaking to him I saw a hole in the right sleeve of his coat, and I said, 'Allen, you are shot,' and he replied, 'Yes; good bye.' He walked away, with blood running from his arm, and he helped to serve ammunition all night. All I could do, as I was lying on the ground, was to encourage the men, and I did so as long as I was able to open my mouth. I lay on my back just behind the biscuit boxes, where Mr Dalton gave me a full round all night, and soon after he did this he was shot through the right shoulder.

Before I fell I heard Private Fagin shout, and I saw him fall. He was shot in the abdomen, and died shortly afterwards. The Zulus came right up to the bags, and I could hear them outside, and could also see many by the burning hospital, and told the men very often to fire away and pot them off.

Private Deakin, who dressed Hitch's wound, was also very busy in firing.

Private Waters, who also came home with us, was a patient in the hospital and was rescued, but received a flesh wound in the shoulder.

Every man fought dearly for his life, but we were all determined to sell our lives like soldiers, and to keep up the credit of our regiment.

Mr Dalton, who has since received a commission, deserved any amount of praise.

43e. *Pontypool Free Press,* 20 September 1879

Corporal Lyons.

Our readers are already aware that our brave townsman, Corporal John Lyons, was badly wounded in the neck, by a Zulu bullet, at Rorke's Drift, on the 22nd of January last. The bullet, which remained in the neck until the 27th of February, causing intense pain, is supposed to be made of zinc or a similar metal; it is round and ungrooved, roughly cast, having a shank left by the hole in the bullet-mould still upon it, measuring 2³⁄₁₆ ins in circumference, and weighs within a trifle of three-quarters of an ounce. The operation was performed by Dr D. Blair-Brown, F.R.C.S., Ed., A.M.D., from whose "Surgical Notes on the Zulu War," published in the *Lancet,* we have extracted the following: –

Case of Gunshot Injury to the Cervical Vertebrae with Lodgement of the Bullet. – No. 1112, Corporal. J. L. …, of the 2nd-24th Regiment, when engaged in the defence of Rorke's Drift, on the night of 22nd January, received a bullet in his neck, near the posterior margin of the sterno-mastoid of the left side, about the upper portion of the middle third of its length. Only one wound, that of entrance, was present. He complained of great pain in the neck on the slightest movement. When in bed the pillow caused an increase of this. He had lost almost all use of his arms and hands, especially the right one, which he describes as "quite dead". Painful "twitchings" were experienced in the arms. Whenever he moved his head from the bed some one had to support it between their hands before he could do so. At Rorke's Drift several surgeons tried to find the bullet, but were unsuccessful. In the above condition he arrived at Helpmakaar on the 26th of January. Next day, assisted by several surgeons, I got him under chloroform, I made a prolonged attempt to find the bullet. The course I found it had taken was in a direct line with the spinal cord. I made a free opening in the middle line, as far down the course as possible, and again attempted to reach the bullet. I found by digital examination now that the processes of two adjacent vertebrae were smashed, and I felt a soft, smooth, cord-like substance under my finger beyond. Pressure on this instantly caused the patient to turn very pale and the pulse to be almost imperceptible, and necessitated the immediate withdrawal of the chloroform and adoption of artificial respiration. I have no doubt but that it was the spinal cord. I took away several pieces of vertebrae which were lying loose, but had to give up attempting to reach the bullet. The case continued much as described for some time. He was sent to the Base Hospital at Ladysmith. On taking over medical charge thereof, on the 27th of February, I found my old patient much in the same condition as before described. He was suffering greatly from the pain in his arms, and wished to have them both off to relieve him from it.

On examination I found a distinct hard substance on firm pressure beneath the ligamentum nuchae, which was not present on former occasions. On consultation with the Surgeon-General of the forces, who happened to be on a tour of inspection at the time, I cut down upon it, and without much difficulty enucleated an ordinary round bullet, with a rather long rough process extending from its smooth surface. The wound healed rapidly; but the original one still continued open and discharged a little pus. In a few days the pain entirely disappeared from his arms, and their use nearly returned. The right arm was not "quite the thing" when he was sent to head-quarters at Pietermaritzburg. He has since, I learn, sailed for the Royal Victoria Hospital at Netley.

Those of our readers who are acquainted with Corporal Lyons will not, perhaps, be surprised to hear that the gallant fellow bore the excruciating pain of the operation without making the slightest murmur, although he was not under the influence of chloroform or any other anaesthetic.

43f. *South Wales Argus*, 3 May 1923

A Newport V.C.
Hero Of Rorke's Drift.
A claim is being sent to the War Office for a Victoria Cross on behalf of Corporal J. Lyons, late of the South Wales Borderers, for conspicuous bravery at Rorke's Drift 44 years ago. Lyons is said to be on the Horse Guards' roll of Victoria Cross heroes, but he has never received the award.

A pathetic feature in connection with the matter is that the gallant old soldier died at Newport on Wednesday without knowing the result of the belated claim. He enlisted in the 57th Foot of the old "Die-hards" in June, 1864, served in New Zealand through the Maori War in 1865–6–7, and, after a subsequent short stay in England volunteered for service for the 63rd Foot in India, and later joined the 24th Foot (South Wales Borderers). He was present at the battle of Haynes Hill, Rabula Heights, and Perie Bush in the Kaffir war in South Africa.

When the Zulu war broke out he embarked for Durban, and marched from there to Pietermaritzburg and on to Rorke's Drift, where on January 22, 1879, he was wounded in the neck by a bullet. He continued to fight and serve out ammunition in spite of his wound. He was 78 years of age, and leaves a widow, two sons, (both of whom are in Australia), and two daughters.

The funeral will take place from Oxford Street, Newport on Saturday morning next.

44. Colour Sergeant George William Mabin, General Staff

44a. *Cape Times* (South Africa), 22 January 1914

"Lest We Forget."
Anniversary of Rorke's Drift.
A Survivor's Story.
How the Defenders Triumphed.
As the 22nd of January comes round, the number of gallant men who took part in the defence of Rorke's Drift and stemmed the tide of invasion which threatened to overwhelm the colony of Natal grows smaller and smaller.

One of them – Mr. G.W. Mabin, of Woodstock – probably the only one remaining in South Africa – was interviewed yesterday by a representative of this journal. Mr. Mabin was at the time of the affair staff-sergeant on General Chelmsford's staff. He accompanied Col. Glynn's column on the invasion of Zululand, and in his capacity as staff clerk found himself at Rorke's Drift on the occasion of that memorable impi attack, which the men of the 24th Regiment, now known as the South Wales Borderers, so gloriously frustrated.

Lord Chelmsford had formed a station at Rorke's Drift, on the Buffalo River, which formed the centre of communication between his base at Helpmakaar and his advance force in Zululand. The post was under the command of Major Spalding, to whom Staff-Sergeant Mabin was appointed clerk.

Lord Chelmsford, with his advance column, consisting of the Second Battalion of the 24th Regiment, Lonsdale's Light Horse, and a battery of artillery, were in Zululand. The post at Rorke's Drift was held by one company of the 24th Regiment, under the command of Lieut. Bromhead. Rorke's Drift was also used as a hospital base for the advance column, and at the time there were a number of patients in charge of the Medical Corps. It will be remembered that the advance column had reached Isandhlwana, twelve miles from Rorke's Drift, and on the morning of the 22nd of January, 1879, the greater portion of this column was out on reconnaissance, under the personal supervision of Lord Chelmsford.

An Eventful Day.

During their absence a large Zulu impi, said to number nearly 20,000, attacked the camp at Isandhlwana, and after a severe fight overpowered the troops, resulting in almost a general massacre, only six escaping with their lives. A portion of the successful impi, numbering, it was computed, between 4,000 to 5,000, made their way to Rorke's Drift, where they arrived at about four o'clock in the afternoon. Prior to their arrival Lieut. Adendorff, of the Natal Native Contingent, who had escaped from Isandhlwana, reached the drift, and gave warning of the approach of the Zulus.

"I was sitting at my office tent door," said Mr. Mabin, "Major Spalding had gone to Helpmakaar that morning with a view to arranging for reinforcements. At the station we did not expect any trouble. Just after three in the afternoon a man, hatless and bootless, rode up on an exhausted horse. He halted at the tent, and I immediately asked what had occurred. He exclaimed, 'Good God, the camp is taken, and they're coming on here.'"

Sergeant-Major Mabin took the bearer of the news to Lieut. Bromhead, who at the time was in charge of the camp. The latter then brought in Lieut. Chard, R.E., who was superintending the working of the ponts on the river half a mile away. Steps were taken at once to put the camp in a state of defence. The windows and doors of the hospital were blocked up with mattresses and other things, loopholes made through the walls both of the hospital and store-house. A wall of mealie and other grain bags was made, enclosing the front of the hospital and running along the edge of the rocky terrace to the stone wall of the kraal. Three or four bullock wagons were utilised to stop gaps between the existing buildings and the barricade of biscuit boxes. Ammunition was then served out.

A Forlorn Hope.

"We had scarcely finished our preparations," went on Mr. Mabin, "when the approaching Zulus were observed coming round the spur of the Oscarberg Mountains. There were 86 of us bearing arms, and we were prepared to sell our lives as dearly as possible."

The enemy were now upon them, and were pouring over the right shoulder of the hill in a dense mass, and making straight for the connecting wall between the store-house and the hospital. But when they got within fifty yards the firing was altogether too hot for them. Some half of them swerved round to the left, and passed the back and right end of the hospital, and then made a desperate attempt to scale the barricade in front of that building. But here too they were repulsed. They dispersed to find cover amongst the bushes and the stone wall below the terrace. The others found shelter amongst the numerous banks, ditches and bushes and poured a continuous fire on the camp.

"The first man I ever killed in my life," said Mr. Mabin, "was a big Zulu, carrying an assegai and shield, and as he advanced he took cover behind anything that presented itself. He dropped behind a rock prior to making another rush, when I covered the rock with my rifle, and as he rose to come on again I pulled the trigger, and he leaped at least five feet into the air and dropped dead."

Mr. Mabin went on to say they afterwards found that the area of defence was too large to be adequately defended by the small force, and about half was discarded, and Lieut. Chard ordered the construction of a biscuit box re-entrenchment which, unfortunately left the hospital outside the lines of defence. But there was nothing else for it if the station was to be saved. Attack after attack was repulsed by the gallant defenders.

Lighted Tufts Of Grass.

"About seven in the evening," went on the narrator, "the Zulus attempted to fire the hospital, lighting tufts of grass and attaching them to their assegais and throwing them on to the thickly-thatched roof of the building, which was soon afire. The flames, as a matter of fact, aided us, because by their light we were able to distinguish the Zulus as they formed into bodies for succeeding rushes."

While the building was in flames many gallant acts were performed in saving and attempting to save patients, the greater part of whom were borne to a place of comparative safety.

The attacks of the Zulus were continuous. Hardly had the defenders repulsed one, than another body would move forward and fling itself on the stockade, and on one or two occasions the gallant body of defenders were almost overwhelmed. The Zulus forced themselves fearlessly up to the points of the bayonets, where they met their fate by bayonet thrust or ball. But the stream of savages was never quite sufficient to swamp the camp, and between nine and ten in the evening their rushes became fewer. At intervals of about twenty minutes, however, fierce assaults on the stockade were kept up.

Then one of the chief buildings, once used for mission work, became the centre of the attack, but the assaults were successfully repelled by the handful of defenders by a steady fire through the loopholes which were constructed earlier in the day. Then attempts were made to set fire to the building, and one of the Zulus, more daring than his fellows, rushed with a lighted assegai, and getting in between the loopholes, reached up and attempted to fire the eaves of the thatched roof. Corporal Attwood, of the Army Service Corps, pushed his carbine through a loophole, and fired downwards on the off chance of getting his man. And so it proved, for on the following morning the Zulu who had made the attempt was found immediately under the wall with his head split open by the bullet.

An Anxious Night.

"Probably upon this incident," said Mr. Mabin, "hung the preservation of the camp." Desultory firing was kept up during the whole of the night, and in the early dawn the enemy was seen to be assembling some six hundred yards away, and this was judged as to be the preparations for the final onslaught. By this time their ammunition was running short, and it was found that only a further 13 rounds per rifle remained.

"Just about this time I was on look-out," said Mr. Mabin, "and discovered a movement on the Zululand side of the river. Owing to the light I could not determine what was happening – whether they were friends or enemies approaching. But in the next ten minutes I found they were mounted men, and to our intense joy it proved to be the General at the head of the remainder of the column, and their approach was the signal for the full flight of the Zulus."

The defenders lost 15 killed, two mortally wounded, and 10 others less seriously hurt. No fewer than 386 of the Zulus were buried in a donga, while many bodies were found day by day in isolated spots. He believed that the besiegers lost quite 500 men.

Mr. Mabin, who was sixty-five last birthday, looks hale and hearty, and certainly belies the number of his years. For his share in the defence of the river post Lord Wolseley promoted him to the warrant rank. After going back to Pietermaritzburg, the trouble with Joubert's Boers developed, and as chief clerk he accompanied Sir George Colley to fields destined to be less glorious than Rorke's Drift, but almost as noteworthy. At Laing's Nek and Ingogo he fought, and one night the ill-prepared force, with seventy rounds and three days' rations marched to Majuba Hill, and scrambling up the crags got into position, where the Boers found them at dawn. The Boers' Council of War decided to attack, and they advanced up the hill fairly well covered. When the ammunition of the British was expended they had only stones to fight with, and they (the Boers) got possession of the crest. Mr.

Mabin was near Colley when the latter fell, shot through the head. Amongst the many medals which Mr. Mabin holds is the gold medal presented on the occasion of the Diamond Jubilee, and this was presented to him for the longest and most meritorious service in South Africa.

44b. *Cape Times,* 3 October 1928

One of the Gallant Band who defended Rorke's Drift. Mr. Mabin, of Cape Town, Still Hale and Hearty.

Mr. George William Mabin, of 20, William-street, Woodstock, who on Friday next will celebrate his 80th birthday, is one of the few men living to-day who formed part of the gallant little garrison which defended Rorke's Drift against the fury of the Zulus on January 22, 1879.

Mr. Mabin enjoys robust health and is wonderfully preserved. He looks many years younger than his age and is still an active man. "I often walk to Cape Town and back and think nothing of it," he told a 'Cape Times' representative who called on him yesterday.

In conversation, Mr. Mabin recalled some of the incidents of the memorable defence of Rorke's Drift – a border Post between Natal and Zululand on the Buffalo River.

"The first shot fired in the Zulu War was on January 13, 1879, just over the border across the Buffalo River," he said. "I was a Staff-Sergt. of the General Staff and was stationed at Rorke's Drift at the time.

"At the outbreak of the trouble with the Zulus the 1st and 2nd Battalions of the 24th Regiment advanced into Zululand, leaving one Company (B. Co.) at Rorke's Drift. Major Spalding was senior officer there and other officers at Rorke's Drift Post were Lieut. Chard, of the Royal Engineers, and Lieut. Bromhead, of the 2/24th, who was in command of B. Co.

"On the morning of January 22, Major Spalding went back to Helpmakaar to hurry on the Company of the 24th Regiment, which was required to protect the ponts. Rumours were then abroad that the Zulus were on the warpath.

"At 3 o'clock in the afternoon of that day I was sitting outside the Staff tent at Rorke's Drift, when a mounted man came up at the gallop. His clothing consisted merely of shirt, trousers and socks. I asked him what was up and he said 'Good God, the camp at Isandhlwana has been rushed by Zulus and nearly all our men have been killed. I've come to warn you. The Zulus are on the way here.'"

Here Mr. Mabin explained that the greater part of the force at Isandhlwana under Lord Chelmsford had that morning proceeded some 10 or 12 miles from the camp on reconnaissance, and during their absence the Zulus had attacked and overpowered the small garrison left behind.

Reverting to the story, he continued: "I immediately rushed up to the camp and informed Lieut. Bromhead of our position. He sent a man hurriedly to recall Lieut. Chard, who was at work on the pontoons about half a mile away, and the rest of us got to work without delay to erect the best barricade possible. Mealie sacks, biscuit boxes and a few wagons were among the most useful things we could lay our hands on.

"We piled these things up, and had no time to cut the bush in front when the first Zulus appeared round the spur of the Oscarsberg. Their numbers increased rapidly, and on they came to the attack, leaping, shouting and firing at us with all sorts of weapons. The majority carried assegais, but many had their own firearms as well as a number of rifles captured at Isandhlwana. Luckily for us they were not good marksmen, but numbers were against us from the beginning."

[The official report estimates the Zulu force to have been 3,000, whereas the total garrison at Rorke's Drift numbered 139, many of whom were non-combatants.]

"All I had was a revolver and ammunition," said Mr. Mabin, "but when the first casualty occurred I took over a rifle. The fight lasted all night and ended at 4 a.m. Many were the rushes made to storm our slender barricade, but the bayonet did useful work. Only two Zulus, I think, managed to get inside and they were quickly dispatched. Seventeen of the garrison were killed and ten wounded, but when relief came at dawn and we went outside we collected about 350 dead Zulus. At the finish, when Col. Baker Russell's Horse and other units under Lord Chelmsford came to our aid we were reduced to 13 rounds of ammunition per man. During the 12 hours' scrap I fired 30 rounds with the revolver and afterwards used 90 rounds with the old Martini Henry.

"I shall never forget when Lord Chelmsford lined us up and thanked us for our gallant defence. After a few words he completely broke down with emotion."

Mr. Mabin was born in Bristol on October 5, 1848. He joined the 2nd Battalion Rifle Brigade on June 1, 1868 and was promoted Acting Sergeant after four years. He then obtained an appointment as temporary clerk at the War Office and later secured an appointment as Military Staff Clerk at Manchester Headquarters of the Northern District. He was later moved to a staff clerkship at Dover, at which station he had previously married. In 1878 he volunteered to serve in South Africa and in recognition of Rorke's Drift was promoted a warrant officer on July 1, 1881 – a rank he continued to hold until his discharge at Aldershot on May 31, 1898, after 30 years' service.

Since his return to South Africa on pension Mr. Mabin, who holds the Zulu War Medal with bar 1878–79, Boer War medals, Meritorious Service Medal with annuity of £10 per annum, and gold medal presented by the Cape Government "for the longest and most meritorious service" (at the time of the Diamond Jubilee) has at various times been employed by the Barrack Department, Cape Town, and by the Pay Department. At present he is living a retired life, and, as already stated, enjoys the best of health.

One of Mr. Mabin's treasured possessions is his soldier's 'Small Book,' in which appears the signature of Prince Arthur of Connaught. The entry was made at Dover on February 29, 1872, when the Prince was a Captain in the Rifle Brigade. During his term as Governor-General of the Union, Prince Arthur renewed acquaintances with Mr. Mabin at Woodstock and was delighted to see this book.

Among his old army colleagues Mr. Mabin is always referred to as "The Fighting Clerk."

44c. An unidentified South African newspaper (possibly the *Natal Mercury*), 22 January 1937

A Survivor Tells the Story of Rorke's Drift

"The Fighting Clerk," as ex-Sergeant-Major Superintending Clerk G.W. Mabin was called in the '80's, is living with his daughter at 20 William Street, Woodstock, Capetown.

Big, heavy-jowled clear-eyed, with a moustache which droops at the corners of his mouth, he still has the bearing of a soldier of the line.

His voice retains the resonant power of that of the sergeant-major of the parade ground. His hearing is good. He walks about, he sees, and he remembers …

In an interview with "The Natal Mercury" he recalled that late afternoon nearly 60 years ago at Rorke's Drift. He was a colour-sergeant then, in the 24th Regiment. He had accompanied colonel Glynn's central column at the invasion of Zululand.

Well he remembers the impi's attack, and the desperate 12-hour battle 104 British soldiers had with 4,000 Zulu warriors. Six times during that night the Zulus got within the entrenchments of the little riverside hospital base camp. Each time they were driven back at bayonet point.

And at dawn Colour-Sergeant Mabin and 86 other weary, dirty, blood-bespattered men gazed at the shambles about them.

Seventeen of the garrison had been killed. Ten had been wounded. And all about them lay the half-naked, war-plumed bodies of 350 of the warriors of Dubulamanzi, Cetewayo's brother.

The rest had fled. And Natal had been saved from invasion …

… One of his most cherished souvenirs of the Battle of Rorke's Drift is a copy of a Natal newspaper published shortly after the battle. It contains a full account of it, running into several columns. And it also has the names of all the soldiers who were there.

"You see, son," he said, "there's a lot of people who say they were at Rorke's Drift during the Zulu War. They probably were – months after the battle. But all our names are here."

Another souvenir is a Rorke's Drift Bible presented to him by a committee of women in England. It is inscribed in gold on the cover as such, with Mr. Mabin's name written on the flyleaf.

44d. *Rockhampton Evening News* (Australia), 9 August 1938

Survivor of Heroic Defence of Rorke's Drift.

One of the last – if not the last – survivors of the heroic defence of Rorke's Drift, during the Zulu War of 1879, is Warrant-Officer George Mabin, of Capetown. He is 90.

Warrant-Officer Mabin comes from Bristol. His sister, 81-year-old Mrs. Florence King, who has lived in Capetown for 47 years, was on a visit to London. She told a London "Star" reporter;

"My brother still receives a pension of £10 a year which was awarded by Queen Victoria, who also gave him a gold medal for his part in the defence during the siege.

"I have often heard him tell the story of the terrible night when the little station at Rorke's Drift was attacked.

"There were only a few soldiers there who had been left to guard the stores and the hospital when during the night 4000 Zulu warriors attacked.

Frantic Defence.

"My brother was on the head-quarters' staff. He told me that a cavalryman, his head bandaged, galloped into the station and gave the alarm. He had come from a nearby station that had been wiped out.

"Frantic preparations of defence were made. The defenders made a bulwark with wagons, rice bags and biscuit boxes.

"They could not see the Zulus until they set fire to the hospital. Then they became targets for the defenders rifles.

"My brother said that he fired his rifle so many times that night that when morning came he could not raise his arm, so bruised was his shoulder by the kicks of the weapon.

"Six times in succession they drove out parties which got within the barricades."

The courage of the little defence force proved a turning point in the war.

44e. *Cape Argus* (South Africa), 24 October 1938

Rorke's Drift Veteran
"Old Dad" Mabin Dies Aged 90
Took Part In Many Battles

"Fighting Clerk" (ex-Sergeant-Major G.W.) Mabin, the last known survivor of the 124 of the defence of Rorke's Drift 59 years ago, died at his home at 20, William-street, Woodstock, in the early hours of yesterday morning. Ailing since August, he reached on October 3 the 90th birthday which he had set his heart on living to celebrate, with the good wishes of his 45 descendants and host of military friends, to whom he was also affectionately known as "Old Dad" Mabin.

Born in Bristol in 1848 Mr. Mabin enlisted in the British Army in 1868, and took part in many historic battles before he retired after 30 years of service. Although it was for his part in the battle of Rorke's Drift that he was most celebrated, it was in the 1881 Boer War that he won the soubriquet of "The Fighting Clerk."

Beside Colley

At the battle of Majuba he was standing only a few feet away from General Colley when that leader fell with a bullet through his forehead.

"Old Dad" Mabin retired from the army in 1898. The later years of his life he spent with a daughter in Woodstock. Active until a few months ago he spent his time between his garden and the Castle and other meeting places of military folk, among whom, regardless of rank, he was held in the greatest affection.

Until his death he remained in full possession of a remarkable memory. He was able to give a most graphic description of how, at dawn on January 23, 1879, 124 grimed and bleeding men stood surveying the shambles around them and the ruin of the little riverside hospital base at Rorke's Drift, which, for 12 hours, they had defended against the repeated onslaughts of 3,000 picked Zulu warriors.

Dubulumanzi's Impi

Among them lay the bodies of nearly 400 black warriors, belonging to the impi of Dubulumanzi, Cetewayo's brother, who had led the attack on Rorke's Drift after 800 British soldiers had been wiped out at Isandhlwana. Among the biscuit tins and mealie sacks of which the Rorke's Drift laager was hurriedly improvised lay the bodies of 17 men who had fallen in the battle which saved Natal from massacre at the hands of Cetewayo's hordes.

Rorke's Drift was a small depot of provisions established with a hospital base on the banks of the Buffalo River to keep the line of communication with Natal open. It was left in charge of two young officers, Lieutenants Chard and Bromhead with 141 men.

The post was attacked by one of the Zulu king's "crack" impis a few hours after 800 men left by Lord Chelmsford at Isandhlwana (the hill of "The Little Hand") had been wiped out.

In that memorable battle "Old Dad" Mabin, who fought also through the thick of Ingogo, Majuba and Laing's Nek, got off with only a slight wound in the shin, caused by a spent bullet.

"Sunset Parade"

At 6 p.m. to-morrow a "Sunset Parade" will be held in memory of "Old Dad" Mabin by the Moths organisation of which he was a life member.

45. 2-24/1731 Private John Manley, 'A' Company, 2/24th Foot

45a. *Beeston Gazette and Echo*, 25 October 1924

Military Funeral.

One of the few survivors of the Rorke's Drift episode, when less than a hundred British soldiers held at bay for 17 hours about 5,000 Zulus, was laid to rest with military honours in the Carlton Cemetery on Wednesday afternoon. The deceased was John Manley, whose home was at 5. Frederick Terrace, Livingstone Street, Nottingham, where he had lived for nine years. He had served 18 years with the colours, twelve with the 24th Foot, now the South Wales Borderers, and six with the 28th Foot.

He left the service with the rank of sergeant, and became in civilian life a painter and decorator.

Many times he has described to his family and relations the drama of Rorke's Drift, where, by the light of a burning hospital, the sick and wounded fought side by side with the hale and hearty, and every man that could raise a finger to help himself was called into the firing line. He himself was in the hospital when the Zulus impis rolled up to the attack, and recalled that many of his fellow patients fought in their shirts so desperate was the situation.

It was not possible to provide a gun carriage at the funeral, but the coffin was draped with the Union Jack, and a bugler who sounded the 'Last Post' over the grave, and a party of bearers were supplied from Normanton Barracks, the depot of the Notts and Derbyshire Regiment.

The first part of the funeral service was conducted at the Church of the Sacred Heart, Main Street, Carlton, and was conducted by Father Austin Williamson, of St. Edward's, Bluebell Hill, where the deceased was accustomed to worship. He leaves a widow and grown-up family.

46. 25B/1284 Private Charles Mason, (Frederick Herbert Brown), 'B' Company, 2/24th Foot

46a. Extract from a letter from Mason to his family [author's collection]

Rork,s Drift Natal South Africa
Feby 8th 1879

Dear Cary Mary & Charly

I write these few lines to you ought this will find you all in good health as it leaves me at present thank God

Dear Cary whe are at war with the Zulus the Regiment crossed the bufloe river into Zulu land on the 10th of January and camped there they had a bit of a skirmish on the 11th of the month but very few negoes ough killed on the 15th the Regt moved further into Zulu land to a place called izila valley that is between two very high hills and camped there there was not much fighting done till the 22nd of January they received orders that the 2nd 24th and 4 guns of artilry, and mounted troups mounted police and voluntiers and carbeniers leaving in camp 5 Companies of the 1st 24th and 1 Company of the 2nd 24th that was G. Company and 2 big guns of oughtio and mounted police and Native contingents and servants and cooks numbering all about 900 well you must understand the enemy had been watching the movents of the troups and early in the morning of the 22nd there was a number of kaffers showed I for the intension of drawing the troups out well the Generall on seeing this advanced in ought of them with the column as I stated before well you must understand there was thousands of Kaffers behind a hill watching the column leave the camp they watched them till they got some 10 miles away then we are told by those who escaped that the enemy sent a small body of kaffers into camp to lay down their arms and give I up well you know that was only done for a blind to see how many there were in camp and how these were situated the troups in camp they lay down their arms and the colonel in command let them go away well from what we hear they whent back again to the main body of the enemy and told them how many was in camp – the tropps that where in camp thought no more about it not thinking they were going to be attacked well there where all over the camp some asleep some washing there clothes others cooking servants busy waiting on the officers

well Dear Cary the alarm was given that the enemy was advancing on them every man flew for his rifle and amanition then they could see that the kaffers where surrounding them they commenced fireing on them whe hear there where about 15 thousand kaffers well every man ought till the last there a few escaped but not many they ought for some hours but all was in vain the kaffers got oughtion of they camp and murdered every poor fellow that was in camp they took the big guns and amanition and rifles and every thing they could get hold of there were 5 boys belonging to the Band poor little fellows they where left in camp the black buggers got the boys and tied them up by the hands to the waggons and butchered them cut their privates off and stuk them in there mouths

Dear Cary I forgot to tell you that my Company was left behind to take charge of the Commersery Stores at Rorks Drift well whe was all busy the time of the fight I was on guard myself that day whe had news the kaffers where coming to attack us well you can guess how whe felt about 100 of us sick and all well whe made a bit of a fire round the Commersery whe managed to make some sort of fort true enough they came to murder us the same as the poor lot in the other camp but they got took in there was about 4-000 of them and 130 of us sick all those that could get out of the hospital got out the best way they could there were two or three poor fellows that were very bad in hospital and whe could not get them out because the kaffers set fire to it and got in the hospital and cut the four fellows up to pieces well we ought bravely from 3 o Clock an the 22nd till day break 23rd when reinforcements came the loss on our side where 13 killed and 4 wounded thank God I am alive myself that is all at present I dare say you have seen in the paper about the cut up of the 1st & 2, 24th 5 Compys of the 1st-24 & 1 Compy of the 2/24 G Compy

Give my kind love to Mary Tom all the children & Charely & Dick & Mr & Mrs Schooley and all the children Dear Cary I have not had my clothes off since the 22nd of Jany

Dear Cary you excuse the writering because I could not get any ink no more at present, from your affectionate Brother Fred. God Bless one and all of you good by

1284 Private Charles Mason
B Company 2/24 Regiment
Rorkes Drift Natal
South Africa

47. Corporal Jesse Handcock Mayor, 1st/3rd Natal Native Contingent

47a. Extract from a letter written by Jesse Mayor to the Colonial Secretary requesting employment, 22 June 1884 [Western Cape Archives and Record Service, Cape Town, South Africa, CO Vol. 4234, Ref. M78]

Sir,

I have the honor to elicit employment under the Government in any suitable capacity.

I am 24 years of age, a fair clerk, of business habits and speak the dutch language. I served through the Gcaleka and Gaika rebellion in the C.M. Rifles for which I received the war-medal with clasp for 1877 & 78, in the Zulu-war in the Natal Native Contingent as a N.C. Officer and was severely wounded in the first engagement fought at Sirayo's stronghold on January the 12th, served also at the defence of Rorke's-drift post after escaping from the hospital there on January the 22nd, 1879. I also served in Lonsdale's Horse during the latter part of the same war, in 1880 & 81 I served as a corporal in Bakers Horse during the disturbance in Pondoswine country and took part in the operations in Griqualand-East and Basutoland.

I hope Sir, that having served my adopted country for so long a time and been severely wounded in its defence, I may be considered to have some claim, and that you will favourably consider this my application.

I have the honor to be, Sir,
Your obedient servant
Jesse Handcock Mayor

48. 2260 Sergeant Frederick Augustus Millne, 2/3rd Foot

48a. *London Evening Standard,* 17 April 1891

Rorke's Drift and Thobal.
To the Editor of the Standard.

Sir, – With regard to the letter in *The Standard* of to-day, I can fully confirm the statement made by Mr. W.J. Humble-Crofts both as to the supply of arms the Zulu regiments had and the time we received information of the taking of the Isandhlwana camp.

I was under the immediate command of Lieutenant Chard, in charge of the stores of the R.E. Pontoon Train of the Third Column at Rorke's Drift. Shortly after one p.m. on the 22d January, 1879, a party of native women and children, with a few decrepit old men, came down to the river, and wanted to be put across, as "Cetewayo had killed all the white men."

After obtaining permission, Daniels and I ferried them over. About an hour after a transport rider, named Stone, galloped down, and told us the camp had been taken. About the same time a trooper of the N.M. Police gave information at Lieutenant Bromhead's camp, near the stores.

That there would have been plenty of time to get away is proved by the fact that the whole of the company of the Natal Native Contingent, together with some mounted Basutos, were well out of sight by the time the attack commenced.

The Zulus had arms of all descriptions, from the old Dutch roer to the Martinis they had taken from the poor fellows of the 24th at Isandhlwana. Quite a large pile of firearms was burnt when the ground was cleared after the fight.

I am, Sir, your obedient servant,
Fredk. A. Millne, late Colour Serjeant,
Second Battalion, The Buffs.
Matlock, April 16.

48b. *Manchester Evening Chronicle,* 2 December 1905

A Life's Adventures.
Story of Rorke's Drift Hero,
Who Drew A Cheque for Forty Thousand Dollars.

On an eventful morning in January, 1879, the remains of a British column moved down from Isandhlwana to Rorke's Drift. The Isandhlwana camp had been, in the forcible language of the Zulus "eaten up," and the savage warriors, primed with victory, made straight for the guard of white men on the Buffalo River. No one in the ranks of what proved to be the relieving force expected to find a living soul at Rorke's Drift, for the Zulus were seen retreating from the place, and volumes of smoke were rising from the hospital.

But the Union Jack was still flying, and a British cheer rang out as Colonel Russell and his men galloped into the beleaguered encampment at the Drift. One of the men who kept the flag flying is in Manchester today, and chatted recently to an "E.C." representative of his experiences on that memorable occasion.

War and Fortune.

Ex-Colour-Sergeant Fred. A. Millne, who is now caretaker of Princess-road Higher Grade School, has seen not only the fortune of war, but also the "war of fortune". One day, when out in the Far East, some Shanghai policemen rushed up to him excitedly with the story that he had drawn the winning number in a lottery, and was worth forty thousands of dollars. It was true. The sergeant is also one of the few men who have seen reports of their own deaths in print. Further he has been shipwrecked. So to the tale.

As a lad of eighteen he joined the 2nd Battalion of the Buffs in 1872 at Dover. He went to Ireland with his Regiment, and later gained the certificate as an instructor in field works at Chatham. Proceeding to South Africa in 1879 he was wrecked in the St. Lawrence on Paternoster reefs. Everybody on board was saved, and the regiment was stationed first at Durban, and then at Pietermaritzburg.

When hostilities became likely with the Zulus, the sergeant was sent with the pontoon stores and equipment of the 3rd column which was to enter Zululand by Rorke's Drift. Arriving there about a week in advance of any other soldier, he accomplished his work, and on the 12th of January, the troops had passed over, and pitched their camps at Isandhlwana.

News of Disaster.

Firing was heard in Rorke's Drift camp on the morning of the 22nd, and about eleven o'clock a party of native women and children with a few decrepit old men, came to the river bank and wanted to be put across, as "Cetewayo had killed all the white men." A transport rider soon after galloped into camp with news of the Isandhlwana disaster. Under the superintendence of Lieutenants Chard and Bromhead, a breastwork of sacks of Indian corn was raised between the hospital and the stone kraals. Wagons were pulled in on the other side. The Natal Native Contingent and some Basutos left for safety.

"While this was going on," said the sergeant, "Daniels and I were getting things in order on our pontoons. We wanted to moor in mid-stream and, if need be, hold them back." Behind that modest statement lurks the heroic. A leading authority of the time interpreted the incident thus – "The pont guards Daniels and Sergeant Millne of the 3rd Buffs, with five or six men, volunteered to moor the ponts in midstream and keep the ford against the whole Zulu vanguard. They volunteered for a more than forlorn hope, for there was not a chance that one of them would survive the encounter. Lieutenant Chard did not accept that offer. He had other uses for such soldiers."

Zulus' Assaults.

"We joined the remainder of the force," continued the sole representative of the Buffs, "and the firing was pretty heavy as we scrambled over into the enclosure. Just after we got into the laager the enemy advanced in force. Silently they came, taking advantage of every bit of cover that presented itself. Their men dropped fast under our fire. A stalwart Induna yelled out an order. It was his last. On came the mass with a rush, shouting 'Usutu, Usutu.'

"They hurled themselves on our feeble defence, to be repulsed by our concentrated fire and by bayonets. Again and again they came on. Assegais clashed against rifle barrels. They shouted their war-cries and we gave British cheers. At first I felt nervous, but the savage instinct, the blood thirst came on top. So close was the conflict that one soldier felled two Zulus with his fists.

Victoria Cross Won.

"All the afternoon the fight waged, and in the evening the hospital was fired by the Zulus fixing burning bunches of grass on their spear and aiming at the thatch. Six times did the Zulus try to rush the place, and in my opinion they would have wiped us out had they not provided the light which enabled us to perceive their movements. A desultory fire was kept up till dawn."

Next morning the little garrison saw more natives advancing and thought they were to have another day's fighting. But Russell's mounted men were also observed coming from the same direction, and the Undi fell back.

Sergt. Millne served afterwards three years with his regiment in Singapore, and took his discharge in Hong Kong in 1883, being appointed instructor to the Shanghai municipal police force. When his engagement was nearly completed he drew half of the winning ticket in a Manila lottery, getting for his six dollars £8,000. "Had I put it in the bank" he said, "I should not be in Manchester now."

Home with his Fortune.
He came home to England and started a big grocery business with a partner.

"It's like this," quoth the ex-soldier, "You've read Mark Twain. In the first instance I have the money and you have the experience; in the second I have the experience."

Married life, however, toned down his disappointment. He was afterwards assistant labour master at Crumpsall Workhouse, and in 1895 took up his present duties.

It was in the regimental paper of the Buffs in August, 1890, that Sergeant Millne was reported as having died on his way home to enjoy his fortune.

Sergeant Millne has a little daughter born on the anniversary of Rorke's Drift. She was christened Ada Rorke. The sergeant figures in the Sixth Standard readers in use at Princess-road, and with such a history is it any wonder that his name is underlined or that the boys occasionally gather round him in admiration and say, "Oh, Mr. Millne, we've been reading about you."

49. 25B/968 Private Thomas Moffatt, 'B' Company, 2/24th Foot

49a. *Runcorn Examiner,* 16 February 1889

A Rorke's Drift Hero in trouble at Runcorn.
Thomas Moffat, a labourer, was brought up at Runcorn Petty Sessions, on Monday, charged with having wounded Michael Rowley, a chemical labourer with intent to do him grevious bodily harm. Mr. J.W. Knowles defended. – It appeared that both men had been soldiers. The prisoner had taken part in the defence of Rorke's Drift, South Africa, and the prosecutor had served his country in Egypt. They lived together at Plant's lodging house, and on Monday afternoon they had some words about the price of 4 pints of ale they had had on the previous day. Without making any threat, the prisoner deliberately took a large bread knife from a box on the table and stabbed Rowley several times on the head. Rowley struggled with the prisoner, and the landlord entering the room, stopped the affray. Afterwards

Rowley went to the surgery of Dr. McDougall who dressed his wounds, and the prisoner was apprehended by P.C. Gosling. Dr. McDougall deposed that when brought to his surgery Rowley's head and face were covered in blood. He had three wounds which penetrated to the bone on his head. Rowley said he wished to be the best of friends with the prisoner and nothing would give him greater pleasure than his release. The Bench committed the prisoner to the Chester Assizes for trial, but admitted him to bail, himself in £40 and two sureties of £20.

[Moffatt was brought before the Assizes at Chester Castle on 7 March 1889, charged with 'Felonious Wounding'. He was duly acquitted and discharged.]

50. 25B/662 Private John Murphy, 'B' Company, 2/24th Foot

50a. *South Wales Argus,* 3 June 1914

Newport veteran's story – 662 J. Murphy.
A rescue from burning hospital:
Survivors of the small Company who gallantly held Rorke's Drift against an overwhelming force of victory flushed Zulus are few in number, but the discovery of one apparently leads to the discovery of others, Private John Williams V.C.; of Cwmbran, was no sooner thrust into the limelight than Private Sam Pitt, of Nantymoel was unearthed, and now it is learned that there is living in Newport another member of the brave band which added such lustre to British arms. Mr. John Murphy, of 41, William Street, Newport, belonged to the old 24th Regt; and after going through the Kaffir War played his part in the Zulu campaign. He tells a very similar story to that narrated by Private Sam Pitt, and January 1879, he declares, has never been, and is not likely ever to be, effaced from his memory.

Handful against thousands:
It was on January 22nd that the messenger from Isandlwana reached them with direful tidings that the British advance force had been almost wiped out. They knew then what to expect, but handful as they were, there were no cowards amongst them, and they determined either to thrash the Zulus

or die fighting to the last. Indeed, he says, there was no other thing to do, for Cetshwayo's warriors had few notions in the way of dealing mercifully with a foe they had the power to slaughter.

To fix up defences worthy of the name did not appear to be a very hopeful task, for they had no fortifications, simply two old mission rooms, one of which was used as a hospital and the other for storage of provisions, ammunitions ect. Apart from invalids, the British force numbered 84, and it was realised that their visitors would make them look a little lot indeed, bags of biscuits and mealies formed a hastily improvised entrenchment and this was all that was between them and the advancing horde.

Early in the afternoon the enemy were sighted, and soon the country around was black with them. In another hour they were within rifle range, and the ghastly fun began. The fire, however, seemed to make no difference, and on they rolled, the defenders having eventually to retire to an inner "fortification." It was a terrible struggle, but nothing to the fight at close quarters as darkness set in. Private Murphy described the fight at length, but as this is a matter of history – familiar, it is to be hoped, to all – the details need not be given further.

Rescue from hospital:

One incident, however, shall be narrated. When the hospital caught fire, and it was necessary to get the inmates out, Private Murphy did his full share of the work, and one difficult task which fell to his lot was pulling through the window a Private named Conolley, who had a broken leg. The next man near that particular spot was shot through the head. Meanwhile the battle continued to rage, but eventually the fine defence prevailed, and the enemy drew off. The British casualties were few, the Zulus had lost hundreds – for in the morning the ground was covered with their dead and dying. Private Murphy was very emphatic on one point, and, though he may be in error it is perhaps worth recording that he thinks the part played by certain officers was unduly extolled at the time and since. They were not he declares, nearly so conspicuous in the fight as they have been made out to be. Murphy (who at Rorke's Drift was slightly wounded in the foot) was 24 years in the army, and then, having reached the age of 60, had to leave, but declares that at the time he felt fit to serve another 24.

51. 25B/1480 Private William Osborne, 'B' Company, 2/24th Foot

51a. *Free Press of Monmouthshire*, 21 January 1927

Rorke's Drift Hero.
Mr William Osborne,
Blaenavon.
Description of the Fight.

Yet another Rorke's Drift hero has been "discovered," and on this occasion at Blaenavon, in the person of Wm. Osborne, who resides with his wife at 79, Cambrian Row. Mr Osborne, who will be 69 on Feb. 20th, saw active service in the Kaffir War of '77, and the Zulu Wars of '78 and '79, in the old 24th Foot (South Wales Borderers).

Born at Duke's Street, Blaenavon, Mr Wm. Osborne (the son of Mr Thomas Osborne, who was employed at the Blaenavon Co.'s Mills), when quite a youngster, joined the Regular Army, and took the Queen's silver coin at Pontypool. He was at once transferred to Brecon and shortly afterwards moved to Chatham. In November of the same year he was put on draft for Africa, and sailed from Portsmouth in the old Himilaya. Mr Osborne distinctly remembers that one of the first jobs when going on board was to empty the ticks of the old straw, which were then taken to the quartermaster for refilling. The voyage, which lasted about five weeks, was a good one, no heavy weather being encountered. Upon landing the troops entrained and travelled via Durban to Kingwilliamstown. From here a march lasting between two and three weeks brought them in touch with the enemy.

The incident at Rorke's Drift is graphically described by Mr Osborne. A fatigue party of about 100 were told off for commissariat duties and preparing the food for the main column. The small company was in the charge of a captain, and no untoward incident happened for some time. The "kitchen" was an outdoor one, adjacent to a house which had been occupied by a Dutchman who carried on the business of a shoemaker. This house, with a thatched roof, had been vacated when the British reached it, the only living things left being a domestic cat and an old sow. Sixteen hoggets (or small pigs) had been drowned, evidently by the Savages, who were afraid of the swine.

"But we saved the old pig," said Mr Osborne, "and had some fine meat from her."

An interesting description of the method of baking the bread was given. Large ant-hills, were dotted all around the place. At the top of each of these a hole would be made, and, at the bottom, a cavity, into which a fire would be placed, and soon the ants would emerge in millions from the hole at the top. The fire would then be taken out and leavened dough placed in the cavity, which would quickly bake. (This is a principle employed even today, and is known as the "Aldershot oven.")

The first intimation that the enemy were approaching the camp was given by one of the company, who had been washing at the river, and it was discovered that the camp, or dump, had been cut off from the main column. Preparations were rapidly made for defending Rorke's House, which, besides being used for a store for food, was also a hospital. Including the "casualties" there were in all about 100 men. The Zulus, numbering between 3,000 and 4,000 and practically naked, attacked the drift with great courage in face of deadly rifle fire. Their weapons were mostly assegais (spears), but that they were in possession of some ammunition is proved by the fact that Corporal Jack Lines (at one time a postman in the Eastern Valley) received a bullet-wound in the back of the neck, "which bullet his wife still possesses," said Mr Osbornc.

"We had seventeen hours of hard fighting," continued the narrator of the story, "If we were all third-class shots it would have been all over with us. They came on in their thousands, and we made them jump! We took six or seven prisoners, but we sent them out into the open again. If you didn't catch 'em smart as they put their hands up, they were gone like a dart! Jack Lines and I were firing together with our ammunition placed on the wall besides us. The corporal was in the act of raising his rifle when his arms dropped helplessly to his sides from a bullet wound in the back of the neck. The enemy set the thatched roof afire, but we pulled the roof off during the night to stop that little game. It was 17 hours before relief came."

Mr Osborne remembers a few of those who were in the engagement, including Captain Browning and Jack Williams, V.C. (Cwmbran).

From Africa Mr Osborne was sent to Gibraltar, and from there to India, where he completed his six years' regular service. He returned to Blaenavon in 1883 at 26 years of age, and began work underground for the Blaenavon Co. After his return he married Miss Martha Whitcombe, daughter of Mr and Mrs Joseph Whitcombe of Abersychan. There is one daughter (Mrs S. Williams) and an adopted son, Mr Wm. Osborne (Wm. Bumell), the latter who figures in Blaenavon billiards circles.

Africa A Great Country.

Asked his opinion of the countries he had visited, Mr Osborne sang the praises of Africa, which, he thought, was the greatest country in the world.

There are two things which he treasures. One is his medal with three bars which Mrs Osborne wears as a brooch, and the other is a Bible, presented by the ladies of the Rorke's Drift Testimonial Fund, and signed by "Miss Wilkinson."

51b. *Western Mail,* 21 February 1931

Blaenavon Veteran.
Another Rorke's Drift Survivor Dead.

Another of the few remaining links with one of the greatest stands in the annals of British military history – the defence of Rorke's Drift by a small band mainly composed of a company of the South Wales Borderers against the Zulu hordes of Cetewayo – has been broken by the death at Blaenavon of Mr. William Osborne, 73 years of age.

After service in the Kaffir and Zulu campaigns, Mr. Osborne was on garrison duty at Gibraltar and in India. He returned to his native Blaenavon in 1883 where he subsequently worked under ground.

There is confusion about proper Rorke's Drift survivors. William Osborne, however, was in the company that actually came through the siege, along with Mr. John Williams (Fielding), the veteran Cwmbran V.C., who received the decoration for valour for rescue work when the Zulus had set fire to the base hospital.

52. 25B/1186 Private Samuel Pitt, 'B' Company, 2/24th Foot

52a. *Western Mail*, 11 May 1914

Another Rorke's Drift Hero.
Nantymoel Man's Story Of Zulu's Attack
It appears that Private John Williams, V.C., of Cwmbran, is not the last survivor of the gallant band which defended Rorke's Drift. There is at least one other in South Wales in the person of Private Sam Pitt, of Nantymoel, who looks hale and hearty enough to go through another campaign, and young enough to enjoy a few more decades of life.

A *Western Mail* man enjoyed an hour or two in the company of Private Pitt. The word "enjoyed" is used advisedly, for to be in Pitt's company is to be quite at ease and interested. He has a pleasant, homely way, and his stories are mellowed with age and ripe experience.

His account of the terrible struggle against overwhelming numbers at Rorke's Drift was perhaps the more thrilling because it was told in simple language.

The Zulus' Attack.
"Our first news that the Zulus were advancing into British territory," he said, "was brought to us on January 22, 1879, by a messenger from Isandhula, where our advance force had been almost annihilated. We at once set about making preparations for a defence. There was no fortifications, merely two old mission rooms, which were used as a hospital and for the storage of provisions and ammunition. Our total strength, apart from invalids, was 85, and there was no time to throw up entrenchments, but we knocked up a rough defence of bags of biscuits and mealies.

"It was about half-past two in the afternoon when we first caught sight of the enemy rounding the bend of a hill from the direction of Isandhula, and the country was soon black with them. We were without artillery, and it was an hour before the enemy was within rifle shot. Then we pounded away for all we were worth, raining bullets among them, but on they came, not fearing death. They were sharp enough, however, to take advantage of every bit of cover they could.

"Fire away as we could, it was impossible to keep them at a distance, and we were forced to retire to an inner enclosure.

"By nine o'clock, when darkness had set in, they got to close quarters, and were gripping our bayonets through the spaces left between the bags for firing. It was 'touch and go' at that time, and how they were kept out was almost miraculous. Just when the fray was at the thickest a loud 'Hoo-hoo' sounded from the hills, and we had quiet for a while. They seemed to lie under cover for a time. Then there was sound all round, and a renewed attack was made.

Hospital In Flames.

"The hospital, which was situated, outside our defences, and from which the invalids had been removed, was ablaze, and in the glare the Zulus held up their dead comrades for us to fire at, the idea, I think, being to get us to expend our ammunition. Somehow or other, we kept them at bay, and only one got over our defences. Needless to say, he did not live long. By-and-bye they took themselves off. We found we had come off luckily with only five casualties.

"In the morning we found the ground strewn with the dead and dying. We reckoned we had accounted for 875, but the school books tell you 400 or 500."

Private Sam Pitt is 58 years of age, and enlisted in the Warwickshire (now the South Wales Borderers) at Cardiff on February 9, 1877. He saw active service in the Kaffir War the same and following years, and in one of the engagements was shot through the head. His total service in the Army and Reserve was twelve years, and his discharge is marked, "Conduct – very good." He holds the South African medal with the clasp, dated 1877–8–9, and an illuminated address presented by the burgesses of Durban.

At the age of 58, he toils as a labourer underground at the Wyndham Colliery, pensionless. Is not this an instance in which the War Office should recognise Pitt's service to his country?

53. Lieutenant Thomas Purvis, 1st/3rd Natal Native Contingent

53a. Extract from a statement by Lieutenant Walter Higginson, 1st/3rd Regiment, Natal Native Contingent [National Archives, London, WO32/7726]

"We got in there [Helpmekaar], about 7 p.m. I found Capt. Stevenson of 2/3rd. Regiment N.N.C. had brought Lieut Purvis up from Rorke's Drift where he had been in hospital as he had been wounded in the arm in the cave fighting on Sunday 12th January, he asked me to help him to take Purvis to Ladysmith, and as I was very wet & hungry and could not get a rifle there, I thought as I was no use, I was just as well away, so at about 9 p.m. we started, and got to Dundee at 3 a.m., from there we pushed on to Ladismith and got there on Friday, being obliged to go slowly on account of Purvis … "

53b. A minute paper, filed by Major General Clifford, enquiring after the state of health of Lieut. Thos. Purvis Natal Native Contingent [Pietermaritzburg Archives Repository, Pietermaritzburg, South Africa, NAB 2264/1879]

Statement of the case of Lieut T. Purvis, N.N.C.

Lieut Purvis aged 27 single an offr in the NNC was present at the actions at Sirayo's Kraal & Rorkes Drift & recd. a bullet wound thro the Deltoid muscle of the left arm. This healed satisfactorily but dysentery of an acute form set in & for this he was invalided. He was passing numerous motions of a dysenteric character with blood great … & accompanied with pain in the abdomen increased on the slightest pressure. This caused great exhaustion [illegible] & debility but the disease succumbed to large doses of Ipecacuanha (3 frs) twice & three times a day proceeded by MXXV of Laudanum other astringents such as Tannin, lead & opium was used with advantages but he still remains weak & debilitated altho the motions are now healthy both in character & number.

His wound has disabled his arm & he suffers great pain from it. His wound & disease was caused in and by the service.

V. Ash AMD Surgeon in charge
Fort Napier 22.4.79.

p.s. This officer is not likely to be fit for service within a less period than a year

54. Surgeon James Henry Reynolds, M.B., Army Medical Department

54a. *Army Medical Department Annual Report for the Year 1878,* Appendix V

Report of the Defence of "Rorke's Drift."
By Surgeon-Major James Henry Reynolds, M.B., V.C.

On January the 22nd at about 12.30 p.m. we were surprised at Rorkes Drift by hearing big guns in our neighbourhood, and almost immediately I commenced climbing up the hill of Oscarberg in company with the Missionary Met and Mr Smith, Army Chaplain. We expected to get a view of what was happening, but on looking across the Buffalo River from the top we discovered that Isandlana Mountain (five miles away) shut from our view the scene of action. The reports of three more big guns were distinctly audible after we completed the ascent, there being, I should say, a quarter of an hour's interval between each of them.

At 1.30 a large body of natives marched over the slopes of Isandlana in our direction, their purpose evidently being to examine ravines and ruined kraals for hiding fugitives.

These men we took for our own Native Contingent. Soon afterwards appeared four horsemen on the Natal side of the river galloping in the direction of our post, one of them was a regular soldier, and feeling they might possibly be messengers for additional medical assistance I hurried down to the hospital and got there as they rode up. They looked awfully scared and I was at once startled to find one of them riding Surgeon-Major Shepard's pony. They shouted frantically, "the camp at Isandlana has been taken by the enemy and all our men in it massacred, that no power could stand against the enormous number of the Zulus, and the only chance for us all was by immediate flight."

Lieutenant Bromhead, Acting Commissary Dalton, and myself forthwith consulted together, Lieutenant Chard not having as yet joined us from the pontoon, and we quickly decided that with barricades well placed around our present position a stand could best be made where we were.

In other words, removing the sick and wounded would have been embarrassing to our movement, and desertion of them was never thought of.

Just at this period Mr. Dalton's energies were invaluable. Without the smallest delay, which would have been so fatal for us, he called upon the men (all eager for doing) to carry the mealie sacks here and there for defences, and it was charming to find in a short time how comparatively protected we had made ourselves. Lieutenant Chard arrived as this work was in progress and gave many useful orders as regards the lines of defence. He approved also of the hospital being taken in, and between the hospital orderlies, convalescent patients (8 or 10) and myself, we loop-holed the building and made a continuation of the commissariat defences round it. The hospital, however, occupied a wretched position having a garden and shrubbery close by, which afterwards proved so favourable to the enemy, but comparing our prospects with that of the Isandlana affair we felt that the mealie barriers might afford us a moderately fair chance. The patients, I must mention, were retained in the hospital although situated at our weak end, as every part of the commissariat house was crowded with stores, and we did not consider either building would be taken unless with the fall of the whole place.

When our plans of temporary defence were nearly completed, I was relieved by seeing Mr. Met, and Mr. Smith safely inside the laager. They had just then returned from the hill where they remained up to a late moment continuing to believe the natives I before alluded to were our men, instead of which they were the very Zulus who fought against us later on at Rorkes Drift. Mr. Smith was at this time looking for his horse and told me afterwards he should have to remain as his Kafir groom had bolted, and apparently taken with him the horse.

Mr. Met was making preparations to ride away.

About 3.30 p.m. the enemy made their first appearance in a large crowd on the hospital side of our post, coming on in skirmishing order at a slow slinging run. We opened fire on them from the hospital at 600 yards, and although the bullets ploughed through their midst and knocked over many there was no check or alteration made in their approach. They seemed quite regardless of the danger, and what struck me as most strange they had no war cry, nor did they at this time fire a single shot in return.

As they got nearer they became more scattered, but the large bulk of them rushed for the hospital and the garden in front of it. My attention being altogether directed for a while to these points I cannot state with authority whether the Zulus whom I shortly afterwards saw in a large number on the opposite or north side of our fort got there by extending this body or if they came independently from the other direction, thereby carrying out their reputed mode of attack in a bull's horn fashion.

However it was, we found ourselves quickly surrounded by the enemy with their strong force holding the garden and shrubbery. From all sides, but especially the latter places, they poured on us a continuous fire, to which our men replied as quickly as they could reload their rifles; again and again the Zulus pressed forward, and retreated, until at last they forced themselves so daringly and in such numbers as to climb over the mealie sacks in front of the hospital, and drove the defenders from there behind an entrenchment of biscuit boxes, hastily formed with much judgment and forethought by Lieutenant Chard, R.E. I discovered afterwards that this officer when planning our defences reckoned on the assistance of the Basutos who deserted at the last moment.

It followed from this that our men at first had to be distributed over so large an area in proportion to our numbers as dangerously to weaken any one point and render it unequal to repel a determined rush, I am convinced but for this entrenchment our fort could not have held out five minutes longer.

A heavy fire from behind it was resumed with renewed confidence and with little confusion or delay, checking successfully the natives, and permitting a semi-flank fire from another part of the laager to play on them destructively. At this time too the loopholes in the hospital were made great use of, so that the combined fire had the desired effect of keeping the Zulus at bay. It was, however only temporary as after a short respite they came on again with redoubled vigour. Some of them gained the hospital verandah and there got hand to hand with our men defending the doors. Once they were driven back from here, to find shelter again in the garden, but others soon pressed forward in their stead, and having occupied the verandah in larger numbers than before pushed their way into the hospital where confusion on our side naturally followed. Everyone tried to escape as best he could, and owing to the rooms not communicating with one another the difficulties were insurmountable. Private Hook, 2/24th Regiment, who was acting hospital cook, and Private Connolly, 2/24th Regiment, a patient in hospital, made their way into the open at the back of the hospital, by breaking a hole in the wall with a pickaxe and then climbing over the sacks into the curtailed laager. Most of the patients escaped through the small window looking into what may be styled the neutral ground. Those who madly tried to get off by leaving the front of the hospital were all killed with the exception of Gunner Howard. He gained with most extraordinary luck a detached rear without being noticed by the enemy, and after dusk, the Zulus still being close about him, he left this retreat to hide himself in the long grass 400 or 500 yards away. He did not rejoin us until daylight the following morning when it was no longer dangerous to move about.

Private Hunter, Natal Mounted Police, was the only one killed of those who made an escape through the small window. He was shot dead while crossing over to the biscuit boxes after his exit through the window, by a fire from the enemy behind mealie sacks.

The only men actually killed in the hospital were three, excluding a Kafir under treatment for a compound fracture of femur. Their names were Sergeant Maxfield, Private Jenkins, both unable to assist in their escape (being debilitated by fever), and Private Adams, who was well able to move about but could not be persuaded to leave his temporary refuge in a small room, and face the danger of an attempt at escape to the laager. During this partial success of the enemy, very heavy firing was being made on our fort from all sides, and it was in this period we lost a large majority of our killed and wounded. The engagement continued more or less until about 7 o'clock p.m. and then when we were beginning to consider our situation rather hopeless the fire from our opponents appreciably slackened giving us some time for reflection. Lieutenant Chard here again shined in resource. Anticipating the Zulus making one more united dash for the fort and possibly gaining an entrance, he converted an immense stack of mealies standing in the middle of our enclosure and originally cone fashioned, into a comparatively safe place for a last retreat. I would explain that the top of the cone was removed and a number of sacks taken out from the heart of what remained, forming a sheltered space, sufficient to accommodate about 40 men, and in a position to make good shooting. Mr. Dunne, Commissariat officer, assisted in this work. Just as it was completed smoke from the hospital appeared and shortly burst into flames. The light given by it, however, proved advantageous to us *(it being now nightfall)*, a matter which the Zulus themselves must have recognised, as no further attack was made from that quarter. During the whole night following desultory firing was carried on by the enemy, and several feigned attacks were made, with much shouting of their war cry, but nothing of a continued or determined effort was again attempted by them. About 6 o'clock a.m. we found, after careful reconnoitring, that all the Zulus, with exception of a couple of stragglers, had left our immediate vicinity, and soon afterwards a large body of men were seen at a distance in Zululand marching towards us. For a long time, and even after redcoats were distinguished through our field-glasses, we believed them to be the enemy, some of them dressed in the kits of those who had fallen at Isandlana. Indeed we could not think otherwise, as the Basuto officer who escaped with his men from Isandlana and retreated on our post the day before reported that the General's party had been broken up into small lots, each trying to get back into the Colony by any route.

Not until the mounted infantry, forming an advanced party, crossed the Buffalo drift, about a quarter of a mile off, were we convinced of our relief. Then we raised a white flag *(for they were not certain of us either, seeing the hospital still smoking)* and gave three cheers, really feeling that it was all right for us.

I do not think it possible that men could have behaved better than did the 2/24th and the Army Hospital Corps *(three)*, who were particularly forward during the whole attack, as well as odds and ends of other regiments who happened to be present at Rorke's Drift on the occasion. It would be difficult to pick out the heroes from our garrison, but Corporal Schiess of the Natal Native Contingent *(a Swede by birth)* came under my notice as the most deserving of praise and recommendation.

54b. A letter written by John Chard in response to a request from Surgeon General J.A. Woolfryes for corroboration of Reynolds' actions at Rorke's Drift (see also Dalton's statement, vol. 1, account 15a) [National Archives, London, WO138/3]

The P.M.O.
S. Africa
Ladysmith
6th April 1879

Sir,

With reference to your letter and statement of Mr Dalton (returned herewith).

I have the honor to state that I did not myself witness the occurrence described by Mr Dalton, – With regard to Mr Dalton's remarks as to Surgeon Reynolds' activity and energy in helping in the work of defence, I can corroborate them entirely.

The wounded were not able to be removed there being no men spare for that purpose.

Surgeon Reynolds without the slightest hesitation attended to these men performing the necessary operations, and placing them under as good cover as could be got, where they fell.

In my official report of the action at Rorke's Drift on the 22 23rd Jany last. I brought Surgeon Reynolds name to the particular notice of his Excellency the Lieut General Commanding for his constant attention to the wounded under fire.

I have the honor to be Sir
Your most obedient servant
John R.M. Chard.
Lt. R.E.

54c. *Natal Mercury*, 28 August 1879

Public Presentation of the Victoria Cross to Two Officers of the 1-24th Regiment.

A special parade of all the troops there encamped was held at Pinetown at 8 a.m. on Tuesday, August 26th. The 17th Lancers, the 1-24th, the 3rd Buffs, and the depot battalions (numbering, all told, upwards of 2000 men) were present. Colonel Glyn having called upon Surgeon-Major Reynolds and Lieutenant Browne, both of the 1-24th regiment to step forward, announced, that by special permission, he had been deputed to present to each of them the decoration – of which any man might well be proud – of the Victoria Cross. To Dr. Reynolds it was awarded for bravery during the defence of Rorke's Drift; and to Lieutenant Browne for heroic conduct in saving the life of one of the mounted infantry under his command at Zlobane. The Colonel then dismounted from his horse and pinned the ribbon and cross upon the breast of each of the recipients; and with evident emotion he congratulated them, and trusted that they might for many years be spared to enjoy the high honour that they had won. The band of the 3rd Buffs performed, and many residents and visitors were present at the interesting ceremony. Amongst the visitors was the Rev. George Smith, the chaplain formerly to Colonel Glyn's column, and latterly to the second division. Mr. Smith, as is well known, took an active part in the defence of Rorke's Drift, rendered good service to the wounded and dying, and performed the last offices of the church over the slain upon the battle field of Ulundi.

We have seen how a brave doctor has been well and properly rewarded; how a V.C. has been added to his well merited promotion, whilst the College in which he was trained have conferred upon him two of its highest degrees.

With the clergyman above referred to how different matters stand! We see no expression of Royal favour – in the shape of an order of merit; no sign of approbation on the part of high dignitaries in ecclesiastical or academical quarters!

54d. *V.C. Magazine,* 30 April 1903

How V.C.s are Won.
A Tale of Rorke's Drift.
Told by Its Last V.C.

This spare, well-dressed gentleman, with silver hair, spectacles, and soft modulated voice, who smokes his cigarette at the club, and discusses the topics of the town with a pleasant relish for life, stood in a ring of mealie sacks by the Buffalo River on the scorching afternoon of January the 22nd, 1879, and helped to unlock the many fingered black hand that had suddenly crept round the mountain and clutched at the flag of England.

Lieutenant-Colonel J. H. Reynolds, V.C., was in those days a man of thirty-five, an Army doctor of Irish birth, a man with many years' knowledge of Africa at his back – a knowledge which proved of great avail when the black hand came round the mountain.

"Tell me," I asked him, "the story as you remember it." There are many people, be it known, who consider that the tale has not yet been told with completeness; in any case, it is a story that will never grow tedious with the telling.

"I remember," he said, smiling, "my feeling of disappointment when Lord Chelmsford marched away with his army, and left me with about a hundred other men to sit still and bite the bullet of inactivity at Rorke's Drift. There was to be no fighting for us, no doctoring for me: the army moved away to gain glory, and we sat down in what Lord Halsbury would call a sort of a base, to envy the other chaps their chances!

"But the dust had hardly cleared away from behind the heels of Chelmsford's force when we heard in the distance the booming of big guns. 'If we can't fight,' said I, 'at least we can look on – and off we went, clambering up the hill called Oscarberg to get a view of the battle. However, when we arrived on the top and looked across the Buffalo River, we discovered – to our indignation with Nature! – that the Isandlana mountain – five miles away – completely cut off the view. The firing we had heard, I must tell you, began at 12.30, and it was an hour after that we saw a body of native troops scrambling about on Isandlana. We took them for our own Native contingent and wondered how the other side was faring. In the midst of our wonderment three horsemen appeared in the distance riding for dear life. I thought they might be coming for some medical aid, and hurried down old Oscarberg to meet them. I was thinking of my chances of going forward to join our victorious army.

"But their tale wore a whiter face. The British force at Isandlana had been wiped away, like a speck from a piece of paper: crushed, beaten, destroyed, massacred by an overwhelming force of Zulus. We must fly for our lives – as quick as we could. I consulted with Bromhead (Chard had not then joined us from the Pontoon) and an ex-colour-sergeant, Dalton by name. The result of this conference was the determination to barricade ourselves with mealie sacks and to await the impi from Isandlana. It was here that Dalton proved something of a god in our ramshackle car. The colour-sergeant returned to him in a minute, and he was here, there and everywhere, quietly getting the men to put their backs into the work, The mind of that man was the working of destiny. Now I must tell you we built a fairly big laager to permit of the friendly Basutos joining us; but when they came and found that to fight with the white man meant fighting to the death – shut up with no means of escape – 'Not for this child!' said Master Basuto, and wishing us the best of good luck, trotted away to the safety of the open.

"Bromhead, at this point, certainly saved the situation by cutting the laager in half by means of biscuit tins. But for that we should have been smashed to pieces – not a doubt of it. He saw the wisdom of concentrating our defence in the nick of time, and accomplished it. But this traverse meant leaving the hospital, with my thirty five patients, outside our laager. So I and a few orderlies set about loopholing it, and rendering it as strong as we could. We had to leave the patients there, for every part of the commissariat house was crowded with stores.

"At 3.30 a swarm of Zulus came round the crook of the mountain at a slow, slinging trot, spreading themselves out in skirmishing order, and made straight at us, an innumerable swarm of blacks. They came in perfect silence – no war-whoops, no dancing, no shouting, and holding their fire. Striking-looking figures, of great physical beauty, the Martini in one hand, the assegai slung across the back – fresh from the massacre of Isandlana, running in perfect silence to wipe out the little body of left-behinds at Rorke's Drift.

"At six hundred yards we opened fire on them from the hospital, and I must confess we were a little put to it by the impotence of our volley. On they came at the same slow, slinging trot, their heads forward, their arms outspread, their bodies poised in a sort of aim at our mealie circus, and all in a dead silence. Here and there a black body doubled up, and went writhing and bouncing into the dust; but the great host came steadily on, spreading out – spreading out – spreading out till they seemed like a giant pair of nut-crackers opening round the little nut of Rorke's Drift. It was nasty, really nasty, the inevitability of that silent closing in upon us.

"Well, the main body got to the hospital, and seized on that position, with its cover of garden and shrubbery, to pour in upon us a galling fire. It was a frightful oversight – the leaving of that garden and shrubbery. Heavens! they rained lead on us at the distance of a cricket pitch or two. We could only withdraw our forces from the hospital into the smaller laager behind the biscuit-tins. One patient refused to run the short distance – persuasion, everything was vain; he preferred rather to stay there and be butchered than to face the ordeal of that brief run. Another patient it was impossible to remove, and we had to leave him there to be killed. Ah! poor fellow! And sometimes, thinking it over, I cannot help feeling that I might somehow or another have devised escape for him. I cannot help feeling it. But it's hard to think coolly in a rush of that kind.

"The rest is just a story of sticking to it. We stood up face to face, white men and black, and blazed at each other till nightfall. They broke in upon us, and we drove them out. They hammered at us, and we struck the hammer up. And then God sent the night and the flag was still flying. We expected another attack, and Chard constructed a cone-shaped stack of mealies in the middle of our laager for a last stand; But the Zulus set fire to the hospital, lighted themselves up for us in lurid flames against the darkness, and we poured in death upon them with a rush that swept them away. Desultory firing was continued throughout the night, but no big rushing attack; and in the morning – they were gone!"

"And how did you win your Cross?"

"Oh! I carried ammunition to the hospital."

"During the attack?"

"Yes."

"That must have been rather nasty."

"It wasn't nice. But – well, it's just a sense of responsibility, that's all. One had to do it, it was one's duty, and a bullet through my helmet was my only wound!"

And he sits in his club thinking of some possible plan whereby he might have saved that single life in the hospital.

54e. *British Medical Journal,* 19 March 1932

Obituary.
J.H. Reynolds, V.C., L.L.D.
Lieut.-Colonel R.A.M.C. (ret)

Lieut.-Colonel James Henry Reynolds, V.C., died on March 4th, age 88. He was born on February 3rd, 1844, the second son of Laurence Reynolds, J.P., of Dalyston House, County Longford and was educated at Castle Knock and at Trinity College, Dublin, where he graduated M.B. and Ch.B. in 1867. He entered the Army as assistant surgeon in 1868, and was posted to the 36th Foot, now the 2nd Battalion of the Worcestershire Regiment. He became surgeon in 1873 upon the abolition of the rank of assistant surgeon, and surgeon major in 1879, by a special promotion for his services at Rorke's Drift. He was then, however only one year short of promotion by length of service in the ordinary course. He became brigade surgeon lieutenant-colonel in December, 1892, and retired in January, 1896. After his retirement he was employed for some time in medical charge of the Royal Army Clothing Factory at Pimlico.

He served in south Africa in the Griqualand expedition of 1875, in the Kaffir war of 1877–78, taking part in the action with the Galekas at Impetu, and in the Zulu war of 1879 when he was one of the three officers in the fort at Rorke's Drift which withstood the attack of the Zulu army after the annihilation of a British force chiefly consisting of the 24th Foot, the South Wales Borderers at Isandhlwana and saved the colony of Natal from invasion by the rush of the triumphant army of Zulus under King Cetewayo. The other two officers were Lieutenant Chard, R.E., and Lieutenant Bromhead, 24th Foot; all three got the V.C. He was also present at the battle of Ulundi, where the Zulu army was completely defeated and the Zulu kingdom brought to an end. He was mentioned in dispatches in the London Gazette of March 15th, 1879, and received the medal with a clasp, as well as the V.C. He was also given the L.L.D. by the Trinity College, Dublin, the Honorary Fellowship of the Royal College of Physicians, Ireland; and the Gold Medal of the British Medical Association. His V.C. was gazetted in June 1879 …

… Colonel Reynolds was one of the three oldest V.C.s who attended the dinner in the Royal Gallery of the House of Lords at which the Prince of Wales presided, on November 9th, 1929. In 1880 he married Elizabeth, daughter of Dr. M'Cormick.

Mr. Walter G. Spencer writes:

Whilst Colonel Reynolds was in charge of the Pimlico Clothing Department, he frequently sent workers to Westminster Hospital for treatment and, later, he came to me about his health, the last time at the beginning of 1929. Then a cancer, for which a grave operation would previously have been called for, disappeared in about ten days under radium. Colonel Reynolds was thus able to walk at the head of the V.C.s at the Thanksgiving Ceremony, and to be present at the dinner in the House of Lords. Our conversations often returned to Rorke's Drift, and from notes I jotted down I have picked out a few of his reminiscences which I have not noticed in print. There were thirty-six patients in hospital, most in different stages of typhoid fever. No preparations had been made for the defence of the station. Reynolds was the senior officer, having been already six years in South Africa; Bromhead and Chard were young subalterns just out from England; Dalton, an army non-commissioned officer, who had rejoined, had had experience in the methods of defence employed by the Boers. When fugitives from Isandhlwana reached Rorke's Drift, it was first proposed to evacuate the place, but Reynolds declared that to be impossible. Even if the convoy could cross the river the ascent of the opposite bank was so long and steep that the Zulus would certainly catch it up. It was Dalton who arranged the defence with mealie bags. When the Zulus came into view there appeared horsemen in scarlet, and the cry was that the cavalry were returning; but Reynolds pointed out that the riders were not rising in their saddles, but sat the horses as did the natives. Coming nearer, the Zulu impi drew up, and ceremoniously took snuff, heralding a charge to the uttermost. A few Zulus got into the garden and into the hospital before two patients in bed could be got within the laager; a third lost his head, took a wrong turning, and was also killed. The remaining thirty-three cases were saved and survived the subsequent stench.

55. 12046 Driver Charles John Robson, 5th (Field) Company, Royal Engineers

55a. A letter written by John Chard, 17 November 1879
[from 'The Noble Sapper on the Box – Charles Robson R.E.',
by L. Stevenson, *Royal Engineers Journal*, August 1995]

Moredon
Taunton
17th November 1879

Driver Charles Robson Royal Engineers, served with me in the 5th Compy R.E. as my batman, for some months before and during the whole of the Zulu Campaign.

His conduct has been very good & he has given me great satisfaction. He was the only Royal Engineer with me at Rorkes Drift on the 22 Jany where he did good service. He was also present at the action of Ulundi.

I sincerely hope he may get on & do well
John R.M. Chard
Capt & Bt. Maj., R.E.

55b. Extract from *Royal Engineers Journal*, 1 November 1879, reporting on John Chard's triumphant arrival in North Curry, Somerset in late October 1879

Major Chard was accompanied by his military servant in full regimentals and the appearance of this soldierly young fellow bearing an armful of Zulu assegais and other trophies of the campaign excited much interest.

55c. *Somerset County Gazette,* 4 October 1879, reporting on a speech made by John Chard at a civic reception in North Curry, Somerset

Reception at North Curry.

Major Chard, in response … He was sorry that Major Bromhead, who was still serving his country in South Africa, and that Dr. Reynolds, who yesterday landed with him at Portsmouth, were not with him on that occasion to see how much was thought of what they did at Rorke's Drift; but he was glad to say that there was one there beside himself (alluding to a driver in the Engineers, named Charles Robson, who was occupying the box-seat) who had the opportunity of seeing how greatly their services were appreciated, and what a splendid reception had been accorded him, for which he thanked them one and all very sincerely …

56. 1-24/1542 Private William Roy, 1/24th Foot

56a. *Dundee Courier,* 8 March 1879

The Disaster At Rorke's Drift.
Narrative Of A Dundee Soldier.

The following letter from a soldier in the 1st Battalion of the 24th Regiment to his parents in Dundee, may be of interest to our readers at the present time. In his last letter (dated January 20) he bitterly regretted being in hospital, and unable to advance with his regiment on the following day. The letter, which is written in pencil, is a follows: –

Rorke's Drift Mission Station,
25th January, 1879.

Dear Father and Mother,

I take the opportunity of writing you a few lines to let you know that I am well, hoping this will find you the same. I am very sorry to inform you that five companies of the 1-24th have been slaughtered, with the whole of the band and staff, and one company of the 2-24th with their band and staff. There was only a bandsman escaped. There were about 20,000 Zulus came down on about 600 Europeans, and they slaughtered the lot except two. It happened to be the 1-24th's turn to stay and look after the camp. The General went out along with the column. After he had got about twelve miles away to meet the enemy they came down on the opposite side to which he thought they would, and before he had time to come back, they had taken the camp and slaughtered the lot. Then they came to where we were.

Happily for me, I was in the hospital with a sore throat. There were twelve months supply of rations at this place. There were only 70 men, sick included. When we heard the rapid firing we fortified the Mission Station as well as we could. The hospital was in the missionary's dwellinghouse, and the sick (about 20 of us) manned that, while the company were inside the fortification. We had only about three-quarters of an hour to secure ourselves as well as we could. They came down upon us about three o'clock in the afternoon. To the best of my calculations there were 6000 or 7000 of them. They very nearly overpowered us. They took the hospital and set fire to it, while I and another old soldier were inside at the back window, and we did not know they had taken it at the front. My rifle got disabled, so I fixed my bayonet and charged out of the house. While we were charging out the old soldier got wounded in the ear. There were about 30 Zulus chasing us, but the men inside the fort shot them before they could harm us. There were four men burned alive in the hospital, they being unable to move with the fever. We kept our position until the morning and then the General came to our assistance.

There are only two of us saved belonging to my company. The other man happened to get wounded in the shoulder.

Give my love to all friends.

Good night, for I must go to my post again.

56b. *Dundee Weekly News,* 5 February 1881

Reward to Rorke's Drift Heroes.

The Ladies' Rorke's Drift Testimonial Fund, as a mark of recognition of the bravery by the small force under Majors Chard and Bromhead in successfully repelling thousands of Zulus on the night of the 22d January, 1879, have just presented a number of Bibles to those who distinguished themselves on that memorable occasion. Among the recipients is Mr. Wm. Roy, Dundee, late Corporal 1-24th Regiment, who, it will be remembered, was along with a few others, decorated by the Queen with the medal for distinguished service on his return from the Zulu War. The Bible which he has received is extremely handsome, and bears in gold letters on the cover the words "Souvenir of Rorke's Drift, January 22–23, 1879." The fly-leaf bears the inscription, "To Wm. Roy, late Corporal 1-24th Regiment, from the Ladies' Rorke's Drift Testimonial Fund." Accompanying the Bible was a kind letter begging acceptance of the gift as a slight token of the appreciation of the heroic defence made by our soldiers at Rorke's Drift entertained by the donors.

56c. *Sydney Daily Telegraph* (Australia), 25 May 1887

The Case of the Asylum Inmate Roy.

To the Editor of the Daily Telegraph

Sir, In reading the report of the Asylum Inquiry Board the case of Roy at the Parramatta Asylum must surely excite the sympathy of the people of New South Wales. Here is a man who has been in the army, served through the Zulu War, and was one of the heroes of Rorke's Drift, at which place, being sick in hospital at the time, he yet, when the building was in flames, broke through the wall and while exposed to the enemy's fire succeeded to rescuing eight of his comrades (four others were burnt to death). During the whole of his service there is not one military entry against him for insubordination or misconduct of any kind. He received two medals, one marked for distinguished conduct on the field, also a Bible containing the Queen's autograph, which was presented to Roy by her Majesty at Windsor, December 1879.

Eight years only have elapsed since then, and he here is an inmate of Parramatta Asylum, paralysed and blind with, in all probability, but a few months to live. The treatment the poor fellow has received while in the asylum, if true – and the board do not discredit the statement – makes one's blood boil to read. Surely something can be done to make the few remaining days of his life less terrible. Personally, I will do what I can to help any movement set on foot for this purpose; and I have faith in my fellow colonists to feel sure that they have only to read the facts as narrated in our issue of Friday last to at once form a Fund for Roy's relief. Our volunteers will, I am sure, nobly help.

Yours, &c
J Neville
Barton, John-street
Ashfield

57. 25B/1185 Private Edward (Edmund) Savage, 'B' Company, 2/24th Foot

57a. *Manchester Weekly Post,* 17 July 1879

The Zulu War.
Interviewing Invalided Soldiers.

Yesterday several privates belonging to the ill-fated 24th Regiment arrived in Brecon from the seat of war.

Private Savage says he was in the hospital at Rorke's Drift when the Zulus came, and experienced that terrible onslaught of the enemy, whom he described as treating the English dead in a horribly cruel manner. Savage describes the warning given to the unfortunate inmates of the hospital. Seeing the danger drawing nearer, though suffering from an injured knee, he jumped out of the window into the fort. He assisted in the defence, lying on his side and taking aim at the Zulus through an opening in the biscuit boxes. Lieutenant Bromhead assisted to open a cartridge box. In doing so, in the dark, Savage cut his hands. He, however, kept 'pegging' away, and did some execution. An officer standing beside him shot dead a Zulu who had made no little havoc in the English ranks. In the night time, when under fire, Savage heard a fellow soldier of the name of Fagan cry out for water, and managed to crawl along to help his disabled comrade-in-arms, who died before daylight next morning. Savage says he never spent such a miserable

1. Frederick Millne, formerly Sergeant with the 2/3rd Foot, 'The Buffs'. '... The men spoke very highly of Chard and another man named, I think, Milne [sic] ... Milne, if that was the man's name, ought to get the V.C., if any man deserved it; for when the men were distracted with thirst and parched with the dust from the thatch and smoke, they went to broach a cask of rum, but this man stood upon it and threatened to shoot the first who touched it. He also volunteered to go with a few men and guard the punt, but was not permitted to do so ...'

RORKE'S DRIFT HERO.

A V.C. Dies in Manchester.

STORY OF A FAMOUS DEFENCE.

MR. JONES.

2. William Jones, VC, B Company, 2/24th, from the *Manchester Evening News*, April 1913.

3. Sergeant Evan Jones, Royal Welsh Fusiliers, photographed in 1919. Born Evan Cosgrove in 1853, Jones was a Private in B Company, 2/24th at the defence of Rorke's Drift. He was stationed in the cattle kraal during the battle, where, according to one source, he knocked down several Zulus with his fists. Jones served a total of 43 years in the army.

4. Ngaikana kaYenge, a veteran of the uThulwana ibutho, photographed in Pietermaritzburg in 1916, age 85. His head-ring has become detached in old age. (Campbell Collections of the University of KwaZulu-Natal)

5. Trooper Henry Lugg, Natal Mounted Police.

6. George William Mabin, photographed in 1938. Mabin, a staff clerk in the General Staff during the Anglo-Zulu War, was also present at the actions at Majuba, Ingogo and Laing's Nek during the Boer War of 1880–81. He went on to complete thirty years' service in the army, mostly in South Africa.

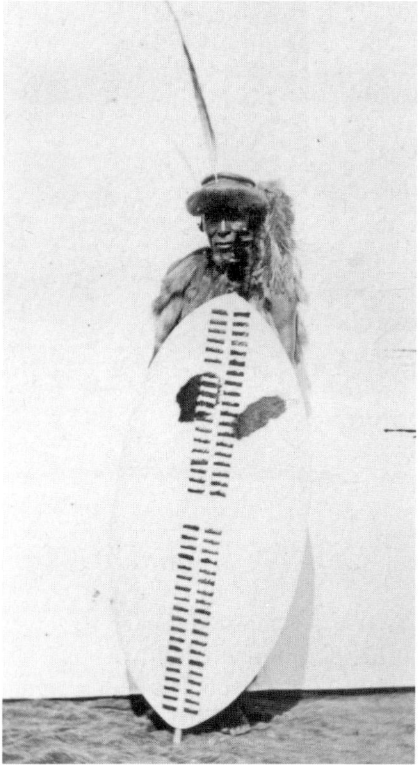

7. A man of a senior Zulu ibutho in full regalia, and carrying the largest size of regimental war shield, the isihlangu. The uThulwana carried shields with a similar pattern of red spots on a white background.

8. As darkness fell, hand-to-hand fighting raged across the perimeter along the front of the post.

9. An eyewitness sketch of the Zulus deploying from columns into lines at the battle of Ulundi; the artist has captured the details of Zulu dress surprisingly well.

10. 'In the name of our God, we have now taken the last step to buying a place for the foundation of our first mission station. After much searching across the colony, and with many prayers for the Lord's help and guidance, we have decided on a place by the Buffalo River, at the very border to Zululand.' Witt's mission station at the beginning of 1879.

11. Oscarsberg rebuilt. James Rorke had used local Zulus to help construct his house at Rorke's Drift; Otto Witt, however, hired several craftsmen from Sweden to go to South Africa to help with the reconstruction of the mission buildings. The small stone church sits over the site of the storehouse.

12. Oscarsberg photographed from the Shiyane. The Swedish mission station grew steadily once the war was over, including additional buildings housing a school and an orphanage. The gardens have been replanted and the natural vegetation is regrowing around the site. Note the new raised wall surrounding the military cemetery.

13. Prince Dabulamanzi kaMpande, photographed at King Cetshwayo's coronation in 1873. Several of the Zulu commanders rode horses at Rorke's Drift. Private George Edwards, 2/24th, amongst others, later claimed to have shot one of the mounted chiefs.

14. 'We are soldiers; we've shown you how we can fight, and I'll show you how we can die' runs the original caption to this illustration which speaks of the British ruthlessness towards defeated Zulus which prevailed throughout the war following the Zulu victory at iSandlwana.

15. Although depicting the aftermath of the battle of Ulundi on 4 July 1879, this image captures something of the ruthless treatment of wounded and fleeing Zulus.

16. An eyewitness sketch of Zulus struck down by volley-fire at the battle of Ulundi; the sight in Otto Witt's garden would have looked much the same on the morning of 23 January.

17. An interesting photograph of the non-commissioned officers of B Company 2/24th photographed in India sometime between 1880 and 1881. Although none are named it is quite likely that some of these men had been defenders of Rorke's Drift. (Royal Welsh Museum, Brecon)

18. In 1910, Frank Bourne was asked to compile a roll of those present at the defence of Rorke's Drift. His roll, containing 112 names, was reproduced in the *South Wales Argus,* 31 January 1929. Bourne later made numerous amendments to this roll, with the number increasing to 148 names. It should be noted, however, that there are inconsistencies between all of the known rolls of defenders, (see Appendix I). As a result, it remains difficult to positively identify all of those who defended Rorke's Drift on 22–23 January 1879.

MILITARY AND MUFTI.

RORKE'S DRIFT ROLL.

LIST OF NAMES TO CLEAR UP CONTROVERSIES.

MANY fading memories among the elder school have been rekindled by the articles and references in the *South Wales Argus* to the anniversary of Isandhlwana and Rorke's Drift, when the 24th Regt. (South Wales Borderers) made immortal history, and the result has been a supply of evidence that there are still a considerable number of veteran campaigners in Monmouthshire who fought in the Zulu War. The fact that they were out with the column on the memorable day saved them from the massacre—after a desperate and unflinching stand by the camp force—at the unfortified position of Isandhlwana Hill, and, for the same reason, they were away from the little stores base and hospital at Rorke's Drift, when the Zulus rushed it for nearly 13 hours before they gave up the attempt to carry the post, so inspiringly and heroically held by a small defending party. Nevertheless, they experienced the rigours of the campaign. It was only the chance of circumstances that they were not engaged in either of those fierce battles where no quarter was given.

Four Gwent men who still survive were definitely in the Rorke's Drift siege, but, because of a certain amount of controversy in other instances, we publish an official roll of the Company of the Borderers, with attachments, who had been left to guard the base. Also it may help in tracing a few others who are in the enjoyment of this life, although they have lost touch with old associations. The quartette of Monmouthshire veterans referred to are John Williams (Fielding), V.C., Cwmbran; Thomas Driscoll, Ebbw Vale; John Jobbins, Pontnewynydd; and Will Osborne, Blaenavon. A further claimant to this distinction has not so far had his case verified. There is, however, a suggestion that the official list omits a few names. It might be that some stragglers drifted into the base after the party had been detailed off for its protection, and, in the excitement of subsequent events, never were recorded.

The roll, by special request, was prepared by Lieut.-Col. F. Bourne (at the time Major), in order to preserve a record, from the Regimental Pay List for January, 1879. It is dated 1910. Lieut.-Col. Bourne was the Colour-Sergeant of the Company that defended Rorke's Drift.

Roll of "B" Company of the 24th Regiment who defended Rorke's Drift against the Zulu attack on the night of January 22-23, 1879.

Lieut. Gonville Bromhead, V.C.

Colour-Sergt. (survivor, now Lieut.-Colonel) F. Bourne, D.C.M.; Sergts. J. L. Windridge, H. L. Gallagher (survivor), G. Smith, A. Saxty; Lance-Sergt. T. Williams.

Corporals J. Taylor, W. W. Allan, V.C., J. French, J. Bush,; Lance-Corpls. J. Halley, W. Bissell, J. Key, G. Sherman.

Drummers P. Hayes, J. Keefe.

Privates J. Ashton, T. Barry, W. Bennett, J. Bly, W. Buck, T. Buckley, T. Burke, P. Caine, W. H. Camp, T. Chester, F. Clayton, T. Cole, T. Collins, T. Connors, H. Connors, G. Davies, W. H. Davies, T. Daw, G. Deacon, W. Deane, W. Dicks, T. Driscoll (survivor), J. Dunbar, G. Edwards, J. Fagan, E. Gee, F. Hitch, V.C., H. Hook, V.C., J. Jobbins (survivor), E. Jones, J. Jones (970), J. Jones (1179), R. Jones, V.C., W. Jones, V.C., P. Judge, P. Kears, M. Kiley, D. Lewis, D. Lloyd, J. Lodge, T. Lynch, H. Martin, C. Mason, M. Minehan, T. Moffatt, F. Morris, A. Morris, T. Morrison, R. Norris, W. Osborne (survivor), S. Parry, T. Robinson, J. Ruck, J. Shergold, J. Smith, W. Tasker, F. Taylor, T. Taylor, M. Tobin, W. G. Todd, R. Tongue, J. Wall, A. Whitton, W. Wilcox, J. Williams, V.C. (1395, survivor), J. Williams (1374), J. Williams (1398), T. Williams.

Attached to the Company.

Members of the 1st Battalion 24th Regiment, patients in hospital: Privates W. Beckett, W. Harrigan, M. Jenkins, W. Nicholas, J. Williams, Roy.

Members of the 2nd Battalion, patients in hospital: Sergt. R. Maxfield; Privates R. Adams, J. Chick, G. Haydon, J. Scanlon.

Also hospital patients: Bombardier Lewis, Royal Artillery; Troopers Hunter and Green, of the Natal Mounted Police; Corporal Mayer of the Natal Native Contingent.

Other attachments: Lieut. John R. M. Chard, R.E., V.C.; Sergt. Milne, The Buffs; Asst.-Commissary Dunne, Acting Commst. Officer Dalton, Acting Storekeeper Byrne, Corpl. Attwood (also with the Commissariat); Army Hospital Corps, Surgeon Reynolds, V.C., and Pte. McMahon; Natal Native Contingent, Corpls. Schiess, V.C., and Scammell; Chaplain, the Rev. C. Smith; also Mr. Daniels, a civilian.

John Williams, of Cwmbran, is the only one of the Rorke's Drift Victoria Cross heroes who survives.

19. James Henry Reynolds, VC, photographed in Dublin in the late 1920s. Reynolds was the last surviving officer from Rorke's Drift. He died on 4 March 1932, at the age of 88.

20. Surgeon Major James Henry Reynolds, VC, Army Medical Department.

21. Lieutenant General Sir Frederic Augustus Thesiger, 2nd Baron Lord Chelmsford, British commander-in-chief in South Africa 1878–79.

22. Brevet Major Henry Spalding, 104th Foot: 'The post was under the command of Major Spalding ... News having arrived that the enemy were advancing on the post and that they would be there in less than an hour, Major Spalding handed over the command to Lieutenant Chard, R.E., and rode to Helpmakaar to bring up the two companies of infantry from that place.'

23. A sketch by Lieutenant Henry C. Harford (99th Foot, adjutant of the 3rd NNC), of men of the NNC at Rorke's Drift on the morning of 23 January. In the centre is Lieutenant Gert Wilhelm Adendorff, who had brought news of iSandlwana to the post the day before. This is the only authenticated portrait of Adendorff yet discovered, and his presence at the post on the 23rd is proof that he had stayed to assist the defence. (Harford family/David Payne)

night in all his life. There was momentary danger of being shot dead, and the likelihood of perishing from cold and hunger. He has no recollections of ever having gone through such hardships as while invalided at Rorke's Drift. After succour arrived he went down country, and as he proceeded his health so much improved that he hopes to be able again to see active service if this is required.

57b. *Western Morning News*, 25 July 1879

The Heroes of Rorke's Drift.

… Edward Savage was one of the defenders of Rorke's Drift. His company B., of the 2nd battalion, remained at the crossing to receive and forward stores under command of Lieuts. Chard and Bromhead and Mr. Dalton, of the Commissariat Department.

On the 22nd of January they spent the morning unloading mealie wagons to fill the store – formerly a chapel. Among the rocks on the rising ground by which the Drift is flanked a detachment of 400 natives belonging to the Natal contingent were quartered. The day was fine, and passed just as usual until three in the afternoon, when three men galloped at a breakneck pace up from the Drift, bringing the news that the camp was taken, and "everybody slaughtered." They were flying to Helpmakaar, and so desperately pushed by the Zulus that one of the party had been struck down as he ran, holding on by the tail of a comrade's horse. "Run for you lives" was all the comfort they could give before they urged their horses beyond the station on the Helpmakaar road. The officers in charge wisely declined the advice, and mapped out the heroic course which has become famous. Of the one-and-twenty wagons received the previous day some were still unloaded and the lines of breastwork having been decided, loads of mealies, biscuit and forage were brought along and each man fell to work building for his life. Forty minutes elapsed before the enemy made an appearance, and then only his scouts were visible, his fording place being some half a mile upstream …

… some men from the hospital, under care of Surgeon Reynolds, were evacuated to a little annexe at the rear of the main building, which had been used as a stable. There carefully ensconced amongst the fodder they were thought most safe from the random shots of the savages. A most fortunate circumstance favoured the defenders. The party of Zulus who first crossed – mounted, as the men of the 24th say – though they outnumbered the English by eight or ten to one, waited on the other side of the rise for reinforcements. Long before they appeared, it should be said, the "loyal natives" had flitted. In their unavoidable absence scout duty was efficiently performed by one of their officers, who again and again galloped up the hill to note the enemy's whereabouts, as well as by Private Hitch, of B company, 2-24th Regiment, who volunteered to watch the Zulus from the roof of the store. There Hitch remained until, apparently with stealth, the Zulus came in sight, marching "like soldiers" in an extended line which reached along both hills on the flanks, and at length with a howl threw off caution and swept down on the fort, dancing, gesticulating, and shouting, and threw themselves against the walls as though to engulph the fabric entire. They had outrun and slaughtered the fugitives of Isandula, and after their 14 mile run came down on the station like hungry wolves. Their first victim was poor Hitch, who got a severe wound in the shoulder from one of the wide-mouthed Kafir guns. The bullet that struck him, Savage says, was like the leg of an iron pot – a lump of iron in fact – just adapted to the weapon, the muzzle of which would admit the four fingers of a man's hand. Hitch is now at Netley. Volley after volley only seemed to bring the blacks to close quarters. Very soon the defenders of the hospital found their ammunition exhausted and quarters untenable. The Zulus dashed in the doors, notwithstanding the flank fire that was poured on the assailants in volleys. Then retreating from room to room by breaking through the walls they made for "the fort," as the enclosure between the buildings was dubbed, some tumbling headlong out of a small window and getting inside the barricade, a few rushing wildly forth into the hands of the enemy, by whom they were instantly speared and afterwards disembowelled with the barbarity peculiar to Zulu warfare. Two others of the party fell in this time – a sergeant and a native, one of the Natal Contingent. Both were in the hospital and refused to leave, the sergeant in his delirium violently resisting every attempt to seize him.

The Zulus seemed bent on plunder at first. When they entered the room where the Kafir was they questioned him minutely as to how, when, and where he was wounded, and after this stabbed him to death. The enemy charged en masse at the enclosure time after time, all the while roaring out threats that they would come in soon, and aiming with assegai and bullet against every form that appeared. The sundown came and no cessation of arms, though two hours more of daylight and the Martini-Henry might have seen the Zulu horde annihilated. The night grew dark and bitterly cold; the men had been on the knee for hours; there was no food for them; no water for the wounded – the supply of the precious fluid being lost with the hospital – the enemy creeping antlike under the walls, or climbing boldly to the top to stab the defenders or half-wresting the bayonet from the grasp of the soldier until he fell back with a bullet through the brain; there was nothing but gloom in the circumstances. By and bye, the savages, savage-like, set fire to the hospital, it being a low thatched building, the roof of which could be reached by the hand. The flames directed the fatal bullets anew; the flames too, lit the way to the water supply in the hospital, and like the noble three who fetched water from Bethlehem there were men who held their lives cheaply to bring their suffering comrades the draught they craved.

Savage, the lad who relates most of the details, had been one of the patients in hospital, and was too weak to carry his accoutrements, but he thought himself too good a man to be left in the hay, and he tottered into the fort with his rifle and belts, and kneeling or sitting got through the night in a manner worthy of his colours. The fight went on until dawn, the Zulus besides rushing and shooting at the stockade, making several attempts to fire the roof of the store. They clung to the walls like leeches, and one fellow by crawling up a buttress almost lit the thatch. He had tied three assegais together and attached to one end a wrapper dipped in oil. Just as he produced his tinder box to ignite the stuff one of the men stationed in the upper storey to prevent such an occurrence detected him. The rifle ball tore away one of his jaws, and he fell to the ground, where two shots more finished him.

At daybreak, no doubt for sufficient reasons, the Zulus drew off taking many of their dead and their wounded with them, but leaving around the enclosure and inside the fort some six hundred dead. Scouts still held the heights, however, and the main body only retreated to the valley beyond, intending, it may be, to re-exalt themselves for a final attempt. Happily, before any material reinforcements reached them the English were reinforced; the remnant of Lord Chelmsford's column, wearied with a long march and dispirited by the anxieties of a night on the slaughter-ground of Isandula, came in sight across the drift, and cheer answered cheer as the red jackets of the 24th were made out.

The Zulus on the heights disappeared wholesale, apparently with only one exception. When Lord Chelmsford arrived at the fort his conflicting emotions almost overcame him as he thanked the heroes who had saved a colony. He would see what could be done for them, he said, and the men understood that a distinguished service medal and a bounty of £30 are in store. Before Lord Chelmsford's arrival they had all had food and water and the other necessaries which were within an ace of becoming superfluities. They had also captured a prisoner, a skulker in one of the kraals which dotted the surrounding heights. The fellow was recognised as the perpetrator of the wanted Zulu barbarity on the body of one of the slain. Moreover, he admitted that he killed and "cut up with assegai," one white man, whose rifle he was carrying. With brief adrift he was sentenced to the gallows and hanged on a bullock beam in the enclosure, to which he walked with a smile – the rope before his eyes.

The victims of Kafir savagery – who were not merely slashed with the assegai, but ripped open from the groin to the breast bone – were speedily committed to the earth, and after that there was the task of burying the Zulus to be performed. To this conversion of the ground near the fort into cemetery, more than to the trials of the night, the sickness of the men invalided home is attributed.

57c. *South Wales Daily Telegram,* 1 August 1879

The Gallant Rorke's Drift Defence and Monmouthshire Men

… It will be recalled to mind several Monmouthshire men took part in the splendid defence which proved so creditable to British arms. There were no more than 80 of the 2nd battalion of the 24th present on the occasion, although a small number of natives friendly to the British cause aided the heroic defence when a hastily formed fort of biscuit boxes and mealie bags was hastily formed to protect the cleverly improvised fortification.

On the ever-memorable day of the attack of the detached handful of men, the two distinguished officers in command were happily informed some hours previously of the approach of the strong body of Zulu warriors, whose precise number has not, and probably never will be, ascertained. These wily savages, well trained in bush-fighting, imagined that they could make an easy prey to their rifles and formidable assegais of the slender garrison at Rorke's Drift. They were probably informed by spies of the small number of British troops against whom they had to contend. It is, however, evident that they imagined after a few previous successes that they could massacre without difficulty the little garrison. We are now quoting the history of the defence from a young invalided soldier named Edward Savage, a native of Newport, who took a prominent part in that famous struggle waged so successfully against thousands of the enemy. We shall quote his own words exemplifying a private soldier's impression of the fearful struggle and magnificent defeat of the barbarian warriors who, with all their shortcomings, have proved abundantly, to our cost, that they are men of mettle, and born soldiers. They can, undoubtedly, prove to be faithful and useful subjects when brought into intimate contact with western civilization.

Private Savage states in his own unvarnished soldiery language as follows; –

"I am a native of Newport, where my young brother and other relatives reside. I have unfortunately lost my father and mother. I enlisted in the 24th Regiment a few years ago, and was ordered with my regiment to the Cape, before hostilities commenced. My officers left me behind in the hospital at Rorke's Drift, from my being invalided by our surgeon, owing to an accident I met in climbing a steep rock with my comrades, who were ordered out for a reconnaissance of the enemy. I fell heavily and seriously injured my knee-cap, and I had been confined in the hospital for nearly a month previous to the attack of the enemy on our position. There were eight or more invalids in the hospital. When we heard that the Zulus were going to attack us, I, in common with all who could move out of the hospital, saw that we had better die as soldiers in our own defence, than be massacred and cut to pieces by savages. I left the couch on which I was resting, and, although very lame, managed with the assistance of a stick to totter to the extempore fort which had been erected for our defence.

True enough, sir, after my services were tendered in such emergency my humble aid was readily accepted by the officer in command. I applied to my superior officer, Lieut. Bromhead, to be placed on the defence, and the Zulu soldiers came down in a large body at half-past three in the afternoon. I found very soon that I could not stand on one leg, as the other became quite useless. I, therefore, lay on my side by a loophole, and fired on the attacking force through an aperture or loop-hole left for the purpose. We had, indeed, hard times of it when the enemy were trying their very best to break into our little fort. Lieutenant Chard, of the artillery, who as in the chief command of about eighty men, under Lieutenant Bromhead, of ours, saw, after some hours of heavy fighting, that we were not strong enough to protect all the fort or retrenchment so hastily put up, and he ordered us to surrender to the enemy about half of the place, as we could be better able to defend the other half next to the hospital and military stores. There were several Monmouthshire men with us; and I can tell you, we fired at the enemy until we were faint for want of nourishment and such fatigue and anxiety from the afternoon until early the next morning. Two Monmouthshire men were killed during the defence. One named Williams, of Newport, was killed by two savages, who asseagaied him dreadfully, as he was leaving the hospital, but they were quickly despatched afterwards by our men, who in broad daylight watched the affair.

I had two months stationed in the Drift before I left it invalided. I felt very much from the exertion when so weak after being in hospital. In that hot climate the dead bodies of about 600 Zulus, whom our fellows buried as soon as they could, tainted the air so badly that I and a number of our men were attacked by fever, and that induced the regimental surgeon to send several of us home on leave until we are fit to resume duty. We were, as invalids, forwarded to the nearest seaport in the Cape, the name of which I do not remember because I was half dead. After a voyage of, I think, thirty-nine days' duration, we arrived at Southampton, and I, with other invalided men, were drafted to the Netley hospital until we recovered sufficiently to go to our homes. I shall not be called upon to return to the army until one of the local army surgeons will certify that I am fit to join my Regiment."

Such is the story of young Savage, who does not appear to be more than 21 years of age, despite his great hardships. He has gained much experience of campaigning in less than one year; and he may well boast and be proud of being one of the 80 men of the 24th, with a few auxiliaries who behaved so admirably at Rorke's Drift.

58. 25B/849 Corporal Alfred Saxty, 'B' Company, 2/24th Foot

58a. *Mid-day Herald* (Singapore), 18 November 1897, believed to have been written by Alfred Saxty

Rorke's Drift.
By one who was there.

The following account has been sent to the "Rangoon Times" by one of the heroes of Rorke's Drift, who is now in Rangoon; –

Allow me to correct a statement in the "Rangoon Times" of the 4th inst. B Company of the 2nd 24th Regiment were left behind at Rorke's Drift to guard the commissariat stores, the officer in charge being Lieut. Bromhead. Some of the men who escaped Isandula informed us that a part of the column had been cut up and everything in camp lost, and that the Zulus were following them up into the Natal colony, when my company was hastily marched down to the stores and entrenched themselves with bags of grain, flour and biscuit boxes, Sergeant-Major Dalton being the first man to commence the work of entrenching. We piled every conceivable thing we could lay our hands upon around the few waggons we had, to make good our defence, and loopholed the stores and hospital. Lieut. Chard being at that time by the punts on the Buffalo River, about a thousand yards away. Lieut. Bromhead sent for him to come at once and bring his men with him, Chard being the senior officer. Information was received at about 2 p.m. and the

Battle Commenced

at about 3.15 p.m. and continued throughout the night except at short intervals. When the Zulus were preparing to charge, on many occasions they made a feints for us to waste our ammunition by shouting "Usuta," their war cry, when charging; but owing to the energy of the officers, aided by the Rev. Mr. Smith, military chaplain, the firing was continued with excellent effect the whole night and yet, on six different occasions, our little fort composed of stores was entered by the Zulus who were driven back again after terrible hand-to-hand struggles. How we lived through that terrible night is a mystery to me. You would think that hell had vomited forth all the fiends below. The hospital was gallantly defended by a handful of men, who, when the hospital was

Set on fire by the Zulus,

had to cut their way through a sun dried brick wall with hatches and bayonets to escape being roasted alive, and then to cross an open space, the zone of fire, to get into the entrenchment. These six men who defended the hospital received the Victoria Cross for their gallant conduct. Trooper Green, of the Natal Mounted Police, was shot down whilst crossing the zone of fire. One Sergeant, Maxwell by name, was left behind in the hospital suffering from enteric fever. Poor fellow, he was unconscious at the time, and he perished in the flames. There was no chance of saving him as the doors were barricaded up from the inside so that the Zulus could not get in. Conductor Byrne was shot dead whilst giving Corporal Lyons a drink of water, who was badly wounded in the shoulder. Byrne, before being killed, went round supplying the men with ammunition. The first man that was killed was Private Cole. We used to call

King Cole.

He was general favourite with officers and men, a civilian butcher to the column. He chanced his life to go to a place called Helpmakaar and was shot dead within a few yards of our little fort and hacked to pieces by the Zulus with stabbing assegais. We could all see it from the fort and I can assure my readers it gave us a very sickening sensation. The same morning as the massacre, 240 Basutos, with a Chief, and a rocket battery under

Colonel Durnford, passed en route to Isandula. After the massacre 37 of the Basutos, who escaped with their Chief, offered their services to us, but our officers fearing that the ammunition might be wasted by the Basutos declined their services. They then checked the advance guard of the enemy, and cleared to Helpmakaar by the waggon track to give information to the two companies of the 1st 24th Regiment who were en route to Rorke's Drift, 12 miles from Helpmakaar, as they were required to protect the punts and pass over stores to the column in front. The 37 Basutos with their Chief returned to Rorke's Drift just as the enemy was retreating, and after they had found that we had held our own against an

Overwhelming force,

they followed the retreating enemy around the hill to the west, which was their only way to retreat; and their way of attack, as the remainder of the column which was out on reconnaissance under Lord Chelmsford was advancing from the eastern side of the hill, and had to ford the Buffalo River to come to Rorke's Drift, the punts having been moored in the centre of the river, to prevent a flank attack on the east side by the Zulus, who might have crossed over on the punts. After Lord Chelmsford had inspected our position and warmly thanked the officers and men for their gallant conduct, he started to strengthen our position, and the Natal Native Pioneers who came with the column, dug holes to bury the dead Zulus, whose bodies had begun to stink, swell and fester in the sun. There were 365 dead Zulus outside the fort, not counting those who were killed inside the fort, and hundreds more who had died from wounds on the plains. So, dear sir, I would like to know where the 80th comes in, in the defence of Rorke's Drift? Some one was heard to say in Rangoon that none of the defenders of Rorke's Drift were alive. But I am one of them and, thank God, very much alive.

59. Corporal Christian Ferdinand 'Frederich' Schiess, 2nd/3rd Natal Native Contingent

59a. A letter written by John Chard to Lord Chelmsford, 22 October 1879 [National Archives, London, WO32/7390]

Beaconsfield Club
Marlborough Gate
S.W.
22nd October 1879.

Sir,

I have the honor in accordance with instructions from the Field Marshal Commanding in Chief, to forward for your approval this my application for the decoration of the Victoria Cross on behalf of Corporal Schiess late Natal Native Contingent in recognition of his gallant conduct on the 22nd–23rd Jany. last at Rorkes Drift.

This man who had been wounded in the attack on Sirayo's Kraal a few days before, was a patient at Rorkes Drift on the 22nd Jany. 1879 – and in spite of his wound (in the foot) he particularly attracted my notice by his activity & devoted gallantry throughout the defence.

Amongst many acts of his I may mention one I myself witnessed. After we had retired to our inner line of defence, the Zulus occupied the wall of mealie bags we had abandoned. Corporal Schiess without any order, crept out along this wall a few feet, to dislodge one in particular of the enemy who was shooting better than usual; on his raising himself to get a shot, the Zulu who was close to him the other side of the wall, fired knocking off his hat. Corpl. Schiess immediately jumped on the wall, & bayonetted the Zulu, & in less time than I take to write it, shot a second and bayonetted a third & then came back to the cover of the inner defence again.

I have the honor to be Sir
Your obedient servant
John R.M. Chard
Capt & Bt. Maj., R.E.

To Major Genl. Lord Chelmsford, G.C.B.
Military Secretary
Forwarded for the very favourable consideration of His Royal Highness the Field Marshal commanding in chief –

Chelmsford
L.G.
Bath 25 October 1879.

59b. *Le Bien Republic* (Switzerland), 21 December 1879

Appenzell. – Un journal anglais signale la distinction acordée par la reine à un Appellenzellois, le caporal Schiess, de Hérisau, de la légion Natal, qui s'est distingué dans la campagne contre les Zoulous en défendant avec 200 soldats la position de Drist, assiégée pendant 11 heures par 4000 Zoulous. Quoique blessé au pied, Schiess se glissa en avant, tua d'abord un Zoulou qui, caché derrière un tronc d'arbre, visait les deux seuls officiers survivants, puis il tua, en outre, deux autres Zoulous qui venaient au secours du premier. Schiess a obtenu la croix Victoria, la plus haute distinction qu'un officier ou soldat anglaise puisse obtenir.

59c. Extract from *Surgical Experiences in the Zulu and Transvaal Wars*, by Surgeon Dugald Blair Brown, Army Medical Department, London, 1882

… Mr F.S., a non-commissioned officer in the Natal Native Contingent Corps, a native of Switzerland, while in a most gallant manner – for which personal bravery he was awarded the Victoria Cross – defending the post at Rorke's Drift, was hit on the ankle by a bullet. The wound was a small one. The projectile struck just over the instep of the left foot, a little anterior to the outer malleolus. When I saw him four days after the injury there was very great swelling of all the tissues in the neighbourhood, both ankle and foot. Poultices were kept regularly applied, and in two days evidence of diffuse suppuration was found, necessitating my making several long incisions into the tissues. After this was done and the poultices continued for some time, he made a very rapid recovery, and regained the use of his joint. The bullet must, in this case, have been an ordinary round one, which had ricocheted off some box or stone and struck the patient in the ankle,

59d. *Natal Witness* (South Africa), 5 February 1880

The Victoria Cross.
Presentation In Maritzburg.
There have been few, if any interesting sights than that witnessed in our Market Square on Tuesday afternoon, when Her Majesty's High Commissioner, a strong muster of Her Majesty's Army, and a large concourse of Her Majesty's subjects assembled to do honour to a hitherto obscure Swiss irregular soldier – Corporal Schiess – late of the Natal Native Contingent. On that night, famous now in history and song, when a handful of British soldiers withstood, as the beetling cliffs of their island home withstand the shocks of the angry sea, the successive assaults of several thousand Zulus behind their "flimsy parapet," as Sir Garnet called it, at Rorke's Drift, Corporal Schiess, the hero of Tuesday afternoon, displayed the most distinguished bravery, and richly merited that cherished trophy of the soldier, the cross given by the gracious Victoria "for valour."…

… His Excellency Sir Garnet Wolseley with his staff, and accompanied by His Excellency Sir Henry Bulwer and Mr. Haden, rode on to the ground. Taking up his position at the base, His Excellency the General called Corporal Schiess to his side. The hero, who had been chaperoned by his later gallant Commandant, was modestly attired in the well-known Lonsdale uniform, in which he did his great service, and looked not a little abashed as, the cynosure of all eyes, he stepped to the front …

… His Excellency Sir Garnet Wolseley then addressed Corporal Schiess as follows: –

Corporal Schiess, I have very great pleasure, in obedience to Her Majesty's commands, in conferring upon you to-day this Victoria Cross, and in doing so, as Her Majesty's representative, in this public manner. This is, as you are well aware, the highest distinction that any soldier or sailor in Her Majesty's service can aspire to, and I am very glad to have this opportunity afforded me to give you this cross in the presence of so many members of the colonial community as an evidence of how anxious Her Majesty is to reward valour and merit, not only in her regular army, but also in the ranks of her colonial troops as well. The extract which has been read from the *London Gazette* describes very accurately the deed for which you are to receive this cross, but I wish to call the special attention of the soldiers to the deed, especially to two distinguishing points which distinguish it in a remarkable manner. First is the fact that you were suffering from a wound previously received, and which many men of a less brave temperament would have been inclined to use as an excuse for remaining in idleness and not taking part in the defence which was made on that occasion. A second and still more remarkable fact is that this deed of valour for which you are now to be decorated was one not of mere passive defence at a loophole, or standing behind a wall where you had been posted; but you went out – sallied out – from that place, and in a most gallant manner, and in front of your defence – the defence of that flimsy parapet on which you had to rely for your lives – distinguished yourself in the manner described.

These circumstances enhance the great pleasure I have on the present occasion in giving you this cross in the name of Her Majesty the Queen …

The Victoria Cross.
After The Ceremony.

… Later on Scheiss' health was drunk by a large party at the Royal Hotel where Col. Lonsdale in a neat speech complimented his former companion-in-arms, and follower, upon his meritorious conduct and on the distinguished ovation of which he had been the subject. In the course of his remarks the gallant Colonel said, "I myself feel the honour that has been done to Schiess today perhaps more than he does, and I am in a better position than the public to estimate the importance of the varied military services of which the part he took in the glorious defence of Rorke's Drift has been but the crown and the completion. Corporal Scheiss was not only a member of my own corps, but had previously during five and a half years faithfully and honourably served the flag of France. He has been but two and a half years in South Africa, but during that time he has succeeded in distinguishing himself in very many battles in the arduous campaigns against the Kafirs in the Cape Colony. If I could wish anything further for him, it would be that he should again find himself in similar scenes of danger to those in which he has reaped so much distinction …"

59e. *Lincoln, Rutland and Stamford Mercury*, 15 April 1881

With Baker's Horse in Basutoland.

We give an extract from a letter received a fortnight ago by Mr. Wm. Barton, of Stamford, from his son, who shortly after landing in South Africa last autumn was, with one or two other Stamfordians, peremptorily called upon to render military service. He was assigned to Baker's Horse, which was destined for employment against the Basutos …

'Fort McKay, Mount Frere, Caffraria, Feb. 2 …

… I have been out the last few days – one of a party repairing the telegraph wires cut by the enemy; not a nice job for five fellows alone and about ten miles from camp. But we had a good man in charge – corporal Schiess, V.C., one of the Rorke's Drift heroes. He is a nice fellow, and we are the best of friends. He was born in the Alps, and is a Swiss. This mountainous country suits him. When we were out the other day we went and looked for some sham chamois. We were unsuccessful, of course. I think if he had seen some of the enemy it would not have been sham. He is a dead shot …'

59f. *Englishman's Overland Mail* (India), 18 December 1883

The Duke of Connaught at Allahabad.
An Incident.

On arrival of the special train at Allahabad on 1st December with Their Royal Highnesses the Duke and Duchess of Connaught (after being presented to the notabilities of the station), the Duke proceeded to inspect the guard of honour composed of a very strong muster of the E.I.R. Volunteers. Glancing over the men his quick eye detected one little fellow, Volunteer F.C. Schiess, in the ranks, on whose breast hung the Victoria

Cross. With that readiness and good feeling so general with the members of the Royal Family, he at once stepped up to him and kindly with interest inquired where and how he had earned the distinguished decoration. The gallant little fellow answered, at "Rorke's Drift, South Africa," such being actually the case. Unfortunately poor Schiess, having his rifle at the present, was unable to grasp the ready hand extended to him by the Duke.

59g. *Natal Witness*, 6 February 1885

Death of a Zulu War V.C.

It may be remembered that Corporal Scheiss V.C., was sent Home from this by the troopship *Serapis*. Word has now been received of the poor fellow's death. It is thus chronicled in the Portsmouth *Times*: –

"Corporal Scheiss served as a volunteer during the last Zulu war, and was present in several engagements, including Rorke's Drift, where he showed conspicuous gallantry, and was awarded the Victoria Cross.

At the close of the war he returned to Natal, where for some time he existed in a state of absolute want. At the time of the arrival of the *Serapis* his abject condition led the inhabitants to raise a sum by subscription to pay for his rations for the voyage home. He was taken on board, but his long exposure told on him, and about the 14th December he died on board."

59h. Extract from the private diary of Lt. Col. W.P. Symons, South Wales Borderers [Royal Welsh Regimental Museum, Brecon]

I saw Corporal Scheiss in November 1891 at Allahabad, India. He had been working in a jeweller's shop, and was just going to Australia. Being afraid to lose his Victoria Cross, he had sent it on already by registered post to his destination.

59i. *Natal Witness*, 2 November 1899

Personalia

Corpl. F. Schiess, Natal Native Forces, was at Rorke's Drift in January 1879. P.G. Crow asks where he is now.

59j. *Natal Witness*, 4 November 1899

Personalia

A correspondent writes that he remembers reading years ago, both in the "*Witness*" and the "*Advertiser*," of Corpl. Scheiss (of Rorke's Drift fame) dying in India destitute.

59k. *Natal Witness*, 6 November 1899

Personalia

A correspondent writes: – I see information is asked of the whereabouts of the late Corpl. Schiess. Immediately after the Zulu War he joined the Telegraph Service as linesman and was stationed at Durban. He left after being decorated with the V.C. He went through the Basuto War later, and returned to Durban invalided and destitute. He was (if my memory serves me correctly) sent to England in one of H.M. transports, and died either in Netley or Haslar Hospitals. The Hon. Mr. Jameson was, I think, the means of his being sent Home. I have a good photo given me by Schiess. Should anyone care for a copy I will get it retaken.

60. 2-24/1387 Sergeant George Smith, 'B' Company, 2/24th Foot

60a. *Brecon County Times*, 29 March 1879

The two following letters are written by Sergt. Smith, who was present at the defence of Rorke's Drift, to his wife, who lives in Little Free street, Brecon.

Rorke's Drift, Natal, 24th January 1879.

My Dear Wife,

I now have the pleasure of writing these few lines to you, hoping to find you all in the enjoyment of the very best health, as I am happy to say it leaves me. I am thankful at having been saved from the cruel slaughter and bloodshed that we had all gone through the last four days. I have some very bad news to tell you. Our regiment, that is the 2-24th, left here five day's ago to go to Cetawayo's kraal, to fight the Zulus. They had left my company at this place to protect the commissariat stores, and encamped about eight miles from here, and on the 22nd the troops went out reconnoitring the country, and had only left one company in camp to protect the ammunition and baggage. They went out about 16 miles, and while they were out the camp was attacked by 6000 of the enemy, and cut to pieces.

The 1st battalion has lost 17 officers killed and missing, and nearly all of the men. The Zulus got hold of four boys of the band 1-24th, and cut them up in bits, and destroyed everything they could lay their hands on, and our colors are missing, and all the ammunition is taken from us. After destroying all they could, they made for Rorke's Drift, and at about 2-30 p.m. on the same day we were attacked by about 3000 of them, and had to build up a fort with bags of meal, oats and boxes of meat and biscuits. How we ever escaped I can hardly tell you. There were only about 100 of us, all told. We kept up a continual firing for 15 hours, from 3 p.m. on the 22nd until 6 a.m. on the 24th when the two battalions of the 24th (what was left of them) came to our relief, and four guns of the Royal artillery. We had 13 men killed and about 8 wounded. Amongst the former was poor Drummer Haydon, that lived at the top of John street. He was stabbed in hospital in 16 places, and his belly cut open right up in two places, and part of his cheek was cut off …

I am afraid poor Mulroy is dead, for there is only about four men of his company left now. Corporal Allen was shot through the shoulder. It is only a flesh wound, and he is coming round very well. Poor Sergeant Williams is said to be killed. One company of ours, No. 7, were cut up to bits. I myself had given up all hopes of escaping. My company was very highly praised for the noble stand they made in keeping the place, and the cool manner in which we defended it, and I heard the general say that the colonel should take the two battalions home again after it was over, and that we were to be formed into one regiment, and a new 2nd Battalion 24th Regiment was to be formed at home. Out of the 1-24th there is only 1 company left, and I fear there will be a good many sore hearts in Brecon, for we have lost Colour-Sergeant Chambers of the 1-24th. His wife is in Cape Town, and her brother, who is in the Royal Artillery, was left in hospital sick with the fever. The Zulus took one of the band boys and hung him up by the chin on a hook, and cut him up in bits. One of our men was shot through the lungs, and he stuck to his post, and fired away for an hour, when he dropped down dead from loss of blood. It is said that Pt. Orlopp, and Sergeant Johnson, who lived in John street are among the slain. I cannot tell you one quarter of the horrors that have taken place. We have lost nearly everything that we had, and we have to return back to Pietermaritzburg to get a fresh supply of clothing, and everything else, for we have only got what we stand up in now.

G. Smith
B Company, 2-24th Regiment,
Rorke's Drift, Natal.

P.S. – We have counted the number of the blacks that were killed and shot by my company, and they were over 800, so that they paid dearly for what they killed of our men.

Rorke's Drift, February 1879

My Dear Wife,

Since I last wrote things have been very quiet. The only thing fresh is that the draft has arrived to make up the company which was cut to pieces in the late fight with the enemy at Isandula. The draft are all quite well, but they don't seem to like the country at all, and they all say they would rather be in the depot at Brecon than be out here. I see another old face in the draft, young Probert, of John-street. He came out as a corporal and is posted to G Company, and also there is a nephew of Mr. Yates, the Landlord of the Clarence Inn, the Watton. Since my last letter I have found out the total number of men killed in the battle of the 22nd. Altogether we have lost about 1,600 men, and the people of Pietermaritzburg are so well pleased at the manner in which my company kept the stores from being taken by the enemy that they think they cannot do enough for us. They have subscribed £150 for us to buy the troops a lot of clothing, and pens, ink, and paper, matches, pipes, and a lot of everything, and sent them to us to be given to the troops at Rorkes Drift. They also sent word that they consider we have been the means of saving the whole of the colony from being taken by the Zulus, and I don't think they were far wrong, for if we had left the place and let the enemy take it nothing would have saved the other parts of the colony from the Zulus' raid.

G. Smith.
B Company, 2-24th Regiment, Rorkes Drift, Natal

60b. *South Wales Daily Telegram,* 27 May 1879

Interesting letter from a sergeant at Rorke's Drift to his friends at Tredegar

"Rorke's Drift, Natal
"South Africa
"25th March 1879

"Dear Friend, I now take the pleasure of writing these few lines to you, hoping that they will find you and your wife in the enjoyment of the very best of health, as I am happy to say that this leaves me at present, thank God for it.

Dear friends, as you can see by this and the newspaper, I am at the seat of war of Zululand. My company that I was in at the time of the great disaster at Isandhlwana, on the 22nd of last January, which was B Company, done our duty well, as the general and all the papers, say was B Company. We were attacked at about three o'clock in the afternoon of the 22nd January, and we kept up the firing until five a.m. The next morning, when the enemy left us we had fourteen men killed, four of our Company, one of A, two of D, one of G, and four of the First Battalion, 24th Regiment and two volunteers; and in killed alone 800 to 1,000 of the enemy. But to see our poor men in the way they are cut open, and parts of their bodies cut away, was sometimes fearful. At the camp of Isandhlwana the sight was much worse. The way the Zulus cut our men was fearful. They took of our little band boys and cut them open down the belly and hung them up just the same as the butchers do the sheep at home. But I cannot tell one half the things they have done, so that I must tell you of the reports that are going the rounds of our camp. One is that 200 of us are to be kept to guard the stores here, and the rest of us to guard a place called Dundee, about 30 miles from here, where there is a large coal-mine with a 9 feet seam of coal about three feet from the surface. Others are to garrison Pietermaritzburg and Durban; and we are to again proceed to Cape Town, and after the war is over, we are to go home to England, which I think we shall do to get re-fitted out, for we have lost everything that we had except what we stand in. I shall be very glad when the time comes to get home, for I am sick of the service, and I want to be out of it, as soon as I get home. I dare say you will get all the news about the war in the papers. There are a good many left to mourn for the loss of a loved one in Wales. I think that I have told you all that there is to tell, so must now conclude with my regards to yourself and wife, and to Mr J. Williams, the carpenter; and to Mr and Mrs North, and Mr and Mrs Spencer, and John Williams, of the Cambrian; and Mr and Mrs Evans, Red Lion; and all kinds of friends in Tredegar; and believe me to remain, yours, &c.,

G. Smith,
No. 1,387, Sergt. G. Smith,
A Comp, 2-24th Regmt.,
Rorke's Drift,
S. Africa."

61. Reverend George Smith, Vicar of St John's, Weston, Mooi River, and St Matthew's, Estcourt, Natal (Church Society for the Propagation of the Gospels)

61a. *Natal Mercury*, 7 April 1879, from a letter written by Rev. George Smith, dated 3 February 1879

The Defence of Rorke's Drift
January 22nd, 1879.
(By an Eye-Witness.)

Descending the steep and circuitous road from Helpmakaar, the valley of the Buffalo River, at and above its junction with the Blood River, is comparatively open; whilst below, on the right, just at Rorke's Drift, a spur of the Biggarsberg shuts it in completely. Upon an elevated terrace of rock (which forms a sort of pedestal for the terminating hill of the range) stood a neat homestead, about three-quarters of a mile from the drift.

The buildings were erected by a former border agent named Rorke, and together with the farm, were recently purchased by the Rev. Otto Witte, on behalf of the Swedish Church, for the purpose of establishing a Zulu Mission; and the fine hill at the back was named Oscarsberg, in honour of the King of Sweden.

The house stood within a few feet of the edge of the rocky terrace, overlooking a well-enclosed garden of two or three acres in extent, planted with standard grape vines, and many fine orange, apricot, apple, peach, quince, fig, pomegranate, and other fruit trees. There was a road running parallel with the front of the house, between the garden and the terrace, with a strong stone wall along the terrace side; whilst the sloping ground, between the walk and the summit of the terrace, was occupied by a grove of fine Cape poplars, some large gum trees, and a luxuriant growth of bushes and shrubs of various kinds.

The dwelling-house standing as above described, was over eighty feet in length, the side wall on the left running back nearly 60 feet.

Forty paces to the left, but with its frontage line of 80 feet running parallel with the extreme back wall of the dwelling-house, was another block of buildings, consisting of large store-rooms, wagon-house, stable, &c. These buildings extended back 52 feet. Almost parallel with the extreme left wall of this block of buildings, with only a space of ten or twelve feet, intervening, a stone wall extended to the edge of the ledge of rocks, forming the right wall of a kraal some 50 feet square, which was divided in half by another similar and parallel wall.

Passing out of the semi-enclosure to the left, between the store-house and the kraal, one saw the neat double-row of tents occupied by B Company, 2-24th Regt., under the command of Lieut. Bromhead; whilst all along at the back, and running parallel with the buildings, juts out another and very precipitous rocky ledge, some 30 or 40 feet high, full of caves, thoroughly overlooking, and within 350 yards of the premises.

The dwelling-house had been fitted up by the medical authorities as a base hospital for the column, and nearly all the rooms, as well as the large verandah in front, which had been carefully screened with blankets, were occupied by patients – 36 in number, including some who had been wounded at the taking of Sirayo's kraals, on January 12th.

The large store house was occupied by the Commissariat department, and was full of provisions of all kinds.

On Wednesday afternoon, January 22nd, after the slaughter at the camp at Isandhlwana, three companies (or regiments) of Zulus were formed upon the neck of land above the late camp, and marched towards Rorke's Drift; each company appeared to be from 1000 to 1500 strong. No. 1 company (we will call it) marched on in advance in open order, and "drove" every mealie garden, firing heavily all the while, killing many Europeans and natives who were trying to escape from Isandhlwana. They crossed the Buffalo River about four miles below Rorke's Drift, just below where the river makes a bend, almost at right angles, between precipitous rocky sides, firing repeatedly into every cave, bush, and crevice that might have afforded shelter for refugees. Being satisfied with the result, so far, they came on to a small green hill, sat down, and – took snuff all round.

Companies 2 and 3 then followed the example of No. 1, keeping some distance apart. They also advanced in open order – after going through various exercises, dividing off (apparently) into hundreds, then into tens, wheeling and quickly reforming; they crossed the river just above the bend, repeatedly firing amongst the bushes and rocks on both sides. They remained a long time in the river, forming a line across it, either for bathing or to assist one another in fording the stream.

By the time they had gained the rising ground upon this side, and had sat down to take snuff, up started 10 men of No. 1, and ran on in advance up the valley, which lies between the high ground at Helpmakaar and the hills at the back of Rorke's Drift.

In the meantime another party of Zulus, who must have crossed the river some miles lower down, had set a European house and a kafir kraal on fire, about four or five miles away at the back of Rorke's Drift.

No. 1 Company followed their advanced guard at an easy pace. No. 2 Company started off, bearing away to their left, apparently to join and support No. 1.

No. 3 Company started off two men straight for Rorke's Drift, who ran as hard as they could, followed by ten others who took it more easily; and then came on the rest, headed and led by two very corpulent Chiefs on horseback.

Whilst these Zulu warriors, reeking with British blood, are pressing on "like a steady rain," to plunder the Government stores, and (incidentally, of course) "wipe out" the handful of men that may attempt to defend them; let us see what preparations for defence have been made by the little band, if only they have been warned in time.

About three p.m. or shortly after, several mounted men arrived from the camp at Isandhlwana, and reported the terrible disaster which had occurred.

Lieut. Bromhead, commanding the company (B) of 2-24th Regt., at once struck his camp, sent down for Lieut. Chard, R.E. (who was engaged with some half-a-dozen men at the ponts on the river), to come up and direct the preparations for defence, as in the absence of Major Spalding, the command of the post devolved upon him.

The windows and doors of the hospital were blocked up with mattresses, &c., loop-holes made through the walls, both of the hospital and store-house. A wall of mealie and other grain bags was made, enclosing the front of the hospital, and running along the edge of the rocky terrace to the stone wall of the kraal, which has been described as coming from the far end of the store-house at right angles to the front of that building, down to the edge of these rocks.

And other mounted men arrived from the late camp, and told of the horrors they had escaped, and the dangers that were about to overwhelm us. Doubtless the poor fellows had seen terrors enough for one day, and were possessed by an earnest desire to warn the people at Helpmakaar in time, and so, like many before, and several after, on they gallopped to carry out their laudable intention.

A praiseworthy effort was made to remove the worst cases in hospital to a place of safety; two wagons were brought up, after some delay, and the patients were being brought out, when it was found that the Zulus were so close upon us that any attempt to take them away in ox wagons would only result in their falling into the enemies' hands. So the two wagons were at once utilised and made to form part of the defensive wall connecting the right hand front corner of the store-house with the left hand back corner of the hospital – about 40 paces long; sacks of mealies forming the remainder, and being also used as barricades underneath and upon the wagons. A barricade, filling up the small space between the left front corner of the store-house and the stone wall of the kraal before referred to, and the blocking up of the gates of the kraal itself made the outer defensive work complete. The men worked with a will, and were much encouraged by the unremitting exertions of both the military officers, the medical officer, and Assistant-Commissary Dalton, all of whom not merely directed but engaged most energetically in the construction of the barricades.

The water cart in the meantime had been hastily filled and brought within the enclosure.

The pontman Daniells and Sergt. Milne, 3rd Buffs, offered to moor the ponts in the middle of the stream and defend them from their decks with a few men. But our defensive force was too small for any to be spared, and these men subsequently did good service within the fort.

About 100 men of Durnford's Horse, who came in from the camp, had been drawn up for an hour or so, up on some rising ground, half a mile off. As soon as firing was heard, they rode off in a body to Helpmakaar, and then a noble body of some 350 loyal natives, who had been left specially to protect this post, and had consumed one or two oxen daily, at the expense of a paternal Government, and had got fat in the process, were seen hurrying away like a flock of sheep to the summit of a distant hill.

The anxiety which had been displayed for the safety of Helpmakaar, Fort Pine, Dundee, and other distant places, had considerably lessened the number of those whose help had naturally been calculated upon for the defence of the place. Seeing this, Lieut. Chard had a retrenchment of a double row of biscuit boxes placed from the right hand front corner of the store-house, straight down, and at right angles to the barricade, running along the ledge of rocks in front, thus dividing our whole enclosure (roughly speaking) in half.

Between this retrenchment and the kraal wall on the left, were two large pyramids of sacks of mealies and oats standing side by side.

About 4.30 p.m., the Zulus came in sight, coming round the right hand end of the large hill in our rear; only about 20 at first appeared, advancing in open order. Their numbers were speedily augmented and their line extended quite across the neck of land from hill to hill. A great number of "dongas," on their line of approach, a stream with steep banks, the garden with all its trees and surroundings, gave them great facilities for getting near us unseen. The garden must have soon been occupied, for one unfortunate Contingent corporal, whose heart must have failed him when he saw the enemy and heard the firing, got over the parapet and tried to make his escape on foot, but a bullet from the garden struck him, and he fell dead within 150 yards of our front wall. An officer of the same corps who had charge of the 350 natives before referred to, was more fortunate, for being mounted, he made good his escape, and "lives to fight another day." But the enemy are upon us now, and are pouring over the right shoulder of the hill in a dense mass, and on they come, making straight for the connecting wall between the store-house and the hospital; but when they get within fifty yards, the firing is altogether too hot for them. Some half of them swerve round to their left, past the back and right end of the hospital, and then make a desperate attempt to scale the barricade in front of that building but here too, they are repulsed, and they disperse, and find cover amongst the bushes and behind the stone wall below the terrace. The others have found shelter amongst numerous banks, ditches, and bushes, and behind a square kafir house and large brick ovens, all at the rear of our enclosure. One of the mounted Chiefs was shot by Private Dunbar, 2-24th, who also killed eight of the enemy, in as many consecutive shots, as they came round a ledge of the hill; and as fresh bodies of Zulus arrive they take possession of the elevated ledge of rocks overlooking our buildings and barricades at the back, and all the caves and crevices are quickly filled, and from these the enemy pour down a continuous fire upon us.

A whisper passes round amongst the men – "poor old King Cole is killed." He was at the front wall, a bullet passed through his head, and then struck the next man upon the bridge of the nose, but the latter was not seriously hurt. Mr. Dalton who is a tall man, was continually going along the barricades, fearlessly exposing himself, and cheering the men, and using his own rifle most effectively. A Zulu ran up near the barricade; Mr. Dalton called out "pot that fellow," and himself aimed *over* the parapet at another, when his rifle dropped, he turned round quite pale, and said that he had been shot. The doctor was by his side at once, and found that a bullet had passed quite through, above the right shoulder. Unable any longer to use his rifle (although he did not cease to direct the fire of the men who were near him), he handed it to Mr. Byrne, who used it well.

Presently, Corporal C. Scammell, N.N.C., who was near Mr. Byrne, was shot through the shoulder and back; he crawled a short distance and handed the remainder of his cartridges to Lieut. Chard, and then expressed his desire for a drink of water; Byrne at once fetched it for him, and whilst giving it him to drink, poor Byrne was shot through the head, and fell dead instantly.

The garden and the road – having the stone wall and thick belt of bush as a screen from the fire of our front defences – were now occupied by a large force of the enemy; they rushed up to the front barricade and soon occupied one side whilst we held the other; they seized hold of the bayonets of our men, and in two instances succeeded in wrenching them off the rifles, but the bold perpetrators were instantly shot. One fellow fired at Corporal Scheiss of the N.N.C. (a Swiss by birth, who was a hospital patient), the charge blowing his hat off; he instantly jumped upon the parapet and bayoneted the man, regained his place and shot another, and then repeating his former exploit, climbed up the sacks and bayoneted a third; a bullet struck him in the instep early in the fight, but he would not allow that his wound was a sufficient reason for leaving his post, yet he has suffered most acutely from it since. Our men at the front wall had the enemy hand to hand, and besides, were being fired upon very heavily from the rocks and caves above us in our rear. Five of our men were here shot dead in a very short space of time; so by six p.m., the order was given for them to retire to our retrenchment of biscuit boxes, from which such a heavy fire was sent along the front of the hospital, that although scores of Zulus jumped over the mealie bags to get into the building, nearly every man perished in that fatal leap; but they rushed to their death like demons, yelling out their war-cry of "Usutu," "Usutu." Shortly after, they succeeded in setting the roof of the hospital on fire, at its further end. As long as we held the front wall, the Zulus failed in their repeated attempts to get into the far end room of the hospital; Lieut. Bromhead, several times, having driven them back with a bayonet charge. When we had retired to the retrenchment, and the hospital had been set on fire, a terrible struggle awaited the brave fellows who were defending it from within. Private Joseph Williams fired from a small window at the far end of the hospital. Next morning fourteen warriors were found dead beneath it, besides others along his line of fire. When their ammunition was expended, he and his companions kept the door with their bayonets, but an entrance was subsequently forced, and he, poor fellow, was seized by the hands, dragged out, and killed before their eyes. His surviving companions were Private John Williams, No. 1395, and two patients. Whilst the Zulus were dragging forth our men's late brave comrade, the latter succeeded in making a hole in the partition with an axe, and got into another room, where they were joined by Private Henry Hook, and he and Williams, turn about, one keeping off the enemy, the other working, succeeded in cutting holes into the next adjoining rooms. One poor fellow, Jenkins, venturing through one of these, was also seized and dragged away, the others escaped through the window looking into the enclosure towards the storehouse, and running the gauntlet of the enemy's fire, most of them got safely within the entrenchment.

Trooper Hunter of N.M.P., a very tall young man, who was a patient in the hospital, was not so fortunate, but fell before he could reach the goal. In another ward Privates 593, Wm. Jones, and 716 Robt. Jones, defended their post until six out of the seven patients in it had been safely removed. The seventh was Sergt. Maxfield, who was ill with fever, and delirious.

Private R. Jones went back to try and carry him out, but the room was full of Zulus. and the poor fellow was dead. The native of Umkungu's tribe who had been shot through the thigh at Sirayo's kraal, was lying unable to move; he said that he "was not afraid of the Zulus, but wanted a gun," When the end room in which he lay was forced, Private Hook heard the Zulus talking with him; next day his charred remains were found amongst the ruins.

Corporal Mayer, N.N.C., who had been wounded under the knee with an assegai, at Sirayo's kraal, Bombardier Lewis, R.A., whose leg and thigh were much swollen from a wagon accident, and Trooper R. S. Green, N.M.P., also a patient, all got out of the little end window within the enclosure. The window being high up, and the Zulus already within the room behind them, each man had a fall in escaping, and had then to crawl (for none of them could walk) through the enemy's fire, inside the retrenchment. Whilst doing this, Green was struck in the thigh with a spent bullet. Some few escaped from the front of the hospital, and ran round to the right to the retrenchment, but two or three were assegaied as they attempted it.

Gunner Howard, R.A., ran out of the hospital, and managed to hide himself in the long grass, on the upper side of the stone wall below our front parapet. He covered himself as well as he could with twigs and grass, and there, in company with a dead pig, and four of our horses (which had been shot where they were tied up), he lay unobserved all night, and came in unharmed at daylight. Another, Private Waters, 1-24th, secreted himself in a cupboard in the hospital, and killed many Zulus who entered the room, he himself getting wounded in the arm. At last he put over him a black cloak, and ran out of the burning building amongst the bushes, in one of which he lay concealed and unharmed until morning, with hundreds of Zulus moving about during the night upon all sides of him.

Whilst the hospital was being thus gallantly defended, Lieutenant Chard and Assistant-Commissary Dunne, with two or three men, succeeded in converting the two large pyramids of sacks of mealie into an oblong and lofty redoubt, and, under heavy fire, blocking up the intervening space between the two with sacks from the top of each, leaving a hollow in the centre for the security of the wounded, and giving another admirable and elevated line of fire all round. About this time the men were obliged to fall back from the outer to the middle, and then to the inner wall of the kraal, forming our left defence.

The Zulus do not appear to have thrown their assegais at all, using them solely for stabbing purposes.

Corporal Allen and Private Hitch both behaved splendidly. They were badly wounded early in the evening, and incapacitated from firing themselves, but never ceased going round and serving out ammunition from the reserve to the fighting men.

The light from the burning hospital was of the greatest service to our men, lighting up the scene for hundreds of yards around; but before ten p.m. it had burned itself out. The rushes and heavy firing of the enemy did not slacken until past midnight, and from that time until daylight, a desultory fire was kept up by them, from the caves above us in our rear, and from the bush and garden in front.

At last daylight dawned, and the enemy retired round the shoulder of the hill by which they had approached. Whilst some remained at their posts, others of our men were sent out to patrol, and returned with about 100 rifles and guns, and some 400 assegais, left by the enemy up on the field; and round our walls, and especially in front of the hospital, the dead Zulus lay piled up in heaps. About 350 were subsequently buried by us. They must have carried off nearly all their wounded with them.

Our loss was 15 killed, two mortally wounded, and 10 others less seriously wounded; but we were not to be left alone, for between 7 a.m. and 8 a.m. the enemy re-appeared in great force, in the same direction as before, when, fortunately, the General, with the remainder of the column, was seen coming in the opposite direction, and, crossing the Buffalo, came straight to our relief, and the Zulus made off as they approached.

Whilst all behaved so gallantly, it was hardly possible to notice other exceptional instances, although all their comrades bore testimony to such in the conduct of Colour-Sergeant Bourne, 2-24th, Sergeant Williams, 2-24th (wounded dangerously – since dead), Sergeant Windridge, 2-24th, and Privates McMahon, A.H.C., and Roy, 1-24th.

It was certainly of the utmost strategical importance that this place should not be taken. Perhaps the safety of the remainder of the column, and of this part of the colony, depended on it.

The determined and successful resistance which by God's help the brave fellows were able to make, seems to have surprised the enemy, who have not shown themselves near the place since.

Whatever signs of approval may be conferred upon the defenders of Rorke's Drift from high quarters, they will never cease to remember the kind and heartfelt expressions of gratitude which have fallen both from the columns of the colonial press and so many of the Natal colonists themselves.

61b. Smith's response to enquiries regarding the death of Corporal W. Anderson, Natal Native Contingent [Pietermaritzburg Archives Repository, Pietermaritzburg, South Africa, NAB 3012/1879]

W. Anderson was killed just outside the laager at Rorkes Drift, at the commencement of the Zulu attack on Jany. 22nd.

I buried him on Jany. 23rd & was told, concerning him, that he was a Corporal in the Natal Native Contingent, who had been left in Hospital; that he had been engaged in working the surf-boats at East London & had been also a performer on the wire slack rope.

He was shot through the head, by the natives who had gained possession of the garden on our front, his body was otherwise untouched.

Geo. Smith
Chaplain
2nd Division

Head Quarters
2nd Division
Upoko Valley
July 16/79

61c. *Woolwich Gazette, and Kentish Advertiser*, 29 March 1879

The following interesting letters have been published: –

"Colonel Glyn's Column, via Helpmakaar,
Natal, S. Africa, Jan. 28, 1879.

"My Dear – We have had an eventful time since I last wrote on the 21st inst. and enclosed the two sketches. On the 22nd we heard from the advanced camp (I was then here – at Rorke's Drift – on the Natal side of the Buffalo river) that the Zulus were awaiting the advance of our column in force, and a battle was imminent.

"So, after luncheon, I took my binocular glasses, and went up a very big hill, and then I heard firing in earnest, and saw crowds of Kaffirs around the distant camp, and coming towards us. I thought they were our native allies, and the more so as I saw some knots of horsemen in uniform galloping in the same direction. I saw several minor battles, the natives driving everything before them. When they got to the foot of the hill I found, but could scarcely realise the fact, that they were the Zulus. Down the hill I went to warn the little garrison, and found them hastily constructing a barricade of sacks of grain round the house (used as a hospital) and the store-house close by, but within twenty minutes the enemy appeared round the hill and opened fire upon us. While half the men returned the fire the rest went on forming a barrier across our oblong enclosure, dividing it in half in case of losing any position. There were about ninety-five men able-bodied, and thirty-five in hospital, a doctor and a parson. It was four o'clock in the afternoon; in about twenty minutes they were crowding in upon our left within 200 yards, and then they made a march forward in a dense mass, and swarmed over the parapet. Driven from that end, our men took up their position behind the biscuit boxes, and mowed them down, but they got shelter from the barricades that we had lost, and our men began to fall. I did what I could in the way of handing ammunition about, and cheering up the men. Between seven and eight p.m. the brutes set the hospital on fire; and by the light of the burning pile our defenders kept up a deadly fire, but had to use great care, as our supply of ammunition was getting low. Then the house burned out, and on past midnight they rushed upon us with their hideous yells and fired from caves and rocks upon the hill above our position. The firing was kept up all night, desultory at times, and then rapid again; and every minute we expected some desperate final rush to storm our position.

But daylight dawned at last, and at about 5.15 a.m., the last shots were fired, and our enemies were gone. We do not know how many wounded or dead were carried off the field, but we found about 200 dead bodies. Our own loss was seventeen killed and twelve wounded. The determined and successful resistance which, by God's help, we were able to make seems to have surprised them; and, although we have been on the alert day and night since, and reinforcements of 500 men have arrived, no fresh attempt has been made by them. But, terrible to relate, the column on that day met with fatal disaster, and it was a mighty wave of victorious barbarity which was checked by our little band …

… everything that I have with me, excepting the clothes that I stand in, were burned in the hospital. My native servant bolted on my own horse, which I have since recovered. I have written to town for a surplice, a shirt, a towel, and some paper and envelopes. As soon as I get the last I will write to you, and tell you how we are getting on. I am afraid that this delay will interfere with my arrangements for a holiday – duty first, and then D.V., a holiday.

Good-bye, God bless you. – Very sincerely yours,

"G.S."

"Colonel Glyn's Column, Rorke's Drift,
"Natal, South Africa, Feb. 4, 1879.

"My Dear ….,

A few days ago I scribbled you a letter in pencil, giving you a very brief account of the terrible reverse our troops had at our advanced camp, nine miles or so from here, on Jan. 22, and how the enemy came on here, flushed with the victory, thinking to take this little post, which had no protection whatever in the way of fortification, and is overlooked by a large hill, covered with rocks and caves, our total strength to guard it being 139 men – including 36 wounded and sick in hospital, and the commissariat clerks, a doctor, and myself. The enemy retreated, after thirteen hours' fighting, with a great loss, our loss being 17 killed and 12 wounded. Some of our poor fellows escaped from the camp when the carnage was at its height, and a few of them got across the Buffalo River at a very precipitous crossing place, six miles from here. The adjutant (Melville) of the 1-24th (with the colours of the regiment) and Lieut. Coghill, of the General's staff, were killed in crossing. I am now (9 a.m.) starting with Major Black, and some mounted Basutos, to try and recover the bodies of these two poor fellows, and give them Christian burial on the spot, and to look for the lost colours of the regiment.

"Afternoon.

"I wrote the above so that, had it been God's will that I should quit this transitory stage in the performance of this morning's duty, you might have heard, from me, the errand upon which I had started. We went to the fatal crossing-place, 27 of us, mounted, 20 being armed with rifles. We passed lots of dead bodies, apparently those of loyal natives, and possibly some of the enemy. We reached the precipitous path leading to the crossing place on the Buffalo River, about eight miles from here, and found the bodies of the adjutant, Melville, of the 1-24th Regiment, and Lieut. Coghill, of the General's staff. We buried them where we found them, with our Church service, and then descended, passing through terrible effluvia of a battlefield, to the river, and there, amidst dead horse, saddles, weapons, &c., about 500 yards below the crossing-place, found the Queen's colours of the 1-24th Regiment, injured by the action of the rapid stream, but otherwise untouched. We bore them home at the head of our small cavalcade in triumph, and arrived at our little fort, where the men poured forth and gave their heartiest cheers, and Colonel Glyn received the lost flag of his regiment with heartfelt gratitude.

"We have just received information (Feb. 6) that a large army left the king's kraal on Feb. 4 to attack us, and that they may be upon us to-night. Thank God our defensive works are improved now, and we have 700 instead of 100 to defend the place – and may God defend the right. Nearly all our native levies have bolted away to their own homes – afraid to meet the Zulu armies – so that, probably, we shall have to remain here, 'just holding our own,' until large reinforcements arrive from England or India. This may interfere with my visit home, but never mind. I may appreciate it all the more when it does come about.

I am, my dear ….., very sincerely yours,

"G.S."

61d. *Croydon Chronicle and East Surrey Advertiser*, 21 February 1880

We have in our midst just now a rather remarkable man who is not often mentioned. I mean the Rev. George Smith whose name is associated with Rorke's Drift. He is a gentle and unobtrusive man, and you would not suspect how "tough a customer" he is. He went out as a missionary to Natal, and was appointed to a parish, where he built two churches and schools. When the war broke out and Army chaplains were wanted he volunteered for service. He is the man who served out the gunpowder at Rorke's Drift, and checked the cursing of one brave fellow with the remark, "Don't swear at the enemy, my man, but fire low!" You may remember that the incident was mentioned in the reports at the time. In Natal, Smith is known as "the fighting parson." He remained at his post throughout the campaign. A few days before Ulundi he volunteered to take Lord Chelmsford's ultimatum to Cetewayo; but the general would not let him run the risk, though the parson's knowledge of the native tongue would have been of great service. He was present at the battle, occupied in burying a mutilated soldier, when the first shot was fired. He came home recently in the Conway Castle, bringing two Zulu lads that he has adopted.

[The two boys were not in fact Zulus but were two former slave boys of the Mang'anja in what is now southern Malawi. They were baptised in 1877 and given the names Edward and Robert Estcourt.]

62. 25B/777 Private Thomas Stevens, 'B' Company, 2/24th Foot

62a. *Merthyr Express*, 29 March 1879

The following is a copy of a letter written by Private E. Stephens, B. Company 2-24th Regiment, dated Rorke's Drift, Feb. 5th, addressed to his parents, who reside at the Robin Hood Inn, Dowlais. We may add that enclosed in the letter is a feather, described by the writer as; "a feather, part of a head-dress of one of the chiefs of the enemy."

Dear Parents,

I now take the opportunity of writing to you a few lines, hoping it will find you in the enjoyment of good health, as thank God, I am happy to say I am. Dear mother, no doubt you will read of our late disaster. I must tell you as near I can. On Sunday, the 12th, our regiment and five companies of the 1-24, and volunteers and natives, crossed the river into Zululand, leaving our company – that's B, and 300 of the native troops behind to guard the stores and provisions. All went well till Tuesday, the 22nd, and horrors, it was an unlucky day of it. Our column went out for an attack, leaving one company of the 2-24th, G. Company, and five companies of the 1st Battalion, and a lot of volunteers to guard the camp.

About two hours after they had gone another party of the enemy attacked the camp. After a long struggle they took possession of the camp, and killed every one of our men, butchered them, and even hung the little boys up by their heels, where they hung the meat; destroyed the waggons and all the clothes and band drums, and even took our colours away; drank all the rum, and even went mad with drink. Well, the General was about 15 miles from them, and could not get to them. This occurred about 10 or 12 miles from where our company is staying. Well, one or two escaped at about two o'clock to our camp, and reported that the Zulus had taken possession of the camp, and they were making for us little lot.

Dear mother, a farthing would have bought our lives. Then we got our guns and ammunition, struck camp, and barricaded the old storehouse as well we could. Some were posted one place and another, and about an hour elapsed when we could see them coming. They say it was 4,000 altogether. Every man went to his post, and all the 300 natives we got ran away, and there was 146 of us altogether. We kept steady firing; it began about three o'clock – kept on for two hours – when they succeeded in setting fire to the little house used as an hospital. It was getting dark then, and we expected help. We thought the General would come to us, but not so. We said we would die brave. We kept it up until day-break, and, thank God, they ran away, and we went around to bury the dead, and we killed a good number, and we lost four, and three wounded.

Dear mother – We worked hard all day, and about three in the afternoon we saw the General and the remainder of the regiment coming. Dear mother, – The General was pleased to see that we had kept the place.

We lost everything. I must tell you that poor Blake and Johnny Shean, and several of the Dowlais lads, is killed, worse luck. Remember me to all friends. I think, we are going back to Pietermaritzburg again. The General has sent to England for more troops. I think we shall stand a good chance of coming home after this is over.

I will send a paper if I can get one. We are sleeping out still; we have no blankets or big coats now, and not a second article to wear. Cheer up! we shall yet meet again. I think B Company will get a good honour and name for what they did – they saved all Natal –

I remain your affectionate son.

E. Stephens. B. Company 2-24th Regt.

62b. *Herefordshire Times*, 12 April 1879. This letter, from 25B/572 Private Thomas Parry, 1/24th, was published in the local Hereford press in April 1879. Thomas Parry is not named in any of the recognised rolls of defenders, nor is he in the list of men of the 1/24th who were present at Rorke's Drift included in the History of the 1st Battalion 24th. Private Thomas Stephens' response to the Parry letter is included below, at 62d.

The Massacre of Isundula

Helpmakaar, Feb 14 1879

Dear Father and Mother,

I now take the first opportunity of writing to you that I have had the last week or two. We have been very busy, the few of us that are left of the 1st/24th Regiment, we have had some very hard fighting, and we have had 600 killed altogether belonging to us.

The way it was done I will try to tell you. On the morning of the 22nd of January there came into the General's camp a native and told him that the Zulus were about 13 miles away. What did he do but take 1,600 and went out to look for them, he left behind five companies of our regiment to look after the camp, with a lot more natives that he has armed to help us.

He had not gone about ten miles from camp before the Zulus began to show themselves on the top of the hill alongside the camp. It was not long before the fight began, when Col. Durnford, of the RE, came up and took our command.

He wanted our Major to let him have two companies to go out to meet them, but he would not let them go, as he had orders to defend the camp; but in a short time Durnford came back and took them, and sent one company out skirmishing to the right of the camp, about a mile away, and there they fell as they extended not one was seen alive afterwards. The Zulus kept coming on in thousands and they fell in heaps, but that made no difference.

They kept walking over the dead bodies of the others till they got within 50 yards of the few poor fellows that were left. Then the native allies turned round and ran away. Then the butchers began their work. They cut our poor fellows up to pieces. Then they made their way down to Rorke's Drift where I was with a company of the 2nd/24th.

We gave them such a warming there they won't forget for some time to come. They kept coming at us all night, but gave it up as a bad job. We killed 400 of them and lost 10 and 9 wounded. The way I came to be with them down there and not at the camp was that one of my horses got lame and I had to stop with him, or else you would not have heard from me any more. My master got shot and then ripped up. He had my horse shot under him first, then he got some one else's, it was a lucky job for me that his horse got lame. I dare say there is a full account in the papers by this time.

There was a lot of poor fellows from about Wales. The companies that are cut up are the N.A.C.E.F.H. Companies. We had our colours lost, but it was brought into camp two days ago. The two officers that saved it got killed about 200 yards from where we are now. We lost altogether 500 or more rank and file and 15 officers. We expect to have a big fight next Monday. We are about 2,500 strong here and in a fort, but the Zulu King tells that if we don't shift out of his country he will eat us all up. So, dear father and mother, I must conclude with best love, and remain your affectionate son.

Tom.

I forgot Ellen is at home. Give my best love to her and William, Mrs Lewis and Johnny

572 Private Thomas Parry. D/Company 1-24th Regiment. Natal, South Africa.

62c. *Merthyr Express,* 12 April 1879

Providential escape of a Merthyr Soldier

This week Mr. Thomas Parry, gardener at the Castle Hotel who had a son in the 24th Regiment at Natal, and had given him up as dead, was overjoyed at the receipt of a letter from the young man reporting himself alive and well, and explaining his providential escape.

He was groom to Colonel Pulleine, whose horse had got lamed, and he took young Parry's horse instead, directing Parry to come along slowly with his own charger. By this exchange Private Parry was delayed on the road so long that he did not reach the camp at all, but was on the march with the lame horse when he met the fugitives, returned to Rorke's Drift, and formed one of the gallant band which repulsed the night attack of the enemy on the evening of the fatal day at Isandula. We hope he will be spared to return to his native country unwounded.

62d. *Merthyr Express,* 19 July 1879

Merthyr Soldiers in the Zulu War.

Sir, – By a paragraph headed "The Zulu War. – Providential Escape of a Merthyr soldier," which appeared in your paper of April 12th, a copy of which I received from my relatives, I was much surprised to learn that a soldier named Parry, of the 24th Regiment, had taken part (according to his own statement) in the defence of the post at Rorke's Drift on the 22nd of January last, after the disaster which took place at Isandhlwana on that day.

Now, Sir, as I belong to B. Company 2nd Battalion 24th Regiment, and was present with the same during the defence referred to, and as I do not care to read of men who were not present or even participated in any way in that memorable affair, misleading their friends and others by misrepresentings, I think I shall be doing justice to yourself and readers, as also to the real defenders in question, if I mention that no soldier or other person of the name of Parry was present at Rorke's Drift on that occasion. If you desire I will gladly forward a correct list of all who were actually concerned therein.

I beg to be, Sir, your humble and respectful servant,

Thomas Stephens

Private 2-24th Regiment, Natal.

63. 25B/104 Private Henry Turner, 1/24th Foot

63a. *Surrey Advertiser and County Times,* 14 May 1883

Shere.

Sad Death of an Isandula Hero.

An inquest was held at the White Horse Inn yesterday (Friday), by the Coroner, Mr. G.F. Roumieu, on the body of Henry Turner, who was found dead in a field at Sherborne Farm on Monday evening last. – Wm. Jubb, bailiff to Captain Mathison, stated that on Monday he employed the deceased to pick stones in a field, and on going there about four o'clock in the afternoon he found him lying in the field dead. – William Carter, labourer, said the deceased had been lodging with him some time, and had delicate health. – Inspector Dennett, Albury, examined the body, but found no marks of violence. Deceased, he said, was a pensioner from the army. He was a very fine man, being over six feet, and formerly belonged to the 24th Regiment. He escaped from the massacre at Isandula, and was present at the fight at Rorke's Drift. Deceased was a steady sober man, and was 32 years of age. – Mr George Fisher, surgeon, Shere, said he had made a post mortem examination, and found deceased was badly affected with congestion of the lungs, to which he attributed death. The jury returned a verdict of "Death from natural causes."

64. 1-24/447 Private John Waters, 1/24th Foot

64a. *Daily Telegraph*, 11 June 1879

The Massacre at Rorke's Drift
Narratives by survivors.

Private Waters tells the following interesting story of his experiences: –

I was special orderly at the hospital at Rorke's Drift, and at this time have seen twenty-one and a quarters years' service. I was in the hospital when Private Evans rode into the camp and reported that the Zulus had massacred the whole column at Isandula. We would hardly believe this at first, but very soon had reason to understand it was only too true. We got as many patients as possible out of the hospital; but we had not time to remove them all. It was an utter impossibility to do that.

Between half-past four and five, as near as I can remember, the Zulus came over the hill, and I saw about fifty of them form a line in skirmishing order, just as British soldiers would do. Their main body was in their rear over the shoulder of the hill. They came about twenty yards, and then opened fire on the hospital. I stopped there firing at the enemy through holes made by other men, and others did the same, but we were not able to prevent the enemy coming right up to the hospital. Some of them came in and set fire to it.

While I was there I took refuge in a cupboard, and Private Beckett, an invalid, came with me. As they were going out I killed many of them, and as I could not stay there long, the place being so suffocating, I put on a black cloak which I had found in the cupboard, and which must have belonged to Mr. Witt, and ran out in the long grass and lay down. The Zulus must have thought I was one of their dead comrades, as they were all round about me, and some trod on me. Beckett had gone out half an hour before me, and he, poor fellow, was assegaied right through his stomach, and went into laager next morning. Dr. Reynolds did all he could to save him, but did not succeed. I got up at daybreak, having expected every minute my life would be taken, and then saw my comrades on the top of the mealie sacks, and I said, "Thank God, I have got my life." I had been shot early in the engagement in the shoulder and knee, and here's the bullet, which was taken out next morning by Dr. Reynolds. I knew many poor fellows who fell at Isandula. I saw Private Harrigan killed. Poor Beckett was buried next morning properly. Round the hospital dead Zulus were piled in heaps.

64b. Extract from John Waters' army service and discharge papers [National Archives, London, WO97/2133]

… Wounded at Rorke's Drift 22/1/79 – bullet entering outer side of arm 6 inches from point of the shoulder & lodging. It was cut out behind shoulder 12 hours after – distance travelled through fleshy part of arm 4 inches. The joint uninjured & bone uninjured …

He has fair power of motion of the injured arm in all directions, but complains of pain in the track of the wound & shoulder when exerting himself …

65. 25B/1395 Private John Williams (John Fielding), 'B' Company, 2/24th Foot

65a. Victoria Cross Register [National Archives, London, WO98/4]

The General Officer Commanding
Gibraltar
13th January 80

Sir,

I have the honour to transmit to you herewith the decoration of the Victoria Cross which The Queen has been pleased to signify Her intention to confer upon Private John Williams, 2nd Battalion 24th Regiment, for his gallant conduct during the recent operations in South Africa, as recorded in the annexed extract of the London Gazette of the 2nd May 1879, and I have received Her Majesty's command to desire that you will take the earliest fitting opportunity after the receipt of this instruction, of presenting, or causing to be presented, to Private John Williams on his arrival at Gibraltar the accompanying decoration in such a public and formal manner as you may consider best adopted to evince Her Majesty's sense of his courageous conduct on the occasion referred to. –

I have to request that you will transmit to me, as soon as practicable, a report of the proceedings which may be adopted on the occasion of the presentation of the enclosed Cross, and copies of any General Order which may be issued, with a view to the same being recorded in the Registry of the decoration, in accordance with Her Majesty's Warrant of the 29th January 1856. –

I have the honour to be, Sir,

Your obedient servant,

65b. *Bangalore Spectator* (India), 11 May 1880

A Brave Soldier.

The *United Service Gazette* tells us the following: –

24th regiment. Private John Williams, 2nd Battalion, was presented with the Victoria Cross, on the 6th inst. at Gibraltar.

He is servant to Major Bromhead: so it is singular that master and man should be similarly decorated …

65c. *Evening Express*, Cardiff, 6 June 1896

A V.C. Man.
Employed at the Cardiff Exhibition.
Brave Conduct at Rorke's Drift Won for Him the Coveted Distinction.

There's a "Victoria Cross" man at Cardiff Exhibition. His name is John Williams; he hails from Cwmbran, and he is 38 years of age. But his hair is prematurely grey, and his features are lined and furrowed, as a result of the terrible experiences he went through on behalf of his country during the Zulu War. He is in Mr. R. P. Culley's employ, as are also a number of Army veterans who have deserved well of their country, but have not always got what they deserve. Pope, writing to Addison in 1714, talked of the ill-fare of many discarded generals – to be first envied and maligned – perhaps praised, and, lastly neglected. This observation, holds good to-day of many of our veteran soldiers. We are not, however, concerned with that matter now. What we want to do is to relate those stirring incidents in which ex-Private John Williams, of Cwmbran, took a prominent part …

"It was the thirteenth time for the regiment – the old 24th – now the South Wales Borderers, to gain the distinction of the V.C.," said ex-Private John Williams, as our reporter examined the medals on his breast, "and eight of us got the decorations – two officers, one corporal, and five privates. Our regiment sailed from Portsmouth to East London, and we went through the Kaffir War before we came into conflict with the Zulus."

"You had a trying time of it, I've no doubt?" said the pressman.

"Yes, very trying." was the modest reply. "The weather was very warm, and we had a lot of difficulties, both officers and men."

"Did you have much trouble with the Kaffirs?"

"Yes. They did not attack us, it is true, but we had to hunt them up, and that put us to a tremendous amount of trouble. It was not until we got to Rorke's Drift, however, that the hand-to-hand work took place. It was for defending the hospital there that we got the crosses. We were only then a garrison of 80 men. We had constructed a laager, and the outside line took in the outbuildings, which were used as a temporary hospital, but, as the 80 men could not spread themselves out over this line we made an inner entrenchment. The onslaught of the Zulus was sudden, but we luckily got warning of their approach from the Rev. Mr. Smith, who saw them coming whilst on the top of the hill. The Zulus attacked us about 3.30 o'clock on the afternoon of the 22nd of January, and we fought them until eight o'clock the next morning, when the column from Isandwla came in sight, and they then beat a hasty retreat. Our garrison was in charge of the supply of stores, and we made our laager of biscuit boxes, mealie bags, and other things that were available. When we heard that the enemy was approaching, Lieut. Chard and Lieut. Bromhead sent out a scouting party, of which I was one. We did our best to check their advance, but at last they came down upon us in a huge body, – yelping and whooping – from 4,000 to 5,000 strong. They were armed for the most part with assegais, but they also had in their possession a lot of our guns. For some hours we managed to keep them off, but, although they failed to break into our laager, they at last got at the hospital and set fire to it. Private Jones, Private Hooke, myself, and several others took up the defence of the hospital, in which there were a number of invalids, and while the Zulus were around the building we had to force our way into the inner room by knocking holes through the walls. The Zulus were causing a terrible din, but we did not take heed of that, and we got all the invalids out with the exception of Sergt. Maxfield, whom Private R. Jones made a gallant attempt to rescue, but the sergeant was killed with assegais before he could carry him off."

"You say the Zulus surrounded the building. Then how did you manage to get the invalids away?"

"We were enabled to do it in this way. A path was kept clear for us by the fire from the forts, which was directed each side of the building, so that we got a passage between the lines of fire. I escaped uninjured – never got so much as a scratch – but Private Hitch was wounded in the shoulder, and Corporal Allen also received a severe wound."

"How many of the Zulus did you kill?"

"Roughly speaking, we killed from 500 to 600, while our loss was only eight."

"Did the Zulus carry their wounded away?"

"As many as they could. The small loss we sustained, I ought to say, was owing to the splendid way in which the small laager was constructed under the superintendentship of Lieutenants Chard and Bromhead. Yes; the Zulus treated any white men who got in their clutches most cruelly. They chopped off their ears and other portions of their bodies, which they carried away as trophies of war. I have seen them cut up a white man with their assegais and mutilate the body in a shocking manner, ripping open the sides and forcing the arms into the gaping wounds. How does it feel to be in war? Well, it's hard to say. Once the fighting commences you forget all about danger, and your mind is simply taken up with popping off as many of the enemy as you can. The rule is to mark your man, and always take care to shoot those who get in front of the main body, because if a gap is once made in your defence you don't know where it will end."

"I have heard it said that every man just before he goes into battle is possessed by a feeling of cowardice, but the brave man is he who is able to subdue that feeling?"

"Yes: I think that describes it. Until the actual fighting commences a man does feel nervous, but once in it one forgets himself." As Williams was at this stage called, the interview ended.

65d. *Windsor Magazine,* December 1900

Famous – But Unknown.
If you go to the Nut and Bolt Works at Cwmbran, South Wales, you may to-day see a middle-aged man (none too strong in health sometimes, from his exertions on that fearful January night), working as a common labourer, in order to earn enough to buy him his daily bread! A man of fair complexion, he is hard-working, honest and respectable. When he is 'dressed-up,' there appears on his coat that little Maltese Cross, with its magic words, "For Valour."

This is John Williams, V.C., the man who saved the patients in the hospital at Rorkes Drift while Hook guarded the door! This is the man who stayed behind in the burning place when surrounded by hordes of Zulus, looking in at the windows watching with savage joy their fiendish work; the man who refused to leave the charnel-house whilst a single sick or wounded soldier was left in it; the man who, with the brave cook, defied the whole host of Zulus to enter that blazing building if they dared! This is the man who at last, smashed through the thick wall and literally dragged the wounded soldiers after him – Hook doing the same – one by one, till he had dropped them all bodily into the yard just below, where the brave Hitch was trying to keep the savages at bay with his rifle-fire, so as to make a clear passage for the patients to cross into safety!

And to-day this man has to earn a scanty living as a common labourer, and to toil as best he can at such hard work as a nut and bolt factory affords, if he wishes to have bread to eat.

We give the successful general a splendid income, and in the end a pension, while to such heroes as Williams we offer nothing better than the workhouse!

65e. *Western Mail,* 22 January 1929

Story of Rorke's Drift.
Stirring Tale of Pte. J. Williams, V.C.

Private John Williams is the last survivor of the ten members of the heroic band who were awarded the Victoria Cross for their share in that memorable night's work. For very many years he has lived in Cwmbran, and to-day, in his 71st year, he is living happily with a married daughter at 21, Cocker-avenue.

He has no affectation about him. He is willing to talk about his memorable experience, but all he says is said in a modest vein.

The name under which he won for himself lasting fame is not his real name. That is John Fielding. He took the name of Williams when he enlisted, but, let it be said, there was no reason of shame behind that, and to-day in Cwmbran he is known to everybody as John Fielding.

"I was born at Abergavenny in 1858," he said, "and enlisted on January 22, 1877 – two years to the day before the fight at Rorke's Drift. We got to South Africa in the beginning of 1878, and after remaining at Bailey's Post for some time were sent up country. While there, by the way, Capt. A.G. Godwin-Austen (whose brother was killed at Isandhlwana), was our captain, and Lieut. Bromhead was our lieutenant. We had a brush with the Kaffirs, and Capt. Austin was wounded and went home. He was shot in the loins by a Hottentot who was up a tree. We very soon settled accounts with him. We had him out of that tree like one o'clock. Well, we moved up to Pietermaritzburg, and thence to Rorke's Drift.

"This, of course, was a mission station, and consisted of a few low buildings. The first lot of the regiment crossed on January 11 to the Bashi Valley and soon had an encounter with the Zulus, and then they moved on to Isandhlwana, and you know what happened there. My company was left at Rorke's Drift in charge of the hospital there, as well as the commissariat.

95 Against 3,000.

"We first heard of the great disaster from Col. Groom, who told us about Lieuts. Melvill and Coghill. We had it, too, from the chaplain, the Rev. W. Smith. He is still living, I believe, but in any case I would like to say what a fine man he was, a true hero, who during the night that followed rendered magnificent service.

"I can see it all now as clearly as I saw it on that day. There were 95 of us at that post, and we knew that 3,000 Zulus, flushed with victory and mad for more slaughter, would soon be upon us. We had just time. It was 3.30 in the afternoon when we saw them begin to round the hill, and never did an enemy seem to have an easier prey. We had had no more than time to improvise barricades with biscuit tins and mealie bags, and now they were upon us.

"What did I feel? I don't know that I felt anything more than all the others felt. In his ordinary life a man often contemplates some possibility and feels that he would be unable to face it, but when it happens he does face it. He finds himself up against it, and goes through with it. That is just about what happened to all of us.

"We knew the seriousness of the affair, but we had no time to sit down and think about it. And now there was the Zulus, and there was one watchword for all of us – we must keep the enemy at bay. I heard that many times during the night that followed.

No Time To Think.

"Besides, when the enemy appeared we had precious little time for thinking. The attack started at 3.30 in the afternoon, and for the next eighteen hours we knew all about it."

Here Pte. John Williams began to show less inclination to talk. One, naturally, wanted him to describe that night of hell and how he helped to save the wounded and the sick. But he would say little more than that it was recorded in the official "Gazette." Therein it is told that –

"Pte. John Williams was posted with Pte. Joseph Williams and Pte. William Horrigan in a distant room of the hospital, which they held for more than an hour, so long as they had a round of ammunition left. As communication was for a time cut off, the Zulus were able to advance and burst open the door. They dragged out Pte. Joseph Williams and two of the patients and assegaied them. Whilst the Zulus were occupied with the slaughter of these men a lull took place, during which Pte. John Williams with the two patients, who were the only men now left alive in this ward, succeeded in knocking a hole in the partition and taking the two patients into the next ward, where he found Pte. Hook. These two men together, one working while the other fought and kept the enemy at bay with his bayonet, broke through three more partitions, and were thus enabled to bring eight patients through a small window into the near line of defence."

"Yes," proceeded Pte. John Williams, "it was a terrible time. All we were concerned with was to keep the enemy at bay and to save the patients if we could. While they were killing poor Joe Williams and Horrigan I was as busy as I could be knocking that hole in the partition."

All he would add was that when his share in the fighting was ended he had just two rounds of ammunition left …

66. 25B/1398 Private Joseph Williams, 'B' Company, 2/24th Foot

66a. *South Wales Argus*, 29 January 1924

Rorke's Drift.
The Story of a Newport Man's gallantry.
How Joseph Williams died.

To the older generation, the story recently told by Private John Williams – and published in the *South Wales Argus* – was a spur to memory. Many of us remember the disaster of Isandhlwana and the heroism of Rorke's Drift; – at the mere mention of those names we hear again the song with which all England rang – "All honour to the Twenty-Fourth" – we recall thrill with which we first heard of the heroism of the men who held out at the Drift. It has led Mr. R. Jenkins, of 4, Raglan-street, Newport, to recall amazing gallantry of one of the defenders who fell. He writes: –

I was much interested to read in your issue of last Friday one more account of the Battle of Rorke's Drift. In this narrative Private John Williams mentions the name of an old playmate of mine – Private Joseph Williams, a man who took a prominent part in the Battle of Isandhlwana at the cost of his life It may be interesting to the rising generation of Newportonians to know that Joseph Williams was a fellow-townsman of theirs. Joe and I were born in close proximity to one another, we went to school together, and we started the battle of life together at a very early age by working in the Dos Works. After a few years of this (both of us were motherless), we started to ferret for our own living. I went to sea, Joe joined the Army – two not very rosy occupations in those days, I can assure you.

Now, we will refer to Joe's gallantry. It appears that Private Joseph Williams was posted on guard single-handed at the door of the temporary hospital and store-room when the Zulus rushed it, coming on in the dusk of the evening. Joe, with bayonet and butt-end of rifle, managed for a short time to keep them at bay, but in beating them and following them up he became surrounded. When poor Joe was found at the dawn of the following morning his body was full of Assegai stabs as there are holes in a riddle. Beside him lay dead 14 Zulus. Joe was supposed to have accounted for the lot. It was reported of him at the time that for single-handed bravery it surpassed everything in the annals of British warfare. His gallantry was recognised by the late Queen Victoria, inasmuch as she forwarded a letter of condolence to his father, accompanied by a sum of money to compensate him for the loss of so gallant a son. May he rest in peace!

66b. *South Wales Argus*, 22 January 1929

How a Newport Man Died.

… Pte. Joseph Williams, referred to, was a Newport man who started life at the Dos Works. It is believed he was on guard single handed at the door when the Zulus rushed it, but, in beating them off with bayonet and butt end of rifle, he was surrounded. When found at dawn next morning his body was riddled with holes from assegais, and beside it were 14 dead Zulus; he is supposed to have accounted for the lot. Queen Victoria forwarded a letter of condolence to his father, accompanied by a sum of money as act of grace for the loss of so brave a son …

67. 2/24 735 Sergeant Joseph Lenford Windridge, 'B' Company, 2/24th Foot

67a. *Birmingham Mail,* 15 March 1879

While two or three Birmingham men have had the misfortune to die upon the battle-field in defending the English column in Zululand, we have the satisfaction of knowing that at least one of our townsmen has escaped the slaughter at Rorke's Drift after conducting himself in a way creditable to himself and to his country.

Lieutenant Chard in his official despatch calls particular attention to the gallant conduct of Sergeant Joseph Windridge during the terribly one-sided struggle at Isandula on the 22nd of January. Windridge, I find, is an old Birmingham man, whose parents live in Granville Street. In his early days he was appointed to learn the printing, and up to 1858 he was employed as a compositor on the Birmingham *Mercury.* When that paper collapsed Windridge abandoned the "stick" and took to the "sword," enlisting in the regiment which has just met with such a melancholy fate. He is one of the survivors, and as his time expires in the course of a few months, his return home is anxiously looked forward to.

68. Pastor Petter Otto Holjer Witt, Swedish Mission Society

68a. A letter from Lt. Col. J.N. Crealock, Assistant Military Secretary, to the Colonial Secretary, Natal, requesting that the Swedish mission station near Rorke's Drift be used for military purposes. [Pietermaritzburg Archives Repository, Pietermaritzburg, South Africa, NAB CSO vol. 679, ref. 1879/172]

To The Hon'ble Colonial Secretary – Natal
1 Jany 1879.

Sir,

I am directed by H.E. the Lt General Commanding to request you will have the goodness to represent to H.E. the Lieut Governor, that in his opinion it is a military necessity that the house and outhouses near Rorkes Drift, the property of Mr De Witte, should be handed over for imperial purposes.

Lord Chelmsford believes that Mr de Witte proposes bringing his family there, which in his opinion should not be permitted, as it is in a very exposed position.

If the Lieut Governor accedes to this request, Lord Chelmsford would suggest that the rent should be decided upon by the Resident Magistrate, and an Officer of the Royal Engineers, and Commissariat Departments; and that the Lieut General should be empowered to take possession of these buildings. He is not aware whether it be necessary to place the border under martial law to enforce this.

Mr de Witte was in negociation with Col. Glyn, but the rent he demanded, viz: – £12 per month for 2 Rooms, and an outhouse, was so exorbitant, that it is evident he is only trying to make a good bargain out of the necessities of the Government.

I have the honor to be,
Sir,
Your most obedient Servant,
J North Crealock
Assistant Military Secretary

68b. *Daily Telegraph and Courier,* 6 March 1879

Plymouth, Wednesday Morning.

I have had a conversation with the missionary Mr. Witt, who arrived here to-night by the Warwick Castle, and proceeded to London, and I am indebted to him for the following statement.

Mr. Witt is a short spare man, with a light beard and moustache. His residence and hospital were close to the scene of the fight at Isandula. He remarked in reference to the statement he had made:

I do not know about the survivors any more than has been already publicly announced. I cannot say whether any more escaped than are now known of.

I was not near enough to the scene of action to gather any exact details of the fight. My position was on a hill on the other side of the river from where the fight was raging. I watched the Zulus descend and draw themselves in long lines between the camp and the river. From where I stood I could also see the English forces advancing to the attack, but I could not see hand-to-hand fighting. I observed that the Zulus were fighting sturdily, and presently I saw that the English were surrounded in a kraal some little distance from the camp. What I was puzzled to learn was the reason why the British troops left their camp to attack, instead of remaining on the defensive. In my opinion they should never have thus advanced. As the fight progressed and I saw that the English were being beaten, I prepared to fly, and had my horse saddled with that object in view. At length I noticed that the Zulus were crossing the river. It was not very deep. The water only reached up to their waists as they forded the stream. I saw that there was no time to be lost, and I dashed away on horseback as hard as I could go, chased by the Zulus who did their best to catch me, but failed. So far as I have been able I have described the fighting which took place correctly. The distance I stood from the fight prevented my observing events more closely.

The following is the statement of Mr. Witt, referred to above:

It was on Jan. 22, 1879. Bright and warm rose the sun over my station, Oscarsburg, situated at the Buffalo River, on the Natal side. At the farm is a drift into the Zulu country, known by the name of Rorke's Drift. Ten minutes' walk from the drift were my houses, two large buildings situate at the border of the Zulus' country, and at the very place where the greatest resistance from the Zulus was expected. Those buildings were found very fit indeed for military purposes, and at the request of the general commanding the forces I left them at his disposal. A large outhouse, 80 by 20 feet, which I used as a church, was turned into a commissariat store, and my dwelling-house, 60 feet by 18, was converted to a hospital, in consequence of which I had to send away my wife and three children. I myself stayed and acted as interpreter between the doctor in charge and the black people. Before the above-mentioned day all was quiet, wagons arriving constantly augmenting the store of provisions, and the only variation in this monotony was the report of skirmishes occurring on this side of the river – but heavy storm is often preceded by sudden calm. The 22nd came and witnessed the battle, in which the warriors on both sides showed, or, perhaps were compelled to show, a courage that cannot be denied neither by contemporaries nor by posterity. Behold, on the one side, 1,000 soldiers, reinforced by equal their number of black, leaving their camp to attack an enemy more than ten times as numerous. Behold, on the other side, this mass of Zulus, who close together and walk straight against the mouth of the cannon. Look, how thousand after thousand are killed, and nevertheless the mass advances without fear, over the dead bodies of comrades against the destroying weapon. Behold, on the one side, a few dozen white troops, the only remainder of the thousand. Look, how they, after having expended all their ammunition, keep close together, trying, yet awhile, to fight for their lives with the bayonets. Behold, on the other side – the blacks – how they are fighting against the intruder and oppressor, fighting for liberty and independence, coming close to the bayonets, and making them harmless by taking the corpses of their brethren and throwing them on the bayonet points. Who wins your warmest sympathy – the captain, who, knowing that he is lost, stops a moment to spike the cannon and die, or the Zulu, who, in his excitement, leaves his fellow soldiers behind, and alone makes the attack on the hospital at Rorke's Drift, resting his gun on the very barricade and firing on those inside? Is your admiration greater for these ninety-five who entered the commissariat store at Oscarsburg and defended it against the 5,000 Zulus than for those 5,000 who fought outside the whole night, trying to overpower the whites, and who withdrew at day break, leaving 1,000 dead, hundreds of whom were lying even on the very verandah of the house? Indeed your admiration ought to be as great for the one as for the other. Where did you find greater courage or contempt of death than theirs?

Doctor R. and myself had in the morning made up our minds to pay a visit to a missionary in the neighbourhood. When about to start at noon we were told that a great fight was taking place over the river. In company of the Chaplain of the Forces we ascended a hill 500ft high, between the station and the river, from where we had an excellent view of what was going on. At a distance of three miles as the crow flies we saw the place where the camp was made. The whole spot swarmed with black figures moving about. Down below, though very hilly and broken, a large flat remained between us and the camp; and on this flat we saw three lines drawn, the one end reaching the camp and the other the river. The whole of it was a shocking sight. The heavy firing from the rifles, mixed with the rolling sound from the big guns and the movements of the lines, all this caused a nervous feeling that something terrifying was going on. What struck us in the beginning was that a good many of the officers of the native contingent had one by one crossed the river some miles below the mission station, and came galloping towards it as fast as the horses could carry them; and, on the left hand side, we noticed some of the mounted natives crossing at the Drift, and driving some cattle before them. Although we could not clearly comprehend this movement, we did not pay much attention to it, our minds being far from dreaming of the real facts.

In the meantime the three lines had drawn themselves more closely to one spot. Here was a large Kaffir kraal, which was gradually surrounded and fired at. How many had entered it I do not know, and will probably never learn, because what was inside there were certainly killed by Zulu bullets. After twenty minutes' heavy firing, the resistance ceased, and the attacking parties divided themselves again. Half of them returned towards the camp, the other half, from 5,000 to 6,000, approaching the river, and the place where I was. Firing every now and then they reached at last the river. There another skirmish took place. The spot where they crossed was half a mile below the Drift, and defended by a few Natal Kaffirs. A tolerably good force could have easily prevented their crossing. Having killed these few Natal Kaffirs, they crossed one by one. This done, they sat down for half an hour in order to get some rest and to strengthen themselves from the snuff-box. Then they separated again, divided into two parties, the one following the course of the river, the other taking its way towards us. We now perceived that the house of a neighbouring farm on the Natal side was on fire; but we were so far from fancying that the Zulus would cross the river that we never had the slightest idea of the real state of things, but still were thinking that the approaching black people were our own troops. They were now so close to us that their bullets could easily have reached us, and we saw that they were all naked. Reality, then, also stood naked for us. The thick mass that swarmed in the camp was the Zulus who had taken possession of it. The light lines firing at the kraal were Zulus; and finally, those who had crossed the river and were approaching were Zulus. The few whites whom we had seen galloping now and then to the Natal side, perhaps were the only survivors of all those who a week before had entered the Zulu country. Our eyes were opened, but why had they not been before? How had the idea of the possibility of a disaster on our side been so far from us that the clearest facts had been unable to make it enter our minds? The officers' flight, the burning farm, the immense masses (say 20,000) moving to and fro in light lines, why had this not long ago told us that the Lord's thoughts are not our thoughts, nor our ways His? These ideas were crossing my mind while we speedily descended the hill, followed by the Zulus.

Arrived at the houses, we saw at once a new proof of the sad truth to which our eyes had just been opened. The tents which surrounded the houses, and were used by a company left there under Major Spalding for the protection of the hospital and the commissariat stores, had been pulled down, and a temporary barricade of meal-sacks was made between the houses, which were a distance of 20 yards one from the other. Here we were met by anxious questions from many lips, "Do the Zulus come here?" and compelled to answer, "In five minutes they will be here." In the same moment the fighting began in the neighbourhood. Though wishing to take part in the defence of my own house, and at the same time in the defence of an important place for the whole colony, yet, my thoughts went to my wife and to my children, who were at a short distance from there, and did not know anything of what was going on. Having seen one part of the Zulus going in that direction, I followed the desire of my heart, saddled my horse, and started to warn my family of what my poor family had had to suffer before. Five days' journey, towards Maritzburg, chased by the Zulus, and frightened by all sorts of reports. I will pass over as of no interest to other people.

The attack on Oscarsburg had been awful. Before I started I saw a Zulu alone at the barricade, kneeling and firing. The whole force drew nearer, and the battle drew on heavier. Soon the hospital was on fire. Our people found it impossible to defend themselves inside the barricade. They must retire within the walls, thus entering the commissariat store. The sick people were brought here, except five who could not be removed, and who were stuck by the Zulus and burnt. That the hospital was put on fire was certainly a great personal loss for me, as all my property was burnt, but it was of great importance for the whole colony, and especially for the people in the commissariat stores, as the flames of the burning house enabled them to aim properly on the Zulus and thus keep them at a fair distance. If the Zulus had known what they ought they should never have put fire to the house, and the heavy darkness of that dreadful night would have made our troops unable to defend themselves as they did.

68c. A letter from Otto Witt to the Board of the Swedish Mission Society, explaining his reasons for departing South Africa in the wake of the disaster at iSandlwana and the destruction of his mission station at Oscarsberg [Church of Sweden Archives, Uppsala, Sweden, ALL:1 – Witt to SKM Board 5/3/1879]

London, March 5th, 1879
To
The Honorable Board of the Swedish Church's Mission, Stockholm

Surely, the sad rumour regarding the English defeat against the Zulus has already reached the Hon. Board. Suddenly and unexpectedly, one of the four regiments marching against the Zulus has been destroyed almost to the last man by the latter. The Zulus have entered the Colony, ravaging, and Oscarsberg has been burned. We barely managed to save our lives. Our suffering during five days on the run, hunted by Zulus day and night, defies description and might have rendered us incapable of intellectual work, had not a longer period of rest among friends helped somewhat to erase the memory of these horrible days.

But not only are the Zulus stronger than the English troops, the Natal kaffers, on whose help one had counted, are rising up to throw off the English yoke, the neighbouring tribes follow their example, and to make matters worse, the Dutch farmers in the Transvaal are using the events to protest against the annexation of their land and are already negotiating with the Zulu King. Such was the situation in Natal, as my people and I reached Durban. Everyone who could escape went there, and we barely managed to secure lodgings for a while, at a high price. But what were we to do in the future? We prepared for the worst. The remaining troops were not able to hold the Zulus at bay, and every day one expected them to attack Maritzburg or Durban. No help from England was to be expected within two months.

Facing these facts, I wondered if not it would be best if my people and I returned to Sweden. If the Lord wants to save the colony from doom, it is hard to see how safety will be restored there within one or maybe two years, and if we during this time were to stay in Durban at a cost of perhaps £2 per day, a trip home would be preferable from an economic point of view. Add to this the necessity to buy things necessary to make a home in the expensive colony. Finally, I feared that the mission's oxen and wagon would be taken from us, if I did not sell them first, maybe I myself would be taken from my family and turned into a soldier. Already during our escape down to Durban, I scrutinised these things and asked the Lord that, if he wanted me to stay, he put obstacles in our path; but since I daily saw how the Lord brought us step by step away from the Zulus, I sold the oxen and the wagon and went aboard along with my people to go home. The last news that reached us, before we set sail, was that all oxen and wagons were to be turned over to the government for use as transport of military supplies, and that no man fit for military service was allowed to leave the colony; instead, they were to join the army.

A Zulu youth, who six months ago had to flee from his country, and who was put into my service for three years by the English government, asked to follow me home to receive further education and baptism, and since I am convinced that it is his honest intention to become a Christian, I approved his request, since I am responsible for him, and since this would give me the opportunity to practice the language of the blacks during my absence from the colony.

Hoping that the Hon. Board will judge my decision to return home as mildly as possible, I intend to leave my family in Helsingborg and appear before the Board as soon as possible.

With the deepest reverence,

Humbly,

Otto Witt

68d. Extract from a list of items, and their estimated values, belonging to the Witt family that were destroyed during the fighting at Rorke's Drift [Church of Sweden Archives, Uppsala, Sweden, SKA 29/12/1879, List of Belongings]

Page 1

8 zulu carpets	30
cloths, ribbons, rags, yarn etc	250
brocades and other loose items	100
oil, kerosene, candles, spices	100
salt, sugar, rice, flour, fruit etc	600
trading items, pearls etc	100
cattle, pigs, hens etc	500
books, sheet music, albums etc	700

Women's clothing

18 chemises, 6 night gowns, 12 night shirts	90
18 night caps, 18 pcs of underwear, 60 pairs of socks	135
6 bodices, 5 peignoirs, 10 wool sweaters	43
2 felt skirts, 6 flannel skirts, 17 white skirts	116
1 silk dress, 4 wool dresses	180
3 cotton dresses, 2 cardigans	50
1 fur lined coat, 2 lined silk gloves	115
3 hats, 1 belt, 12 pairs of cufflinks	35
18 collars, 36 handkerchiefs, 12 aprons	39
3 pairs of boots, 9 shawls, 1 umbrella	134
1 parasol, 4 kerchiefs, 1 sewing machine	52

Children's clothing

3 shirts, 2 wool sweaters, 5 flannel skirts	43
3 pairs of underpants, 2 p. flannel trousers, 2 p. wool socks	17
18 pairs of cotton socks, 5 pairs of boots	41
18 dresses, 12 aprons, 36 diapers	117
4 hats, 1 cradle net	45
Christening costume in Irish embroidery (gift)	400

Men's clothing	
1 winter greatcoat, 1 raincoat	125
4 sets of clothing, 2 thin cardigans	500
3 bright coats, 1 frock, 2 hats	70

68e. Extract from Witt's letter accepting compensation for damages to his property at Rorke's Drift [Pietermaritzburg Archives Repository, Pietermaritzburg, South Africa, NAB CSO vol. 949]

Rev. Otto Witt, Rorke's Drift.
Accepts on behalf of the Swedish Mission society, the sum of £450 in compensation for the damage done during the Zulu War & £200 for himself personally.
Acknowledged 13.2.84

To G Nicholls, Esq., Act Ass. Col. Secrety.
Rorke's Drift, Feb. 9. 1884

Sir,

I beg to inform you that I am in receipt of your letter of Feb. 4th stating that the Lord Commissioner's of Her Majesty's Treasury have been pleased to sanction the payment of the sum of £450 on account of damage done during the Zulu War to the Swedish Mission House at Rorke's Drift, and of the sum of £200 to me personally.

Further I beg to state that I will accept the above named amount viz £450 and £200 in full satisfaction of all demands in connection with these claims, as well from the side of the Mission Society as from my own side.

Please be good enough to inform me what I have to do in order to get possession of the money.

I have &c.
(signed) Otto Witt

69. 25B/1316 Private Caleb Wood, 'B' Company, 2/24th Foot

69a. *Derbyshire Times*, 27 December 1913

Rorke's Drift.
Story of British Valour Retold
By Ilkeston Veteran Who Was There.

Who has not heard of the noble stand made by a fragment of the British Army at Rorke's Drift during the Zulu War of 1877–9 against a host of fierce natives? Many of us have read the thrilling story of the gallant little band who for hours held thousands at bay, and our imagination has been fired and our enthusiasm for British pluck has burned when we have seen that terrible struggle portrayed in colour by the skilled hand of the artist. But the crowning experience of the present generation, is to hear the story of that awful struggle from the lips of one who in daylight and darkness stood behind the wall of corn sacks with fixed bayonet defying assegais and bullets, and helping to form the line of fire and steel which kept the yelling blacks at bay.

Such a one was Caleb Wood, of 55 Lower Chapel Street, Ilkeston, who served his country in that famous regiment the 24th Foot, now known as the South Wales Borderers, and is the proud possessor of a medal with clasp for the Kaffir War and Zulu War in South Africa. The 24th has a proud record dating from the famous Battle of Blenheim, with a host of famous battles to its credit, including engagements in the Peninsular war, India, South Africa and Burma.

Our hero was born in 1858, in Ruddington, Notts., where as a boy he worked as a stockinger at a hand frame. At the age of 19 he enlisted as a soldier in company with Robt. Tongue, another Ruddington youth, and both these young recruits were destined early to experience the rigours of campaign work. Wood as a private of the 25th Brigade 2nd (24th) Regiment, joined the depot at Brecon, South Wales, after going through the recruit's course. Eventually he was drafted to his regiment at Chatham where they were equipped for the Kaffir war. They journeyed to Portsmouth and embarked on the "Himalaya." …

... War Against The Zulus

War was declared against the King of the Zulus, and the services of the 24th Regiment were required. They embarked at East London for Natal, and landed at Durban. They marched to Pietermaritzburg for inspection and equipment ready for active service. The colonel in command in the interval of waiting did not let them idle their time, but gave them plenty of bayonet exercise. "And a good thing for some of us," said Private Wood when telling us his further experiences, "for soon after we had to make good use of our steel." After a few weeks the regiment went on the line of march, and reached Grey Town, and then passed on to Helpmakar where the 1st Battalion 24th, and the 2nd Battalion met for the first time since the battle of Chillianwallah in 1849. A singular incident took place here. Some of the officers of the 1st Battalion invited the 2nd Battalion officers to join them at mess. When the wine came on one proposed a toast, and in doing so expressed the hope that they would have better luck this time than they had at Chillianwallah. Strange to say not one of them was alive a month later.

From Helpmakar the 24th moved on to the celebrated Rorke's Drift, a mission station, on the banks of the Buffalo River, and on the border of Zululand. On the 11th January 1879 the men bearing arms were the 1st and 2nd Battalions of the 24th Regiment, a battery of artillery and a rocket battery numbering 2,600 men, under General Thesiger. All the troops crossed the river within an hour and a half except B. Company of the 2nd 24th, including Private Wood. There were thus left about 110 men with those in the hospital, and they had no captain, he having been wounded in an engagement with the Kaffirs a short time before.

"We pitched our tents," said Private Wood, "at the foot of the mountain in the rear of the storehouse at Rorke's Drift. Meanwhile the column was very busy. We could see them making preparations to march into the Barshee Valley to make an attack upon the stronghold of one of the Zulu chiefs named Doublemanza. In a few hours they returned victorious. Then after a day or two they struck camp and proceeded to Isandhlwana." Quoting from the records of his Battalion our hero says: – On 20th January, 1879, the scouts brought news into the camp that a great number of Zulus had been seen a few miles out. The order was given for part of the column to go out very early next morning to make an attack on them. The remainder were to stay in the camp and form a laager with the wagons, for some reason the latter was not done. Meanwhile the General with his men continued to follow up the enemy for many miles, at last they came to a halt and lay down for a rest. Previous to this a mounted officer had been sent back to camp to order provisions, but when he got near the place he found it in the enemy's possession, and at once rode back to the General with the awful news. Riding between the lines, the commandant spoke these words: "Now my men, we have had a hard day, but we have, I am sorry to say, a still harder night before us. Whilst we have been out the enemy has taken possession of the camp, and we must take it back at the point of the bayonet. I know I can depend on you doing your duty and being a credit to your country, so take a little rest, then fill your water bottles ready, for we must get back if possible before darkness overtakes us." The men gave three cheers to show that they could be relied upon, and when the order was given to fall in they commenced the return journey silently but determined to fight to the bitter end.

At last they reached the brow of the hill and the order was given for the artillery to unlimber and prepare for action. Shell after shell went screaming through the air, and then the "cease fire" sounded. A double line of infantry went charging through the camp, tripping over the bodies of their dead comrades. They reached the opposite hill and then gave vent to cheers to let it be known they had accomplished the task set them. They all thought the same fate had befallen the detachment at Rorke's Drift, but that was not the case.

At Rorke's Drift

We now come to the eventful day which made Rorke's Drift celebrated in British military annals. "On 22nd January, 1879" said Wood, continuing his personal narrative, "I and a few of my comrades were on fatigue duty a short distance from the camp, burying some dead cattle when we heard the artillery firing at Isandhlwana, and also the sound of infantry volleys. One man said 'Hark! Them's our big guns if I'm not mistaken.'

'Ah, and our chaps as well,' said another. 'My word, they're giving them something to go with. It sounds to me as if our chaps are mowing them down. It's just what I thought: we shan't be able to say a word, we shall be like a lot of dummies.' Having finished our work we returned to camp and had dinner. We were settling down for the afternoon when one of the cooks described a mounted man coming as fast as he could from Isandhlwana. We wondered what was the matter. Then we saw another coming as fast as his horse could get over the ground. The first horseman shouted 'They're coming' and rode on to Helpmakar, but the second dismounted and asked to be shown to the officer's tent. Lieut. Bromhead came out and asked him what was the matter. 'Half the battalion that was left in the camp at Isandhlwana are massacred,' replied the man, 'and the Zulus are on their way to Rorke's Drift.' The officer gave the order to 'Stand to arms' and a message was sent to Lieut. Chard, an Engineer officer, to bring a small party from the pontoon bridge a short distance away. When we had fallen in the officer told us what had happened, and said whatever occurred there, we should stand firm to the last man. Our commander was a gentleman we all respected, for he shared and endured the same hardships with his men. I cannot speak too highly of Lieut. Bromhead. Our next order was to take up positions round the hospital, but first ground arms. 'Now then,' was the word, 'all hands take hold of the sacks of corn and build a wall from the corner of the hospital to the storehouse.' This was soon done. 'Now another from the hospital to the cattle kraal.' This was our fortification. Scarcely was this complete when a mounted man who was out scouting for our benefit rode in with the news that the Zulus, about 3,000 strong, were just behind the hill. We fell in between the hospital and the storehouse and fixed our rifle sights at 400 yards.

A Hundred Against Three Thousand.

"Then the Zulus made their appearance. A man named Hitch climbed to the top of the storehouse for a better view, and exclaiming 'Oh, there is a lot,' he fired the first shot. The enemy soon showed themselves, Lieut. Bromhead gave the order for three volleys, and at the first volley the ranks of the Zulus went down as though they had been cut off at the knees. We had only a chance to fire one more volley when there came an order to fix bayonets. Some of the enemy had got inside the defences, but they were never able to get out again. Then the battle began in real earnest. There was a fight for the hospital We tried to get the sick out of the building, and did our best but could not save all. The men who won the Victoria Cross did good work, but we covered them whilst it was being done with our rifles and bayonets. There was one little man amongst us whom the soldiers used to chaff about his size telling him he would make a nice soldier to defend his country. His height was only about 4 feet 10 inches, and he was a carpenter employed by the Government to attend to the pontoon bridge. One of the officers lent him a sword and relied upon his revolver only. The little man stood against the wall for some time with his sword ready for anything. At last, he got his chance. A Zulu put his head above the wall and the diminutive carpenter brought him down, remarking 'There, shouldn't I make a soldier' as he waved his sword triumphantly in the air. One brave man moved about among us unarmed all the succeeding night doing good work by serving out ammunition. This was the Rev. George Smith. How he escaped I do not know. He was constantly giving encouragement, first to one man and then another.

Hospital Fired

"Very soon the enemy got possession of the hospital, and after losing a few men we had to retreat behind another wall of defence that had hastily been constructed. The hospital was set on fire. A young man named Joseph Williams, had stood at the door of the building and had killed fourteen Zulus when he was dragged out and despatched by the infuriated enemy. The remnant of the little band who had guarded the hospital made their way to the inner wall of defence. When the Zulus became so thick round the hospital, one soldier named Marshall, whom we had all regarded as peculiar and different from the others of us, stood his ground for a second or two while we were taking up our position ten yards away. We shouted 'Come here, you silly.' When he saw where we were he turned about and came, but at the risk of his life, for he was followed by the enemy. Hastily turning round with his fixed bayonet he brought three Zulus down with the point from the guard. Then charge after charge was made by the Zulus, but they were met by our fire, the men going down it seemed in bunches. One soldier named J. Fagan, aged about 21, was mortally wounded by a rifle shot, and fell, but got up again, as if he knew not what had happened to him, fired two shots and then collapsed and died.

24. Sixty-eight members of B Company, 2/24th, under the caption 'Defenders of Rorke's Drift', photographed at Pinetown in November 1879. Gonville Bromhead, VC, stands far left, next to Colour Sergeant Frank Bourne. (Ron Sheeley collection)

25. Charles Robson with his family in early 1917. Robson held the rank of Driver in the Royal Engineers and served as John Chard's batman from 1878 to 1880.

26. 'I was one of the number, and in addition to defending the building, our duty was to rescue the sick. We had scarcely taken our place in the hospital before two of the six men were killed in front of the building, leaving only four of us to hold the building and get the sick men out. This was done by two men carrying the sick while my comrade, R. Jones, and I kept the doors with our bayonets, all our ammunition being expended' – William Jones, VC.

27. Corporal William Roy, DCM, 1/24th. After his discharge from the army, Roy emigrated to Australia in 1883. He died in Parramatta, Sydney in 1890, age 35. (Ron Sheeley collection)

28. 'Don't swear boys, but shoot them': the Reverend George Smith, Army Chaplains Department, photographed in the late 1880s.

29. Two surviving 1879 war shields from the uThulwana ibutho. Regimental war-shields were the property of the state rather than the individual and were issued when an ibutho assembled for war – the hides reflected a uniform pattern for each ibutho, the uThulwana's being white with red spots. Both the large isihlangu pattern (right) and smaller umbhumbhulozu pattern (left) were carried in action, even within the same ibutho – it is therefore possible that these particular shields might have been at Rorke's Drift.

30. Drummer Arthur Sears, A Company, 2/24th. It is most likely that Sears was a patient in the hospital at the time of the battle. Three of Arthur's brothers served with the 24th.

31. A Zulu induna (state official or officer) wearing several tokens of his status, notably a bunch of scarlet and green feathers from the purple-crested lourie, and a necklace of leopard claws.

32. A Zulu man wearing the isicoco, the head-ring which marked the status of a married man. All of the amabutho who fought at Rorke's Drift were married, and of a similar age to this man.

33. Young Zulus in full regalia. Each ibutho wore a distinctive costume on ceremonial occasions, but this was largely discarded for active service. Regimental war shields in 1879 were larger than those carried here.

34. The mission station some months after the battle. The original defences have been replaced by high stone walls and the storehouse roof – stripped of its thatch on 23 January – has been covered with a large tarpaulin. In the foreground are two meat frames for stretching cattle hides. It was upon these frames that several Zulus were hanged after the battle. From a painting by Lieutenant W.W. Lloyd, 24th Foot. (Rattray collection)

35. King Cetshwayo kaMpande, photographed in captivity after the war. Although the king did not personally take part in the fighting in 1879, he was of the age group of the uThulwana ibutho, and had served with them as a young man. The uThulwana enjoyed a high reputation because of the number of high-status individuals in its ranks.

36. 'Guilty or Not Guilty? These two prisoners at Helpmakaar, who were captured just after the engagement of Isandlwhana as spies, and were suspected of torturing the poor little drummer boys of the 1st Battalion 24th Regiment. They were made fast to a wagon by ropes, but having been caught in the act of trying to escape, were, for greater security, made fast to a tent-pole to await trial.' *The Graphic*, 29 March 1879.

37. 'What's that on the wall? It was a flag ...' The remnants of No. 3 column arrive back at Rorke's Drift on the morning of 23 January.

38. Pastor Otto Witt and Prince Mkhwelantaba Joseph KaMathaka Zulu waseGazini photographed upon their arrival in London in 1879. Mkhwelantaba was later ordained as a priest in Sweden. He returned to South Africa in 1885 taking up a post back at Oscarsberg. (Church of Sweden Archives)

39. Zulu men taking snuff; the men of the uThulwana would have looked much like this, and are recorded to have taken snuff after crossing the Mzinyathi River and before attacking the post; the snuff was likely to have included powdered medicines which were believed to have protective powers on going into battle.

40. Seven men of the 24th Regiment who were awarded the Victoria Cross, photographed in Brecon in 1897. From the left, standing: Robert Jones, Henry Hook, William Jones; seated: David Bell (awarded for his actions at the Little Andaman Islands in 1867), Edward Stevenson Browne, (Khambula, Anglo-Zulu War 1879), Frederick Hitch and John Williams.

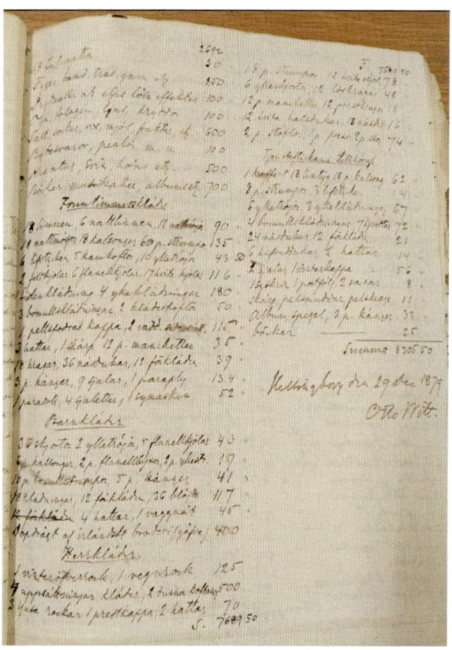

41. A page from Otto Witt's list of belongings lost in the destruction of his house at Oscarsberg. It took five years of negotiation before Witt received compensation for his losses. (Church of Sweden Archives, Uppsala)

42. John Williams, VC, B Company, 2/24th, photographed in 1920. Williams, real name John Fielding, re-joined the army at the start of the First World War. He was discharged unfit for further service in May 1920 at the age of 63.

Black Darkness and Cold Steel.

"The fighting was fierce during the afternoon, but more so after dark. We were so pressed on that Evan Jones hit out with his fists, and let me say he knew how to use them. When our ammunition began to run short the order was given to use cold steel. We stood back from the wall and received the enemy's charges with the bayonet at the "shorten arms," a point which it is almost impossible for any man to turn aside, for there is so much weight behind it. This was very well to stop the first ranks, but points from the guard in quick succession was the method we adopted. We were amazed at the determination of the enemy. One of our men said to about half-a-dozen of us during a calm in the fight; 'Now, lads, listen to me. Let us all stand firm where we are. We may as well die on this side of the wall as on the other; that is if we have got to die. I don't think we shall live to see the light of another day; but we may if we stand firm and never mind how many there are trying to get in. Hark! They are coming. One volley, then step back and shorten arms. Give them the same again.' This type of thing went on for some time till the Zulus began to alter their mode of attack. Some, taking advantage of what cover they could, made as much noise as possible for the purpose of drawing our fire while others of them made an attack on the other side of our position. It was a good move, but did not come off successfully, thanks to someone in the storehouse who gave us warning.

"This battle had various effects on our men. Some who had always been ready to crack a joke could not now seem to speak a word. One man, unbearably vexed at our position, cried like a child, fought like a lion, and swore like a demon. Somewhere, about three o'clock (in the morning), the Zulus began to retire to the hills a short distance away. Their firing got very slack – just a shot now and again from their old Brown Bess's. They were evidently getting tired of their job.

'Now chaps,' said Corporal Bessel, 'What do you say if we fill a pipe and have a smoke?'

'Right-o!' we replied. 'Keep a sharp look-out and we can have a few draws each.' The pipe was filled, and oh! how nice it was. It seemed to be the best bit of tobacco I had ever had. Whilst the first was getting his draw, his comrades impatient to get their turn, said 'Now then, hand it over; you're going black in the face.' There were six of us to that pipe, but presently down it went. 'They're coming again' was the cry, 'Get ready for them.' This was the best and the last assault, and the men came over from the other side and helped us resist it. Many Zulus fell that time, and a few of our men as well. The enemy retreated again to the hills. A few shots were exchanged as daylight began to appear, and then firing ceased altogether.

"Relieved!"

"We mounted the walls of defence to get as distant a view as we could, and between five and six o'clock we saw our General returning with the remainder of his men. As soon as they got near enough to be signalled to Lieutenant Bromhead gave order to the two signalmen to get to the roof of the storehouse and send a message. The signal was 'Come at all possible speed. The enemy's on our left rear.' In half-an-hour they were with us, and meanwhile, the Zulus, having observed their approach, had beaten a hasty retreat into their own country. Then, and not till then, did we see the effect of the battle. Our losses were 15 killed and 17 wounded, while the Zulus left 350 dead, their losses in wounded being unknown.

"The men who fought at Rorke's Drift were 91 of B. Company, 2nd 24th Foot, 6 of the 1st 24th Foot, 2 Army Service Corps, 1 Army Hospital Corps, 1 Artillery, 1 Carrington's Light Horse, Chaplain of the Forces (Rev. George Smith), and one civilian."

The veteran whose story is thus told closes his exciting narrative by quoting the following lines:

> "But the body takes its honour or dishonour from the soul,
> And their names are writ in fire upon our nation's long deed roll.
> Yet let no name of any name be set above the rest,
> Where all are braver than the brave, each better than the best."

A Grey-Haired Veteran.

Caleb Wood is now a grey-haired veteran with grown-up sons, but he is still alert and active, and works as a lace operative. He left the army in 1883, and served ten years in the Army Reserve. He also "went up" at the call of his country during the South African War and did garrison duty at Newport,

Monmouth. The desire came hot upon him to return to the scenes of his old campaigning days. Tongue, his old companion in enlistment, still lives in Ruddington, but is unfortunately an invalid. Possibly these two old comrades are the only survivors in the Midlands of that gallant band who held the fierce hordes of Zulu's at bay at the mission station on the Buffalo River, and when occasionally they meet they still compare notes and live over again that thrilling afternoon and night behind the wall of corn bags at Rorke's Drift.

69b. *Nottingham Daily Express,* 23 July 1914

Ilkeston Hero of Rorke's Drift.
Thrilling Story of Night Fight with Zulus.
True British Pluck.
(Express Special.)

Such is the softening influence of the hands of time on the rugged incidents of war and Empire-building that Isandlwana and Rorke's Drift, the one with its bitterness and the other with its splendour, are now little more than memories of the middle-aged. Yet a representative of the "Express" who, on a bright summer's afternoon not long ago at Ilkeston, handled a yellow piece of skin felt those two incidents of British history very near and very real. The faded strip of skin was a piece of the head of the drum played on the night of January 21st, 1879, scarcely twelve hours before the terrible massacre at the "The Place of the Little Hand." It is the property of Mr. Caleb Wood, of 36, Lower Chapel-street, one of the remnant of heroes who held Rorke's Drift against gigantic odds, immediately after Isandlwana. He is proud, too, of that relic, but prouder still of the story of how he and hardly a hundred comrades held out the Zulu hordes, there on the Natal side of the Buffalo River, through one long afternoon and night, till Chelmsford's relief came at daybreak.

A true appreciation of that night's heroism yet remains to be written, but even as it is the man-in-the-street has a hazy idea that Rorke's Drift and the men of Rorke's Drift have somewhere a page of history as bright as any in the chronicle of British arms. However, be that as it may, it was with extreme modesty and self-effacement that Mr. Wood told his story in the quiet of his own parlour.

Born in the parish of Ruddington, Mr. Wood enlisted on February 26th, 1877, at Nottingham, joining the old 24th (Warwickshire) Regiment, now the South Wales Borderers.

Mr. Wood's first engagement was at Tabarandodi where, along with the 90th, they took some 300 women and children prisoners, more for the sake of their captives' own protection than anything else.

The battle itself was not a brilliant affair.

Following this brush with the enemy Mr. Wood's company, under Lieutenant Bromhead, were joined by the Natal Carbineers and a few more companies of infantry, the whole proceeding to Mount Camp, where a second battle was fought in the "bush".

Cause of the War.

"I don't reckon it was a war, that Kaffir business," said Mr. Wood, "but at any rate, soon afterwards the chief who caused the trouble died and was buried with military honours by the English. Peace was declared with the Kaffirs, but it was not long before war broke out between the English and the King of the Zulus, Cetewayo." Cetewayo was the fourth King of the Zulus and great nephew of Chaka, who was practically the founder of the Zulu race. When the latter came to his chieftainship in 1813 his people were a single tribe living between the eastern slopes of the Drackensburgs and the coast. In fifteen years they had become the greatest Black power in Africa and had invincibly swept the country on every side, killing, one authority estimates, more than a million human beings, and adding vast tracts to their territory. It was little wonder, therefore, that after fifty years' supremacy almost they should, in the general conflict of British, Boer, and Black interests, have become a serious factor in the politics of South Africa. Sir Bartle Frere regarded the Zulu war as necessary in the interests of self-defence, and an ultimatum that Cetewayo should disband his army was issued. This, by virtue of the Zulu character, was almost an impossibility, even had the King been disposed to carry it into effect. Hence, the Zulu war.

"We boarded a vessel at East London for Natal," said Mr. Wood. "Disembarking at Durban, we made our way to Pietermaritzburg, where we were re-equipped with arms and ammunition, rigged out with clothing, boots and accoutrement. The process finished, we marched to Greytown, which lies on the way to Rorke's Drift, and then to Helpmakaar, where a singular incident took place. I was in the 2nd battalion of the 24th, and it was at Helpmakaar that this battalion met their comrades of the 1st for the first time since the massacre of Chillianwallah in the Punjaub in '49. To celebrate the meeting the officers of the 1st invited the officers of the 2nd to join them at mess as they had a bottle of wine left over from Christmas. So a few of the younger men joined together and had a bit of a festival, and one officer in proposing a toast said that he hoped the regiment would have better luck than they had at Chillianwallah, where they had suffered so terribly. Not a man who drunk that toast was alive a month after!

"A few days afterwards we marched on to Rorke's Drift – a farmhouse and storehouse on the Natal side of the Buffalo River, which divides that country from Zululand. The place took its name from Jim Rorke, a farmer, who had lived there. I don't remember ever having seen him, but we used his house for a hospital, and the storehouse for storing arms and ammunition.

1,300 Massacred.

"On January 11th, 1879, we fell in – both 1st and 2nd battalions – somewhere about 2,600 strong, and in an hour and a half all these men had crossed except my company – B. We were about 104 in number, and under the command of Lieutenant Broomhead. The main body who had crossed the river soon got to grips with the Zulus, for in the afternoon we could hear the rattle of their firearms and see the smoke rising. The main body returned that evening and camped on the opposite side of the river from us, while we pitched our tents behind the storehouse. The next day they struck camp and proceeded to Isandlwana. As the crow flies from Rorke's Drift to Isandlwana is not more than five or six miles, but owing to the mountains, it is a pretty long zig-zag march.

"Well, I had better give you some idea of the state of things and what happened at Isandlwana. On January 21st the General in command, Lord Chelmsford, had received accounts from scouts that the Zulus had been seen in numbers over the hills a short distance away, and accordingly he gave orders for half the column, about 1,600, to fall in at about three in the morning. The other half remained in camp and should have been in readiness. We believe his orders would be the same as they always were – that they should go into laager, but for some reason or another this was not done. The probability is that had it been done they would have been able to resist the Zulus and thus have saved their lives. The General with his half column followed a small body of Zulus, but there was no fighting. As the day was advancing he decided to camp for the night and accordingly despatched a mounted messenger to Isandlwana for provisions. In due course this messenger returned to the General with the terrible information that the Zulus were in possession of the camp at Isandlwana. A little later the men rose and marched back again. As they reached the brow of the hill overlooking Isandlwana they realised the worst. Their camp was in possession of the Zulus, who greatly outnumbered the British, and about thirteen hundred of their comrades had been massacred. Darkness fell as they gathered on the hill and the General gave orders for the artillery to be brought forward and about four or five field pieces were brought into action. The 'Cease fire' was sounded after a few shells had been fired through the camp, and the infantry was brought up in double line. The order was given for 'Fix bayonets' and the men charged through the camp, tripping over the bodies of their dead comrades. So they reached the hill on the other side, and without provisions lay there until morning, when the General said: 'There's nothing for it: we must proceed to Rorke's Drift though I expect they have suffered the same.'

Sport!

"Meanwhile, at Rorke's Drift, we had been having a very easy time. On the 22nd I and some of my mates were out burying some cattle – cattle often die out there and you have to bury them quickly for your own health's sake – when we heard the rattle of firearms at Isandlwana. We were cursing our fortune as being left out of it again while the others were having all the sport. Sport they called it!

"We had returned to camp, and after dinner were settling down for the afternoon, which means it was time for the cards to come out, when Fred Hitch, one of the cooks – the man we buried in London a while back – shouted, 'There's a fellow coming across yonder as fast as his horse can get him over the ground!' We looked and saw a horseman riding for all he was worth in our direction from Isandlwana. He was followed in a second or two by another. The first one rode straight past shouting, 'Look out! They are coming.' The second man dismounted as he reached us and asked to see the officer in charge. We took him to Broomhead's tent, and as we were all mighty interested I can tell you, we stood round to hear his story. 'The regiment's massacred at Isandlwana,' we heard him say, 'but we were bathing in the river and so made our escape.' As soon as Broomhead heard that he shouted 'Stand to arms!' and we fell in in our shirt sleeves. He marched us down to the hospital and put us in skirmishing order, but a civilian, employed by the Government, I think, who was with us, suggested that it would be better to build a wall around with the mealie bags that were stacked there. Using the corners of the buildings for the angles, we built a wall all round four feet high, and, what's more, did it in twenty minutes, officers and men working like niggers. We were joined by Lieutenant Chard and one or two Engineers from the pontoon bridges, and another civilian who was with us acted as scout by riding to the top of the hill and telling us how near the Zulus were getting. Later, Private Hitch climbed on to the roof of the storehouse to have a look over the hill at the rear. He sighted the Zulus first, and with a remark as to their great number he fired a shot at them. As soon as he did so they showed themselves; we fired two volleys, but before we could fire the third the order was to 'Fix bayonets!' and receive them at shortened arms. The first charge brought some of them in, but those Zulus never got out again. In a few minutes it became a fight for the hospital, so that we could save the men who were hurt and sick. The roof of the place was of thatch, a fact which soon commended itself to the Zulus, and one of them set it on fire. It has been said that all the men in the hospital were saved, but this is not so – though most of them must have been – because I buried the charred remains of a man myself.

Warm Work Indeed.

"All the afternoon and night it was a hand to hand fight, the Zulus using their assegais, and we our bayonets. They were big fellows, the savages, and did not seem to fear death at all. They would charge at night up to the wall and seize hold of your bayonet, and wrestle with it. At one place their bodies were piled up to a height of four or five feet. They must have died in hundreds, while our losses were only about fifteen killed. After about two or three hours of incessant fighting in the night we began to think it was a case with us, and that we would never see the light of day again.

"The fight never slackened or waned for hours. Fighting side by side with me was Robert Tongue, who now lives at Ruddington, and one man I know, Joseph Williams, killed fourteen Zulus himself in a very short time. But they were determined men, and absolutely didn't fear death at all. It was a terrific struggle, but at daybreak they drew off, and we saw the General and men. Broomhead sent a man to the top of the store house to signal 'Come at all possible speed, the enemy is on our left rear.' We were relieved, and from that day to this I have never again seen thc Zulus.

"How did we do it? Ah! that's always been a puzzle to me. I can't tell you how it was done, except that every man stood firm like a rock. We fired 36 boxes of ammunition, and there's a good many thousands of rounds in each box, so you can understand it was warm work."

Warm work indeed! and such as none but heroes could have dreamt of, let alone execute. The veldt has seen many a combat, but none greater than this, and few of the little tokens issued by the War Office have been welded to deeds of greater gallantry or more fittingly displaying the individual greatness of the British soldier.

70. By an unidentified defender

70a. *The Lancet,* 8 March 1879

The Gallant Defence at Rorke's Drift.

One of the wounded men states as follows: –

"After the niggers surrounded us we fought like tigers. I saw Dr. Reynolds (A.M.D.) blazing away at them, cheering the ones that were hit, running to the fellow, dressing his wounds, then fighting away like a hero. He and the Hospital Corps men defended the hospital to the last moment. When the Zulus got in they charged through them and got into the laager behind waggons and mealie bags, where they all fought like true Britons until daylight. They made several sorties, and drove them off splendidly."

Surgeon Reynolds, writing the next day, reporting the loss of hospital stores, never mentions a single word about himself, but simply states, "I am glad to say that the men of the A.H.C. behaved splendidly; and I am almost certain that Lieutenant Hall, A.H.C., and several men were killed." They were with Dr. Shepherd. But for the magnificent defence by that one brave company, the victorious Zulus would have swept down upon Greytown, and would certainly have destroyed Helpmakaar, laying everything to waste before them.

71. By an unidentified defender

71a. Extract from an unidentified South African newspaper, c. 1879

We have been kindly permitted to make the following extract from a private letter, written by an officer who was present at the defence of Rorke's Drift: –

"Rorke's Drift was splendidly defended. Not a man in it who did not fight for his life from the very commencement of the attack made upon us. The people who escaped from Sandhlwana and came to inform us of the disaster there assured us again and again there was no chance for our escape from certain death, except by rushing away without a moment's reflection: that the Zulus were in myriads; that they had taken our camp only seven miles away, which was then running with the blood of nearly 1,000 white men, not one of whom had escaped. I assure you that these people, four or five of them, coming in madly in ones and two, shouted and screamed at the pitch of their voices all the miseries which had just taken place at Sandhlwana and, worst of all, in the midst of our men. However, by the time the Zulus did come, all our panic was over, and you cannot imagine a lot of men settling down to their work more coolly and methodically. Firing commenced from our men at about 700 yards, and I really think we did more damage then in proportion than afterwards; every shot seemed to fall among the enemy; but the devils did not care for us or our guns. They came on trotting, as if nothing extraordinary were happening, and without returning a shot until they arrived at our laager.

Our business at this time became very, very desperate. It was all round the hospital, and the slaughter of the Zulus in the morning in this vicinity showed how well our labour told, and how desperately the brutes fought. I can't conceive any human courage equal to theirs; it amounts simply to madness. But there is one thing seems worthy of notice in their mode of fighting. They shoot comparatively little, but believe in their own overwhelming crowd breaking down any opposition by firearms or other weapons, and they go in purely for doing the 'eating up' dodge, at which, I admit, they are very clever. On the other hand, I think the Zulus must have suffered severely, and some of their mad ardour must have cooled a bit. They cannot continue to fight as they have done. A few defeats will demoralize them, and then they will sink in character to the level of the common Kafir."

CHAPTER 2

'It was beastly': The Treatment of Zulu Wounded after the Battle

BY IAN KNIGHT

Early on the morning of 22 January 1879, half a day before the cataclysmic clashes at iSandlwana and Rorke's Drift, British troops under Lt. Col. Charles Pearson defeated a Zulu force attempting to contain their advance on the banks of the Nyezane River. Pearson's force had been caught on the march. The Zulu attacks, poorly co-ordinated, allowed Pearson to deploy and concentrate his firepower on one element of the Zulu force, causing it to break and withdraw. The battle had lasted less than an hour. Whilst Pearson had lost just ten men killed and sixteen wounded, Zulu dead numbered upwards of 400 men.[1]

Although the Zulus had carried away their wounded where they could, many more had been abandoned and, as the British regrouped at the end of the battle, some of the Natal volunteer troops took the opportunity to examine the ground where the Zulus had advanced. They found many wounded lying out in the grass in the hot sun, not able to get away. Since Pearson himself was preparing to continue his advance, there was no time to tend to the Zulu wounded, let alone take them with him. Many of the volunteers, who had not been in action before, were moved by the spectacle. A Captain Robarts of the Durban Mounted Rifles wrote:

> We had the leisure to look at the wounded men, and very pitiful it was to see the poor fellows lying with fearful wounds. They were very quiet, and seemed to bear

> pain well, no groaning or crying out. We could not do anything for them except give them water to drink. Some of them were very anxious to be taken by us … Of course it was impossible …
>
> The vedettes found a great many dead and wounded up on the ridge – one of them had crawled at least a quarter of a mile with a broken leg. One poor fellow was in an antbear hole about 70 yards from the vedettes in front of them, and they did not see him for a long time until he called out – asking them to find him. He also wanted to be taken but of course it was impossible.
>
> It is a fearful thing to see a wounded man uncared for … The excitement is all right enough while it is on – but I do not like to think of those poor fellows left.[2]

The devastating effect of mechanised weapons on men armed with nothing more than shields, spears and antiquated firearms, left many who saw it feeling decidedly uncomfortable, yet those sobering expressions of compassion would not last the night in Zululand. Later that same evening, Lord Chelmsford's force, which had been looking for the Zulu army some twelve miles in advance of iSandlwana, returned to the camp they had left that morning to find it utterly devastated.

Before them lay the bodies of the men they had left behind, strewn amongst dead mules, horses and oxen, and hundreds of Zulu dead. This was the reality of an overwhelming Zulu victory. It was late evening and the smoke from burning tents drifted into the sunset. As they approached the camp, Chelmsford's men could see large bodies of victorious Zulus on the skyline, carrying away their trophies from the battle. Chelmsford's men were exhausted – some had marched almost thirty miles in the hot summer sun that day – and fatigue, coupled with shock at the defeat and a real sense of dread that they, too, were in danger, left no room for the sort of compassion their comrades had felt at Nyezane. Here and there, as Chelmsford's men passed over the iSandlwana battlefield, picking their way through the dead in the dark, they came across wounded Zulus, or men who had found alcohol in the camp, and had drunk themselves into unconsciousness. Without hesitation, the Zulus were killed. Lieutenant John Maxwell of the 3rd Natal Native Contingent (NNC) recalled, 'On a buck waggon we came across some of the enemy drunk, about eight or ten. Some of the 24th being close by then, I shouted to them. They mounted the waggons and put the bayonet through them.'[3] Private Herbert Plant, of the 1/24th, attached to the Mounted Infantry, reported a similar incident: 'Lieut. Walsh went to a Mounted Infantry waggon, and found three Zulus lying asleep. He ran his sword through one, and one of the Mounted Infantry shot the other, but the third man escaped.'[4]

Chelmsford's men would spend a harrowing night on the battlefield. It was so dark that men lay down to sleep, only to find in the morning that they had been lying next to the bodies of the slain. Maxwell himself, on doing the rounds to inspect the NNC sentries, tripped and fell down a slope; putting his hands out in front of him, he fetched up against something mushy and, when a staff officer held up a lantern, Maxwell found himself 'with my hands inside what turned out to be the body of a 24th man'.[5] A heavy smell of blood and death hung over the battlefield, and at times during the night a drunken Zulu called out incoherently, and an injured animal whinnied in pain. Several times there were false alarms; few men got any sleep.

That overwrought atmosphere, that sense of traumatic horror and dread, would hang over the survivors of the column for weeks to come, and at a stroke it transformed the image of the Zulus among their enemy. The British had begun the war with an air of breezy self-confidence and presumption. Modern weapons and military discipline would ensure them an easy victory over an enemy who was unworthy of their respect, perhaps even to be pitied in the inequality of their struggle.

iSandlwana changed everything. That nightmarish glimpse of the true horror and savagery of war against the Zulus, determined to defend their country, led many in the British ranks to fear their new enemy. Now with the Zulus re-imagined as ferocious and bloodthirsty bogeymen, credited with the ability to move impossible distances through the dark veld and to strike with audacious, lurid ferocity, the British learned a short sharp lesson about respecting their enemies. It was this fear and urge for vengeance that underpinned perhaps the most controversial aspect of the battle of Rorke's Drift: the killing of the Zulu wounded from the battle.

* * *

The Zulus had begun to abandon the attack and withdraw from the battlefield in the small hours of the morning of the 23rd. The defenders had noticed that after midnight the Zulu attacks became more sporadic, eventually dying away to a spluttering firefight which ceased altogether an hour before dawn. The Zulus had begun 22 January at the far end of the bivouac in the Ngwebeni valley, north of iSandlwana, then crossed miles of terrain, and the Mzinyathi River, before beginning the battle. After hours of intermittent fighting, the men were not only tired but, when the capture of the hospital building brought no quick victory, also increasingly convinced that the attack was hopeless. It is impossible, now, to say how organised the Zulu withdrawal was; certainly Lord Chelmsford's men had passed large bodies of warriors on the road from iSandlwana to Rorke's Drift hours before, suggesting that a substantial portion of the amabutho had retired in comparatively good order. It was, however, a particularly dark night, and the terrain – being on the Natal side of the border – was unfamiliar to the Zulus, even without the disorienting effect of the flames and gunfire. How effective any command decision to withdraw can have been under the circumstances is debatable. The identity of the men seen on kwaSingqindi hill, opposite the post, shortly after dawn on the 23rd is also open to question; whether they were an organised rearguard or elements regrouping who had detached themselves to loot the river valley before the fight, or even mat-carriers watching the battle from a safe distance – they were undoubtedly the last to leave.

The Zulu army had no organised system of casualty evacuation. It fell to a man's friends, comrades or brothers to try and carry him out of action, at least to a safe place where his wounds could perhaps be washed, and bound with grass by way of bandages. Then it was simply a question of helping him as best as possible on the long walk to his home, where local izinyanga – traditional healers – might attempt to debride and clean his wounds, bind up broken bones with splints and apply herbal poultices to open wounds. During the later battles of the war, when the Zulus were defeated, it was often those helping wounded men, and the wounded themselves, who suffered most from the rigours of any British pursuit, since they could not get away quickly enough. Sometimes the wounded were abandoned when the retreating army met a physical obstacle across which the casualties could not be easily carried.

Although there was no pressure on the retreating army after Rorke's Drift, it was still difficult for the Zulus to evacuate their casualties effectively. Not only were many of those who fell close to the British barricades still exposed to enemy fire, and might be hit again during subsequent attacks or during any attempt to carry them away, but the darkness and the orchard and bush surrounding the post made it difficult to locate many of the injured. Although it is clear that some were evacuated, either supported by their comrades or dragged away on shields, many were left to fend for themselves. Inured by their hardy outdoor lifestyle to a degree of pain which would have incapacitated many of their British counterparts, large numbers of Zulus crawled away in the darkness to find shelter where they could, either in the undergrowth or in the crevices among the rocks on the lower slopes of Shiyane. Some were immediately exposed by the sunrise of the morning of the 23rd, whilst others were only found days afterwards. When they were found, for the most part, the British or their African allies killed them.

At first light Chard's men, too, were exhausted and acutely vulnerable. Many of them were battered and bloody after hours of fighting, their fingers scorched by the hot barrels of the Martini-Henrys and their shoulders bruised by the repetitive firing, and although 'each man had a good supply of ammunition in his pouches or pockets, we had only about a box and a half left besides'.[6] As the sun rose over the battlefield, at first the only Zulus in sight were the dead sprawled across the barricades or out in the garden beyond – many bearing horrendous close-range gunshot injuries – and the wounded who moved here and there among them. To the garrison, still expecting the attacks to resume at any moment, these men presented an active threat, as Henry Hook found out. Chard had ordered that the bodies of the Zulus lying around the barricades be dragged aside – presumably to repair the barricades and clear a field of fire, should the Zulus return – and Hook had wandered away from the post,

> and was walking up the dry bed of a little stream near the drift, with my own rifle in my hand and a bunch of assegais over my left shoulder. Suddenly I came across an unarmed Zulu, lying on the ground, apparently dead, but bleeding from the leg. Thinking it strange that a dead man should bleed, I hesitated, and wondered whether I should go on, as other Zulus might be lurking about. But I resumed my

> task. Just as I was passing, the supposed dead man he seized the butt of my rifle and tried to drag it away. The bunch of assegais rattled to the earth.
>
> The Zulu suddenly released his grasp of the rifle with one hand, and with the other fiercely endeavoured to drag me down. The fight was short and sharp; but it ended by the Zulu being stuck in the chest with the butt and knocked to the ground.
>
> The rest was over quickly.
>
> After that we were not allowed to go on with our task except in twos and threes.[7]

Similarly, Trooper Harry Lugg of the Natal Mounted Police, who had been a patient in the hospital before the battle but had taken an active part in the defence, was 'moving about among the dead and dying after the fight was over [when] a warrior suddenly rose up from the ground and jammed his "gas pipe" against him, but it misfired, whereupon Henry closed with his man and stabbed him to death [with a hunting knife]'.[8] Chard himself noted:

> One Zulu had remained in the kraal and fired a shot among us (without doing any damage) as we stood up on the walls, and ran off in the direction of the River. Although many shots were fired at him as he ran, I am glad to say the plucky fellow got off.[9]

However, a few of the defenders reported 'prisoners' being taken; Hook said several wounded were brought in. At least one Zulu prisoner – 'Umtyololo' – 'was found wounded at Rorke's Drift' and was interviewed by Mr Drummond, Chelmsford's interpreter.[10] He gave a lengthy account of the movements of the Zulu army in the build-up to iSandlwana. According to Lt. Archibald Milne, Royal Navy, attached to Lord Chelmsford's staff, 'a private of the 2/24th took from one of the prisoners captured at Rorkes Drift some of his own property taken at Isandhlwana the day previous'.[11]

Around 7 a.m. – about three hours after daybreak – a Zulu force appeared on the slopes of kwaSingqindi, opposite the mission. Chard called his patrols in and the men prepared for another attack; instead, however, the Zulus rose up and moved away out of sight, disappearing behind the shoulder of Shiyane in the direction from which the impi had first come.

Shortly afterwards the men at Rorke's Drift saw troops approaching from the direction of the drift; it was Lord Chelmsford's men, returning from iSandlwana.

The arrival of Chelmsford's column, at about 8.30 a.m. on the 23rd, marked the effective end of the battle. As they crossed the river, several men noticed a pile of bloody Zulu shields on the Natal bank, where the Zulus had tried to evacuate some of their wounded, abandoning the shields in the face of the river.[12] It is clear that from the moment they arrived, Chelmsford's men, too, had no qualms about killing any of the Zulu wounded they found. Gunner Abraham Evans, who had been a patient in the hospital, was standing near Chard on the parapet when Lord Chelmsford himself

> came and spoke to Lt. Chard, thanking him for the way we held the position during the night. Shortly after this our brave men followed up to the laager and into the bush, where they found heaps of dead bodies, and I shall never forget the sound of the click as they fixed bayonets, and there took some revenge for Isandhlwana.[13]

Lord Chelmsford himself had strongly warned both his regulars and auxiliaries in Zululand against mistreating non-combatants at the start of the war. Indeed Chelmsford had ordered the release of several Zulu prisoners taken at the homestead of Sihayo kaXongo at the start of his advance into Zululand. Nevertheless, as Evans recognised, the situation was not now a normal one, and the night spent among the disembowelled dead at iSandlwana had worked many of Chelmsford's men into a cold fury. Although attempts were later made to attribute the subsequent excesses entirely to the auxiliaries of the NNC, it is clear that European troops – both Natal volunteers and British regulars – were involved. Lieutenant Maxwell recalled that, after spending a short while wandering the battlefield and marvelling at the evidence of the fight, he

> walked to the front again, and to my astonishment perceived a Kethla, or ringed native, hanging to the crossbeam that had been erected some days previously for the butchers. It appeared he had been found under suspicious circumstances in the neighbourhood, and so met his end in rather a summary manner.[14]

The scaffold – a simple cross bar raised on two poles, had indeed been constructed a few days before the battle on the orders of Lt. Smith-Dorrien, 95th Regiment, who was attached to the column transport. It had been built to stretch raw hides that were used to repair broken wagon-traces. Smith-Dorrien had been present at iSandlwana during the attack – he had managed to escape and fled to Helpmekaar, the next post down the line of communication. When he returned to Rorke's Drift, he was appalled to see the dead Zulu still hanging on the makeshift gibbet, and even more so to be accused of having authorised the lynching. 'It was found that it was a case of lynch law performed by the incensed men', he wrote, 'who were bitter at the loss of their comrades.'[15]

Although no one was ever officially called to account for the incident, one of the defenders, Private Edward Savage, 2/24th, provided fairly telling evidence:

> Before Lord Chelmsford's arrival they had all had food and water and the other necessaries which were within an ace of becoming superfluities. They had also captured a prisoner, a skulker in one of the kraals which dotted the surrounding heights. The fellow was recognised as the perpetrator of the wanted Zulu barbarity on the body of one of the slain. Moreover, he admitted that he killed and "cut up with assegai," one white man, whose rifle he was carrying. With brief adrift he was sentenced to the gallows and hanged on a bullock beam in the enclosure, to which he walked with a smile – the rope before his eyes.[16]

Many years later, Frank Bourne recalled another version of what might have happened:

> One Zulu who was alive had been left for dead.
>
> Later in the day Lieutenant Bromhead sent for me and said, very urgently, 'Where's that man who was here just now with a prisoner? Find that man and bring him here.'
>
> I went round asking 'Who's the man who's got a prisoner?' They said, 'Ashton, of course.' Ashton was a lusty Irishman. I found Ashton.
>
> 'What have you done with your prisoner?' I said. He pointed to a tree from which the Zulu's body was hanging.

> 'I took him in to Lieutenant Bromhead', said the innocent Irishman, 'and he told me to get the hell out of here with him, and I did.'[17]

Bourne himself, it seems, did not report Ashton at the time.

It should be noted that Bourne recalled that the Zulu was hung from a tree, rather than the meat frame. At first glance this could be attributed to a lapse in memory – Bourne's account was written in 1938 – some fifty years after the battle. Yet, other eyewitnesses reported seeing a Zulu hanging from a tree. Lt. Henry Curling, Royal Artillery, had escaped from iSandlwana, making his way to Helpmekaar by nightfall. On the following day he set off back down to Rorke's Drift hoping to find other survivors from his battery. He arrived just as it was getting dark, but noticed that 'a Zulu spy was hanging from one of the trees in the garden, and the whole place was one mass of men.' Curling returned to Helpmekaar the next morning, sharing his observations in a letter to his mother a week later.[18] Bernhard Kraft, a German farmer who had been employed by Otto Witt to tend the crops and garden at Oscarsberg, although not present at the defence, returned to the mission station in early March 1879. Writing to a missionary friend, Kraft expressed his shock at the state of the place: 'Zulu bodies are buried in and around the garden,' he wrote, adding that 'the large thorn tree [dornbaum] situated in front of the house on the way to Mubris' kraal' had been used as a 'gallows' for hanging Zulu spies.[19]

It is quite likely then, allowing for the very confused and heightened state of affairs and varying reports from eyewitnesses, that a second Zulu was hung on 23 January. As Smith-Dorrien later confirmed, 'other incidents of the same sort occurred in the next few days before law and order were re-established.'[20]

In the afternoon there was a further serious incident. Once the column had arrived at the post, an attempt was made to secure the wider area, and a vedette, probably of mounted infantry, was sent out to watch the line by which the Zulus had approached the mission. Exactly where they were posted is a matter of conjecture, but it seems they were on the shoulder of Shiyane hill to the south, where the ground falls away to give a view of the Mzinyathi valley downstream. Near here were a number of mealie patches – and these were found to be full of wounded Zulus, presumably men who had managed to stagger or crawl that far but, unable to go any further, were hoping to hide in the long green stalks.

Initially, it seems, at least one officer with the Mounted Infantry was moved to compassion by their plight. In a piece published in *The Sketch* as late as 1906, apparently in an attempt to counter the by-then widespread belief that the Zulu wounded had been killed without compunction, an anonymous writer gave details of his own encounters. The writer was probably Nathanial Newnham-Davis, who contributed regularly to the paper, and as a young lieutenant had been attached to the Mounted Infantry:

> I was with the relieving force, and when the troops for the duties of the day were told off I was sent out on picquet. There were a number of wounded Zulus in the mealie fields round the farm at Rorke's Drift, and the first one we found was an old man, with a ringed head and greying hair, a man of the veteran regiments. He had no fight left in him, and I had him picked up and sent into camp. No harm happened to him, I can certify, for I saw him off the premises myself next day, watched him get across the drift with the aid of two gourds, and saw him hobble into the cover of a kopje whence, no doubt, he trekked at nightfall to join his friends and relations.
>
> My next wounded man was a very different customer. He announced his presence with a light assegai, thrown with much skill, which whizzed past my ear, just missing me. He was one of the men of the king's regiments, with a white and brown shield, and was under the shelter of a rock in a place of vantage. I told a Basuto who was with me to inform him that we did not wish to kill him, and, though my knowledge of Zulu was limited, I assured him so myself. He only showed his teeth, and got his biggest assegai into stabbing position. The Basuto saw that he had been shot through the stomach, and suggested that in an hour he would be too stiff to be dangerous; and when I came back through the mealie field an hour later, and approached the rock very cautiously, I found that the Basuto had been a good prophet: the man had died of his wound. Had he not been as unreasonable as a trapped tiger-cat, he might have been in condition to join my personally despatched tour across the [Mzinyathi] River the next day.[21]

Captain Henry Hallam Parr, of Chelmsford's staff – who was afterwards indignant at the attempts 'at one time made to blacken the character of the remainder of No. 3 Column … with accusations of having put an end to the wounded' – recalled that a small number of Zulus were treated by the British surgeons:

> I myself saw three wounded Zulus at Rorke's Drift. Two of them were found on the morning of the 23rd, and were brought in by some men of the 24th and treated by one of the surgeons in the column; the third was found half-starving in a kraal some days afterwards, having crept there disabled by a leg wound.[22]

Perhaps, as Newnham-Davis and Hallam Parr believed, these men were later released; perhaps they were among those later killed. In any case, Newnham-Davis' man well have been the only man found in the mealie fields to have survived. Shortly after the mounted vedettes had taken up their position, a battalion of the 3rd NNC arrived to support them, and according to their commander, Captain George Hamilton Browne,

> it was discovered that a large number of wounded and worn out Zulus had taken refuge or had hidden in the mealie fields near the laager. My two companies of Zulus [i.e., Zulu émigrés of the iziGqoza faction serving in the NNC] with some of my non-coms and a few of the 24th quickly drew these fields and killed them with the bayonet, butt and assegai. It was beastly but there was nothing else to do. War is war and savage war is the worst of the lot. Moreover our men were worked up into a pitch of fury by the sights they had seen in the morning, and the mutilated bodies of our poor fellows lying in front of the hospital building.[23]

It is difficult to tell whether Hamilton Browne – whose own approach to war was notably ruthless – had authorised these killings, or whether, given that they were clearly organised and involved more than his own command, they were ordered from above. Either way, Lord Chelmsford was still present at Rorke's Drift at this point, and must at least have been aware of them.

In mitigation, it is perhaps true that, whatever the tide of opinion in the ranks, British options were limited. Chelmsford's command had lost all their tents at iSandlwana and would face weeks of sleeping out in the open, often in the rain. Even had they wanted to, there were few enough options for containing prisoners. Moreover, the Centre Column's medical depot had also been destroyed at iSandlwana, as had the base hospital at Rorke's Drift. Chelmsford had taken two ambulances out with him to Mangeni, and these were now required to provide medical support for his entire surviving column. Although it might have been possible to send walking wounded prisoners up to Helpmekaar, there was in reality little that could be done to help those who could not move.

While the NNC were sweeping the mealie fields clear of wounded, the task of burying the battlefield dead had begun. A hole was dug in the ground, the Zulu weapons were tipped into it, and wood from Otto Witt's orchard was cut down, thrown over them, and set on fire. The NNC dug two long pits,[24] while the men of the 24th tied reims around the bodies and dragged them there to tip in. According to a Trooper Clarke of the NMP, at least one Zulu was thought to be alive when he was interred; given the ruthlessness with which any showing signs of resistance had been shot or stabbed, it seems likely this man was unconscious but breathing – and no one cared to help him.[25]

On the evening of the 23rd the men of the 3rd NNC were ordered to bivouac on the slopes of the Shiyane hill while the rest of the command huddled around the ruined mission. There were no tents, and the men snatched what sleep they could on the wet ground. There was a false alarm during the night, and the white officers and NCOs of the NNC promptly decamped to the mission, leaving their men on the exposed hillside. The night passed nervously, in hourly expectation of a Zulu attack, and by morning the morale of the NNC had completely collapsed. Their commander, Commandant Rupert Lonsdale, addressed them, asking how many were prepared to stay in the field; when only a few said they would, he decided to disband the regiment entirely. Their officers collected the red headbands which distinguished them as being in British service, and the few firearms among them, and they were dismissed. After witnessing at iSandlwana what the Zulus could do, they were delighted to go. Many had been recruited among African groups from the Msinga district in Natal which lay beyond Helpmekaar and the Biggarsberg ridge, and they set off in a body to go home. No one had told the garrison at Helpmekaar of their passing, however, and there was an uncomfortable moment when they approached, and the Helpmekaar garrison thought they were Zulus.

Fortunately, only a few ineffective shots were fired by outposts before they passed by.

Lord Chelmsford also left Rorke's Drift on 23 January, riding off with his staff and escort to Pietermaritzburg to break the news of iSandlwana. At the same time Chelmsford's artillery and the mounted Colonial Volunteers were ordered up to Helpmekaar to add to the defensive position which was rapidly being constructed there.

The command left at Rorke's Drift consisted largely of the 2nd Battalion, 24th Regiment – including B Company, who had defended the post – and the white officers and NCOs of the NNC, who were formed into an ad hoc mounted unit for patrolling and vedette work. The troops were now under the command of Col. Richard Glyn, who had been nominally commander of the Centre Column, although his authority had been largely overshadowed by Lord Chelmsford's presence. Glyn was an officer of the 24th who had served with the 24th officers killed at iSandlwana, and the loss of the first battalion had shaken him deeply. He had become morose, irritable and rather nervous, and over the next fortnight the command took its cue from him. While stone was collected from the Shiyane terraces and used to transform the surviving storehouse into a more secure fortification, life remained unpleasant, with no shelter from the weather and the smell of the Zulu dead hanging on the wind, particularly when it blew from the line of their retreat. Glyn's daily orders forbade the garrison from going far from the confines of the fort, specifically, 'NC Officers and men are permitted to go as far from the fort as the Gibbet Tree,'[26] which added to the prevailing sense of nervousness.

Against this background there were a number of further summary executions of Zulu personnel. During their operations at Mangeni on the 22nd, Chelmsford's men had captured a handful of Zulu prisoners (Trooper Symons of the Natal Carbineers, who was instrumental in the capture of some of these prisoners – to the point of preventing several of them being stabbed by members of the NNC – stated that nine prisoners were taken) and had brought them back with them into Natal.[27] The Bishop of Natal, John William Colenso, who was an indefatigable critic of British actions in Zululand, identified one of those captured Zulus as one of Matshana's indunas named 'Njuba'.[28] According to Frances Colenso, the bishop's daughter, all of the captive Zulus were later shot and killed. It is not clear when this incident took place, but the reference to the involvement of the Natal Carbineers in the story suggests it was on the 24th, before the mounted troops departed, and quite possibly shortly after Chelmsford himself had left Rorke's Drift:

> It was intended to set them free, and they were told to run for their lives, but they were shot down and killed, within sight and sound of the whole force. An eye-witness – an officer – described the affair to the present writer, saying that the men whom he saw killed numbered 'not more than seven, nor less than five.' He said that he was standing with others in the camp, and hearing shots close behind him, he turned, and saw the prisoners in question in the act of falling beneath the shots and stabs of a party of our men. The latter, indeed, were men belonging to the Native Contingent, but they were supposed to be under white control, and should not have been able to obtain possession of the prisoners under any circumstances.[29]

Once this story became known, there were attempts to discredit it. In 1907 the same anonymous contributor to *The Sketch* – presumably Newnham-Davis again – recalled a conversation he had later in Natal with a lady in Pietermaritzburg who may well have been Frances Colenso herself:

> After the relief of Rorke's Drift, in the Zulu War, some Zulu prisoners had been taken and were put under guard. There was no enclosure of any kind in which to keep them confined, for the space inside the stone walls held so gallantly by the company of the 24th was required by the hospital authorities. The prisoners were warned by the interpreters and by some of the Natal Carabineers who spoke the Zulu language that if they attempted to escape they would be shot. The sight of the Blood River and Zululand on the other side was too much for two of the prisoners. They watched their chance and ran for freedom. They were both shot dead before they reached the river bank. I heard the shots, and saw what had happened. Many months later, when the war was ended, I found myself at a dinner party in Pietermaritzburg, sitting next to a lady who, when she found out that I had been at Rorke's Drift at the time of its relief began to cross examine me as to the shooting of the prisoners. I soon found that an attempt was being

> made to entrap me into some support of a statement made by the lady that the prisoners had been told to run away in order that their guards might fire at them. I protested very earnestly against this, for it so happened that some of the men who had been on guard over the prisoners were personal friends of mine. I knew them to be humane men, and they had told me how much they regretted that duty had compelled them to shoot the escaping men.[30]

Despite Newnham-Davis' determination to spring to the defence of Chelmsford's men, his protestations do not quite ring true, not least because of his attempt to diminish the number of Zulus involved. Colenso's source had been adamant that between five and seven Zulus had been shot down in this way, and overall Colenso estimated that as many as twenty men had been shot in this manner altogether. Trooper Symons of the Natal Carbineers was shocked to hear all nine Zulu prisoners had been killed and that a wounded man he had personally captured at Mangeni 'was seen being shot by a mounted officer with a revolver'. The Regimental History of the Natal Mounted Police commented simply that 'there were many wounded Zulus, but none recovered, and several who tried to escape were shot. One actually got back across Rorke's Drift, although dozens of shots were fired at him, but he was followed by a mounted infantryman and killed.'[31]

In the fortnight after Chelmsford's departure tensions at the post remained high but most of the Zulu wounded had been found by this point. The disbandment of the NNC provoked the few other Africans with the column to desert, and the command at Rorke's Drift was now almost entirely without any African contingent. As a result, in the febrile atmosphere which prevailed, any passing African was liable to be regarded with suspicion as a Zulu spy, and to be executed.

Hamilton Browne described how, perhaps a week after the fight, he was tasked with capturing a Zulu scout who had been observing the camp from a hill on the Natal bank, possibly kwaSingqindi. Attempts to capture him had proved futile as the man slipped away as soon as he saw any patrol advance in his direction, Browne guessed that the man had taken the same route every day and, searching for his tracks, found a possible route across the river below Shiyane which led through mealie fields towards the hill where the Zulu posted himself. Browne and two of his officers posted themselves before dawn in ambush, and sure enough when it grew light they saw the Zulu working stealthily through the mealies. The three men charged at him on horseback, and overtook and captured the Zulu before he could reach the river:

> His field kit consisted of the usual Zulu outfit, one skin apron in front and one behind, with the usual charm etc, but there was one etc. he had no right to wear and that was a piece of turkey-red cloth bound around his head. This was the uniform of the Natal Native Contingent and on Duncombe demanding why he wore it, he answered, so as to deceive the red soldiers if he chanced to meet any. This was a fatal admission as it at once turned him into a spy.[32]

Browne took him back to the fort, where he was interrogated. The Zulu refused to give any usual information, and a sergeant brought him back to Hamilton Browne. Browne breezily admitted that he had just barked his shin when the sergeant asked what was to be done with the 'spy': 'Oh,' replied Browne, 'hang the bally spy!' – and the man was strung up on the same scaffold used for the earlier lynchings.[33]

Lieutenant H. 'Charlie' Harford, a young officer of the 99th Regiment seconded as adjutant of the 3rd NNC, also found himself accused of ordering the hanging:

> and one morning Major Black and I were sitting outside, warming ourselves in the sun and chatting, when we saw the most extraordinary-looking object suspended on the scaffold, and wondered what an earth it could be. Presently, a Private of the 24th came up from that direction, and Black asked him what the thing was, and he said it was a [Zulu] spy that had been hanged. 'Good Heavens!', said Black, 'By whose orders was he hung?' 'Captain Harford, sir,' was the reply, so we went down at once to look into the matter. The poor wretch, who was an old, wizened-up, grey-headed native, had apparently been dead for some hours, and must have been hung some time during the night, but by whom it was never discovered. Every possible inquiry was made, but not a soul knew anything about it and nothing was known of the native or where he had come from.[34]

Although the story of the red headband on the 'spy' told by Hamilton Browne sounds like a convenient excuse to justify the man's death, it is not inherently impossible. The Zulu military system did allow for bold intelligence gathering, in which individuals volunteered to infiltrate the enemy camp, and no doubt the Zulus were as interested to try to interpret British movements on the Natal side of the river as the British were theirs on the Zulu side.

Whatever the real degree of Zulu scouting, however, there is no doubt that for the best part of a month after the battle the British were in great fear of it along the Mzinyathi valley; not just at Rorke's Drift, but at Helpmekaar too. *The Graphic* went so far as to publish an engraving of two Zulus, shackled to a crossbeam, and under guard at Helpmekaar on suspicion of having been involved in the death and mutilation of 'little drummer boys' of the 24th at iSandlwana.[35] How any individuals could have been recognised in the confusion of the battle by men who were not themselves there remains a mystery; in any case, the story of the 'little drummer boys' was a myth, the product of the charged atmosphere after the battle, since the youngest bands boy killed at iSandlwana was fifteen, and the average age of the drummers was twenty-three. Who these men were, whether they were really Zulus or simply hapless citizens of the colony of Natal who were in the wrong place at the wrong time, and what became of them, is not recorded.

There was undoubtedly, however, as strict an atmosphere prevailing at Helpmekaar as there was at Rorke's Drift. Henry Curling, the artillery officer who had escaped iSandlwana, noted that 'Their spies are everywhere', and that 'all spies taken are shot; we have disposed of three or four already'.[36] Lt. William W. Lloyd, 1/24th, added, 'I pity any Kaffirs that fall into our hands.'[37] Finally matters came to a head: Civil Surgeon Lewis Reynolds noted in his diary that on 27 January, 'A prisoner who was taken yesterday was tried by court-martial today, & found to be a Zulu spy, and was shot by 10 Basutos. He jumped into his grave to try and escape the bullets, without avail.'[38]

A trooper of the Buffalo Border Guard reported a similar story:

> A few days ago, after our return into Natal, we caught a Zulu spy; he was sentenced to be shot, and I was one of six told off to dig the wretch's grave. He was placed at one end of the grave, and six of our Natal Kaffirs shot him standing

at the opposite end of the grave. We stood within five yards of the savage, and saw his brains blown out.[39]

How many Zulus were killed at either Helpmekaar or Rorke's Drift after the battle is, of course, impossible to say, not least because they are not mentioned in any official reports. At Helpmekaar, taking Curling's comment as the basis, perhaps half a dozen men were shot; at Rorke's Drift a handful of men were hanged and a number shot, but it is impossible to guess how many wounded were summarily killed. Given the intensity of the fighting, and the fact that the Zulus managed to evacuate at least some of their wounded, the total, despite the numerous references to the deed, may not have run to more than a few dozen. Nevertheless, even allowing for the overwrought atmosphere at the camp, and the practical difficulties of securing treatment for enemy wounded or maintaining prisoners, the incident remains at odds with the heroic image of the battle which has prevailed ever since.

And what of those wounded who were carried away by their friends and somehow made it home again? How many of them there were will also never be known, and among the Zulus their story was regarded as little more than a footnote to the success at iSandlwana. Nevertheless, there were some – perhaps many. In 1902 Harry Lugg:

> was carrying out inspections of war graves at [Rorke's Drift] and at Isandlwana, where by chance he met an old warrior bearing a number of obvious war scars. A bullet had seared his scalp, another his left shoulder, and two through the calf of his leg, all received at Rorke's Drift.[40]

As late as the early 1960s, Mike McCabe, who was then a small boy living with his ex-pat parents in Durban, but who later went on to become a colonel in the Royal Engineers and a scholar of the Anglo-Zulu War, was taken on a picnic to the iSandlwana battlefield. Here he met an elderly Zulu who explained that he had been a mat-carrier for his father at Rorke's Drift and had watched the battle throughout the night from kwaSingqindi. He recalled the darkness of the night broken by the flames from the burning hospital, and the constant crackle and flash of the British musketry. The following morning, he found his father had been wounded and had been carried away by his friends. A bullet had passed through his side, but he had survived and lived to a great age. Years later, the old Zulu recalled, his father had developed a hard and painful swelling on his hip. Eventually the man had sought the help of an inyanga, a traditional healer, who had lanced the swelling – and removed a misshapen Martini-Henry bullet which had lodged there ever since the battle.

CHAPTER 3

'"What's that on the wall?" It's a man waving a flag': No. 3 Column Returns to Rorke's Drift

A correspondent of the *Natal Witness*

Natal Witness, c. January 1879

Lord Chelmsford's Return to Isandhlwana.

... we marched steadily forward to Rorke's Drift, the smoke rising from the missionaries' house on the other side suggesting to us further disaster. As, however we neared the river, men could be seen manning the walls of an old ruin next to the building used as a commissariat store, some of them waving coats, &c., and Colonel Russell, with the Mounted Infantry, was ordered to ford the river, and go straight up to them. Our belief in Zulu cunning had by this time got so strong that it was not until the mounted men reached the building, and were received by true English cheers that we were fully persuaded it was not a trick. The fact that the pont ropes were untouched also proved to us that the Zulus could not have had everything their own way; and it was with anxiety to reach our men, and hear their news, that we watched the Carbineers, who had crossed at the ford, cast off the ropes, and prepare to tug us over. Little time was occupied in so doing, or in reaching the commissariat store, and the cheers which burst forth from our men as the General cantered up and said, "Thank you all very much for your very gallant defence," were pleasant to hear. A gallant defence it indeed had been – eighty men, ten of whom were sick in hospital, had beaten off and thoroughly defeated some 3000 Zulus, flushed with their late victory. They had hardly had half an hour's warning, during which to make what preparations were possible for defending an extremely weak position. Fortunately there were plenty of sacks of mealies, &c., to be had, and temporary fortifications were rapidly constructed with them. From 3 a.m. to 5 a.m. the Zulus came on again and again with undaunted pluck. They succeeded in taking the hospital and burning it, though, in doing so, they lost ten times the number they killed; and they charged up to the very walls, and attempted to unscrew the bayonets which met them. Greater bravery than that displayed on either side could not have been, but the little body of English soldiers behind their frail rampart knew they were fighting to hold a most important post, and never hesitated for an instant; whereas the Zulus, who no doubt thought they could easily cut up a handful of men like those opposed to them, after their recent achievement, were beginning to find out their mistake. The engagement, however, continued the whole live-long night, the Zulus once and again attempting to take the place by storm. At last, fairly discouraged, they retreated just as dawn was breaking. Our loss, as may be imagined, was severe; out of eighty men one fourth had fallen, thirteen killed and nine wounded, of whom some have since died; but if our loss was severe, that of the enemy must have been something enormous. They had come on again and again in broad daylight, and by the light of the burning house, up to the very muzzles of the guns, and their dead were heaped up in scores all round the barricade. Within 300 yards of the spot, our burying parties counted 351 bodies, whilst on the road they had taken in retreat the dead and wounded lay thick. That in this engagement the enemy lost 500 killed and 200 or 300 wounded is, I think, a very moderate calculation, and the lesson taught them by that gallant company of the 24th is one they will not soon forget. I fully believe the loss the Zulus incurred in taking our camp, which I cannot estimate at less than 2000 to 3000 men in killed and wounded, added to their repulse and loss at Rorke's Drift, will have a very great effect on their minds, nor do I anticipate that they will run the risk of incurring such again, unless under circumstances exceptionably favourable to themselves …

Lieutenant General Sir Frederic A. Thesiger, Lord Chelmsford, KCB

A letter from Lord Chelmsford to the Secretary of State for War, 8 February 1879 [National Archives, London, WO32/7710]. See also the response to this letter by Colonel, the Hon. F.A. Stanley, in Vol. 1, Appendix I.

From the Lt. General Commandg. in S. Africa to the Rt. Honble. the S of State
Durban, Natal,
8th February 1879

Sir,

It is with much satisfaction that I have the honor to forward the report of the successful defence of Rorke's drift post on the 22d & 23d January.

The defeat of the Zulus at this post, & the very heavy loss suffered by them, has to a great extent neutralized the effects of the disaster at Insandlana, and it no doubt saved Natal from a serious invasion.

The cool determined courage displayed by the gallant garrison is beyond all praise & will I feel sure receive ample recognition.

As at the present moment the lesson taught by this defence is most valuable, I have thought it advisable to publish, for general information the report in question, which I trust will meet with your approval.

I have the honor to be Sir
your most obedt. Servant
Chelmsford LG

From reports received since the date of Lt. Chard's letter, it appears that the Zulu loss was greater than he knew of at that time.

A letter from Lord Chelmsford to the Military Secretary, Whitehall, which accompanied the original recommendations for the award of the first Victoria Crosses to members of the Rorke's Drift garrison [National Archives, London, WO32/7390]

Military Secretary
Submitted for the favourable consideration of his Royal Highness the Field Marshal commanding in Chief.

I would express a hope that the gallant conduct of Lt Chard R.E. and Lt Bromhead 2/24th may be taken with consideration in view, of possible, that these two officers should receive the Victoria Cross –

Had it not been for their fine example and excellent behaviour, under most trying circumstances, it may be assumed that the defence of Rorke's drift post would not have been conducted with that intelligence and tenacity which so essentially characterised it –

Whilst in no way desiring to deteriorate from the individual conduct of any of those who took part in this gallant defence, I cannot help feeling that its success must in all fairness be in a great measure attributable to these two young officers who exercised the chief commands on the occasion in question –

Chelmsford LG
PMBurg 23-2-79

Lieutenant George S. Banister, 2/24th Foot

Extract from a letter from George Banister to his father [Royal Welsh Regimental Museum, Brecon]

Rorke's Drift, Natal, 27th January 1879

My Dear Father, …

… When we reached the top of the last rising ground between us and Rorke's Drift our hearts again sank, for where our little camp of one Company used to be was now to be seen nothing but a column of smoke and no tents. Then we gave up all hope for Gunny Bromhead and his

Company who had been left there. We crossed the river in the punts, which to our surprise had not been destroyed, but before our turn came we heard a cheer from those who had gone first to the house, which had been used as a store. But how much or how little it meant of course we could not tell. At last we crossed and went up there and found old Gunny as cheery as ever and not a scratch about him. All round was a scene of awful confusion. What had been a hospital was a misshapen mass of smoking cinders – dead niggers everywhere. Some horsemen, who escaped from Isandhlwana, brought the news that our camp was sacked and that they were coming to polish off Rorke's Drift, and then galloped off to Helpmakaar advising everyone to do likewise.

Gunny and a Lieutenant of Engineers immediately set to work to strike the tents and with the bags of oats and mealies in store to erect breast works, and generally place the house in a state of defence, loopholed the walls. They worked well you may be sure but, before they had been more than an hour and a half at it, one Zulu was seen on a high hill close behind the house. Everyone immediately got to their places, and the next moment about 1,000 came round the corner of the hill thinking they'd just walk over the place. But they got such a hot fire that, though from their numbers the advance was not checked, yet it was diverted and streamed round to the front of what must now be called the Fort. This was between 4 and 5 in the evening, and from time to time to 5 the next morning the firing never ceased, nor did they flag in making most desperate assaults. The Hospital was held for a long time but being an advanced post, they were driven out, all the sick that could get about tried to escape back into the Fort and some succeeded and others were helped, but several were caught and done for. One wretched fellow lost his head and rushed right out into the thick of them, he must have got about 100 yards before he fell stabbed all over. Our fellows took the Hospital at the point of the bayonet three or four times and were as often turned out, the end being that the building was set on fire.

Had they succeeded in firing the roof of the House it would have been a case with them all, but though they made the most desperate and gallant efforts to do so, could not succeed. One Zulu went very close, he had actually got his torch within a few inches when luckily a rifle was got to bear on him and half his head was blown off. The next morning there he still was propped in some marvellous way against the wall as if he were still making an effort to climb up. Over and over again our fellows thought it was all over for with them that they could not keep the brutes off, for they were reinforced several times during the night, and they piled themselves one on top of each other at some of their rushes. But each time they were beaten back, cheer upon cheer rose from our fellows. So one way or another the night passed away and the day dawned, and then they finally retired. The ground was strewn with their corpses most of them lying at the very walls, and a good many killed by the bayonet.

The Hospital was the worst place for there were several of ours mixed up. Our loss was very slight considering all things: 9 killed and 5 wounded. Taken alround I think it one of the most grand and gallant things ever done. We all attribute no opposition being offered to our retreat the good effect of this one Company holding out against such fearful odds. Taking everyone the garrison numbered 100 men, and at the lowest computation there must have been over 2,000 against them.

The Colonel took me aside and said "I promised you the I of M'ship and it is still yours as I never go back on my word, but I should like to do something for Bromhead, and it is about the only thing he is fit for, so would you let him have it, and take the Adjutantcy?"…

Trooper William J. Clarke, Natal Mounted Police

Extract from Clarke's own reminiscences entitled 'My Career in South Africa, (c. 1878–1919)' [Killie Campbell Africana Library, KwaZulu-Natal, South Africa, Clarke Papers, File 1]

… On reaching the summit of the hill overlooking the Drift, we could see men moving about round the hospital, so Colonel Russell sent on the Mounted Infantry to reconnoitre. After they had crossed the river we saw them gallop up to the buildings and we then knew that the Zulus had been unsuccessful. As we approached the Commissariat Store the first dead man we came across was a N.C.O. of the N.N.C. who had attempted to run away and had been shot by our own men before the fight had commenced.

One of the N.M.P., Trooper Hunter, had been killed in the space between the Hospital and the Commissariat Store. Hunter had shot his assailant dead while receiving two assegais in his chest. When we searched his pockets before burying him we found two pounds of gold. Altogether we buried 375 dead Zulus and some wounded were thrown into the grave.

Seeing the manner in which our wounded had been mutilated after being dragged from the Hospital (men who were wounded in the skirmish on the 12th January) we were very bitter and did not spare wounded Zulus. One man of the 24th, in escaping from the burning hospital, had rushed through the Zulus in the darkness and had hidden in a cave within a few yards of the spot where the mutilations took place and which he witnessed. Another man had dashed into a mealie garden and had remained there unseen.

As soon as we had off-saddled we were paraded to draw rations and a tot of rum, the first food I had had since the morning of the 20th, nearly three days ago. I managed to consume a 2lb. tin of corned beef and a 3lb. loaf of bread whilst walking round looking at the slaughter.

One man, Sergeant Maxwell, of the 24th, had been burnt alive. As soon as we had buried all the dead, we laid down and slept until evening …

Major Cornelius F. Clery, 32nd Foot

Extract from a private letter from Major Clery to Lady Allison [from *Nothing Remains but to Fight*, by Ian Knight, London, 1993]

Wolf's Hill
Zululand
16 May 1879

My dear Lady Alison, …

… Reputations are being made and lost here in an almost comical fashion, from the highest downwards. At the risk of being looked on as very ill-natured and scandalous, I will have a little gossip with you on this subject.

Well, Chard and Bromhead to begin with: both are almost typical in their separate corps of what would be termed the very dull class. Bromhead is a great favourite in his regiment and a capital fellow at everything except soldiering. So little was he held to be qualified in this way from unconquerable indolence that he had to be reported confidentially as hopeless. This is confidential, as I was told it by his commanding officer. I was about a month with him at Rorke's Drift after Isandhlwana, and the height of his enjoyment seemed to be to sit all day on a stone on the ground smoking a most uninviting-looking pipe. The only thing that seemed equal to moving him in any way was any allusion to the defence of Rorke's Drift. This used to have a sort of electrical effect on him, for he would jump up and off he would go, and not a word could be got out of him. When I told him he should send me an official report on the affair it seemed to have a most distressing effect on him. I used to find him hiding away in corners with a friend helping him to complete this account, and the only thing that afterwards helped to lessen the compassion I felt for all this, was my own labour when perusing this composition – to understand what it was all about. So you can fancy there was not one who knew him who envied him his distinction, for his modesty about himself was, and is, excessive.

Chard there is very little to say about except that he too is a 'very good fellow' – but very uninteresting. The fact is that until the accounts came out from England nobody had thought of the Rorke's Drift affair except as one in which the private soldiers of the 24th behaved so well. For as a matter of fact they all stayed to defend the place because there was nowhere else to go, and in defending it they fought most determinedly …

Lieutenant Colonel Henry J. Degacher, 2/24th Foot

An official letter from Lt. Col. Degacher to Col. Glyn, Officer Commanding No. 3 Column [National Archives, London, WO32/7390]. See also Bromhead's official letter, in Vol. 1, 7a

From Officer Comdg. 2/24th Regt.
For Staff Officer 3rd Column.
Rorke's Drift, Natal 15.2.79

Sir,

I have the pleasure of forwarding the enclosed letter from Lt. Gonville Bromhead 2/24th Regt. and beg that the Officer Comdg. the Column will be so good as to forward the same to H.E. the Lt. General Commanding the troops in South Africa, in the hope that the conspicuous gallantry of the men named in the margin and mentioned in Lt. Bromhead's letter, may be brought by H.R.H. the Commander-in Chief to the notice of Her Majesty the Queen, and be deemed worthy of the Victoria Cross being awarded them

No. 1395 Pte John Williams 2/24th Regt.
No. 1373 Pte Henry Hook 2/24th Regt.
No. 593 Pte William Jones 2/24th Regt.
No. 716 Pte Robert Jones 2/24th Regt.
No. 1240 Corpl Wm Allen 2/24th Regt.
No. 1362 Pte Frederick Hitch 2/24th Regt.

I have the honor to be
Sir
Your most obedt. servant
H.J. Degacher
Lt. Colonel
Commandg. 2/24th Regt.

Rorke's Drift 17 Feby.
DA.G. P.M.B.

Submitted R.J. Glyn. Colonel
Commanding 3rd Column

Captain Allan Gardner, 14th Hussars

Nairnshire Telegraph, 2 April 1879

"… After crossing the river we rode for our old camp at Helpmakaar. I forgot to say that, when all was over, I sent an order to the company at Rorke's Drift – some eighty men – to fortify the house, and that all was lost, and that they must defend themselves and fight to the last. Every one also had forgotten them, and the happiest moment of my life was when I returned here, the officer coming up and thanking me for the warning. They knew nothing of what was going on, but at once made preparations, and fought splendidly all the night, killing some 400 and driving the enemy off."

Lieutenant and Adjutant Henry C. Harford, 99th Foot, attached to 1st/3rd Natal Native Contingent

Extracts from *The Zulu War Journal of Colonel Henry Harford, C.B.*, edited by D. Child, Pietermaritzburg, 1978 [by kind permission of the Local History Museum, Durban, South Africa]

… When the general advance took place, a few of our Natives under a corporal named Schiess were left at Rorke's Drift as part of the Garrison of the Fort under Lieutenant Bromhead, of the 2nd Battalion, 24th Regiment, and Lieutenant Chard, of the Royal Engineers. Schiess was subsequently awarded the Victoria Cross for very conspicuous bravery. Some of the men of the 24th Regiment told me that he fought like a tiger and at one time, when some Zulus actually managed to clutch hold of his bayonet, he got it out of their hands and, springing over the parapet, bayonetted some six or seven of them straight away …

… Throughout the night we could see the intermittent flashes of light from the firing at the Rorke's Drift post, which was only some three of four miles off in a straight line, though twelve miles by road. Everyone felt anxious for the fate of the little garrison after what had happened in the Camp, and longed for daylight to march to their relief …

… As we approached the Drift and reached the hill overlooking the river and the Post, the excitement became intense, all eyes were strained and field-glasses raised, to see if there was any sign of life in the Fort. Then, as we drew nearer, a man was seen on the bared roof of one of the buildings, signalling with a flag, which was hailed with a tremendous cheer from the whole Column as we knew then that the garrison had not been wiped out.

The General and his staff galloped off at once to the Fort and the troops got in by degrees, the selecting of their camping grounds taking some little time. We were the last to get in, and for some time it was quite impossible to keep the men in hand. They were all round the surroundings of the Fort in a second, crowding about the Zulu dead who were lying thick everywhere, partly, no doubt, from curiosity but I dare say some may have been looking out to identify friends or relations as many of the Natal Kaffirs are refugees from Zululand.

Commandant Lonsdale having gone to interview the General and to get something to eat, I also strolled into the Fort and helped myself bountifully to some biscuits, several boxes of which the thoughtful Commissariat Officers, Dunne and Dalton, had hauled out and opened for us hungry souls. What a Godsend it was, as it was over two days and two nights since most of us had had a mouthful of food. Hunger, however, luckily does not affect one like thirst, and one could have gone on much longer as there was plenty of good water.

As I ate biscuits I wandered about the Fort, looking at the wreckage which gave the appearance and feeling of devastation after a hurricane, with the dead bodies thrown in, the only thing that remained whole being a circular miniature fortress constructed of bags of mealies in the centre. Several of our dead lay just where they had fallen, and one of them – a youngster in the Natal Mounted Police – a very fine specimen of humanity, struck me particularly. Having given our natives ample time to exhaust their curiosity, they were got together and marched off to the position allotted to us at the back of the Fort, behind the Itchiane hill to guard the valley up which the Zulus had made their attacks, well hidden until the last moment. Outposts were at once posted and Mounted Patrols sent out, and the remainder of the troops not thus occupied were told off to clear the surroundings of the Fort and renovate the defences. As many of our men as could be supplied with picks and shovels were set to work to dig pits and bury the dead Zulus, and the remainder brought in stones for reconstructing and strengthening the barricades. Altogether, it was a stiff day, and officers and men worked alike …

… With the disbandment of our men, the officers and N.C.O.'s of the Contingent were brought into the Fort and given the N.E. corner of it to hold, and a very tight fit it was for everyone as the place was overcrowded with the number of men in occupation. To make matters worse we had a lot of rain, and the interior of the Fort became a simple quagmire from the tramping of so many feet. Fatigue parties were employed for the best part of the day in carrying liquid mud away and emptying the slush outside. In this state of filth we lived and ate and slept for more than two months, no-one being in possession of anything more than a blanket and the clothes that he stood up in. An exception was made, however, with B Company, 2nd battalion 24th Regiment, who had made such a gallant defence, and they were housed in the attic of Rorke's house with a tarpaulin thrown over the rafters (from which the thatch had been removed) to shelter them from the wet, a well-deserved honour. However, even they had their troubles in trying to keep dry, as the tarpaulin often bagged in between the rafters with a collection of water which had to be ejected, and I shall not easily forget one particular night when Dr. Reynolds, who got the V.C., and I met in the dark having been literally washed out of our sleeping place, and mooched about, endeavouring to find a more sheltered spot. Suddenly we hit upon the idea of lying down under the eaves of B. Company's roof, so coiled ourselves up in our soaking wet blankets, thanking our stars that at all events there would be no river running under us, when presently swish came about half a ton of water clean on top of us – B. Company were emptying their tarpaulin! It was useless moving, as we could not better ourselves, and wet as we were, thanks to the temperature of the atmosphere and the heat from our bodies, were comfortably warm as long as we lay still …

… Some 300 or 400 yards behind the Fort, and overlooking it, was Itchiane hill from the summit of which a splendid panorama of the country for a great many miles round could be obtained, and where, after the arrival of the relief column a heliograph station was established. On the morning of the Isandhlwana fight, the Rev. W. Smith went up there to see what was going on, as he had heard the guns in the distance, and a day or so after we got in he took me up to explain to me what he had seen. On the "neck" just below Isandhlwana hill he saw the artillery firing, and presently a large body of Natives moving round the hill towards them. Thinking it was our Contingent, he said to himself, "Well done, Lonsdale!", as they were moving with such precision. Then shortly after, he noticed a number of horsemen galloping for their lives, away on his right, making towards the Drift, which made him think that Lord Chelmsford's column were being driven back, and almost at the same time large numbers of Natives appeared away to his left front, coming up from the river very leisurely and massing in the valley. After taking a look at these, and seeing that none of them wore the red head-band of Lonsdale's men, his first impulse was to go down and parley with them, but noticing that their numbers were considerably increasing he hastened down the hill again to inform Chard and Bromhead who, however, had already received warning that a Zulu impi was advancing on the Fort. The horsemen he had seen were fugitives from the Camp and had passed the Post before he got down, and be it to their everlasting shame and dishonour, galloped on as hard as they could, refusing to stop a moment to assist the garrison, and merely shouted out that the Zulus were close on them. How far their flight took them, I don't think was ever ascertained.

The part which the Rev. Mr. Smith played in the defence, and the splendid example he set throughout that terrible night, ought to have earned for him the V.C. The same with the Acting Commissariat Officer, Mr. James Dalton, who in the absence of Lieutenant Chard, R.E., (who was down at the river superintending Pontoon work at the moment when warning was received of the nearness of the Zulus), devised all the rapid arrangements for the defence as well as working like a Trojan himself with the men at the barricades and did much gallant work during the night. All this was gratefully acknowledged by Lieutenant Chard in his report to the Commander-in-Chief after the fight, but neither Dalton nor Smith received any further distinction than promotion. Mr Thomas Atkins is the best judge of gallant deeds, and when he applauds you may be certain that he is right and does so with good reason, and I noticed that directly Mr Smith or Mr Dalton showed themselves they received an ovation from the men, which was unmistakable.

Among the six or seven young soldiers of the 24th who garrisoned the hospital and received the V.C. for defending it against such tremendous odds, and removing most of the sick while absolutely surrounded by Zulus, was one named Hook, who was taken on as servant by Major Black, whose shrill voice with its Scotch accent could be heard above the Fort calling for "H-o-o-k!" many times a day. So the men had their little joke, and whenever Hook was called for they themselves shouted for Hook and then yelled out, "I think he's hooked it, sir!", which always caused great merriment.

The following astounding incident of Colonel Harness's servant's escape from the hands of the Zulus was told me by one of the garrison; Colonel Harness, C.R.A. of the 3rd Column, had been obliged to leave his servant behind sick at Rorke's Drift when the Column crossed into Zululand, and on the night of the attack on the Fort he happened to be outside the barricades at the moment when the Zulus made their sudden rush on the hospital. As he would to a certainty have been shot down by the fire of our own men had he attempted in the darkness to run in and clamber back again, he quickly bolted under a small hand-cart that had accidentally been left propped up outside against the back of the hospital wall and which (luckily for him, but unfortunately for the garrison), was in such a position as to be completely out of the line of fire. Here he remained throughout the night, wrapped up in his blanket, with the Zulus swarming all round him – many of them actually jumping on to the cart to try and get on to the roof of the hospital, which some of them succeeded in doing and setting fire to it. But none of them, curiously enough, made any attempt to move the cart, in which case he would have been done for. In the morning, however, when the Zulus had decamped and all firing had ceased, to the great astonishment of the garrison he walked in safe and sound, after about as terrifying an experience as any man could have gone through.

By another lucky coincidence, too, the whole garrison had escaped a terrible catastrophe as only a very short distance away at the back of the Fort, between it and the Itchiane hill, a large hay rick had been left standing, there being no time to clear it away before the Zulus commenced their attack, which if they had fired it would have smoked everyone out and rendered the Fort enterable; but luckily, in their eagerness to wipe out the garrison with the assegai, it was left untouched …

… Occasionally I rode out by myself to take a look round, and one afternoon about a mile from the Fort came across a portmanteau torn in half and empty, but lying by the side of it was a Bible, and a few feet further on a silver watch, which I restored to their rightful owner, the Rev. Mr Smith, when I got back, and very pleased he was to have them in his possession again. The portmanteau itself was far too damaged to be of any further use, so was left where it was.

The same day, I think it was, I came across the body of a very fine specimen of a Zulu in the skeleton stage, which I took Surgeon Reynolds out to have a look at. He too was impressed with the stature and splendid proportions, and brought away one or two bones of scientific interest, and the soles of the feet which had become detached and were just like solid pieces of horn. I also took one of the collar bones and the lesser bones of one of the arms, which I intended some day to give to the Durban Museum …

… In front of the Fort and some 600 or 700 yards down the slope of the hill, a scaffold had been put up by the Commissariat Department on which the carcasses of the cattle were hung up previous to issue, and one morning Major Black and I were sitting outside, warming ourselves in the sun and chatting, when we saw a most extraordinary-looking object suspended on the scaffold, and wondered what on earth it could be. Presently, a Private of the 24th came up from that direction, and Black asked him what the thing was, and he said that it was a Kaffir spy that had been hanged. "Good Heavens!," said Black, "By whose orders was he hung?" "Captain Harford, sir," was the reply, so we went down at once to look into the matter. The poor wretch, who was an old, wizened-up, grey-headed Native, had apparently been dead for some hours, and must have been hung some time during the night, but by whom it was never discovered. Every possible enquiry was made, but not a soul knew anything about it and nothing was known of the Native or where he could have come from …

1481 Private John James, 2/24th Foot

South Wales Daily News, 29 March 1879

Rorke's Drift
February 2 1879

... Dear Mother, after they done slaughtering us there, they went down to where B company was with Commissary – about 12,000 of them, and they set fire to it, but our boys had the best of them here. They killed about 1,000 of them, the loss on our side was 11 killed and two wounded. William Osborne had a narrow escape. They had to fight hard for their lives that night. William Osborne, Edward Murray, S. Parry, and William Davies, all send their kind love to you. George Slasher got killed in the battle. So no more at present from your loving son, John James.

Thank God that I am alive to tell the news.

Private John James, 1481, G Company 2-24th Regt. Natal, South Africa.

Lieutenant Henry G. Mainwaring, 2/24th Foot

Extract from 'Isandhlwana Prelude and Aftermath, 22nd January 1895', written by Mainwaring [Royal Welsh Regimental Museum, Brecon]

... On arriving in sight of Rorke's Drift, we saw the house in flames, also far over the country we observed various homesteads ablaze. This led us to believe that the Zulus had invaded Natal. We naturally thought that the garrison had fallen. Great therefore was our relief when the cavalry, who were the first to cross the river, galloped up to the house and sent up a ringing cheer. Soon afterwards, the infantry crossed by the Pontoons and I shall never forget seeing 'Gonny' Bromhead (then Lieutenant) come out to meet us as we formed in quarter column outside the gate. He told me afterwards he felt as if he was walking on air as he never expected to see daylight again. After giving me some food Bromhead took me round the scene of the fight. In front of the verandah outside the hospital and near the two blue gum trees the Zulu bodies were lying three deep. 'Gonny' especially pointed out a young Zulu Induna with a plume head-dress, telling me that he was a very gallant man, and had headed a charge three times. 'But we got him the third time' he added. Inside the hospital he pointed out the remains of Sergeant Maxwell who I knew well – a good fellow.

Within the yard and right in front of the Rorke's Drift house was an inner defence – a sort of redoubt. This was suggested by Lieutenant Chard. It consisted of a circular pile of mealie bags, about 20 feet high. I climbed up to the top and looked down into the well space inside and there saw a soldier lying – dead as I first thought but after calling up 'Gonny' we found he was fast asleep from exhaustion. As a matter of fact we were all well played out.

But there was much to be done. The dead were buried – we lost 15 men and we buried between 300 to 400 Zulus …

Lieutenant John Maxwell, 2nd/3rd Natal Native Contingent

Extract from *Reminiscences of the Zulu War*, by John Maxwell, edited by Leonie Twentyman Jones, Cape Town, 1979

… We were anxious to reach Rorke's Drift not knowing how matters stood there. Firing had been heard distinctly during the night from that direction, and we pushed on with that object, enemy being in sight on each side of the road, until we arrived within some five miles of the drift. And then a number were made out on the Shean, the mountain at the back of the missionary's house, the place left occupied by a company of the 2nd 24th Regiment, stores, a few invalids and some of the Commissariat. And what was then of great moment, we expected our breakfast.

Those that had glasses eagerly scanned the place, but I was looking at the river which seemed to be a perfect torrent. The ponts appeared all right, so the Infantry would have no difficulty in crossing. We received orders to march on a spot further up the river, and to cross in the best manner we could. After a very rough time of it in the river, we found ourselves across all right with the exception of a soaking and marched on the house. By this time we could distinguish several soldiers waving their hats and apparently very glad at our appearance. On approaching nearer we saw several dead bodies of the enemy lying about, which at once told us the place had been attacked. It was 8 o'clock when we arrived at the front of the place, scattered over which we saw about 2 hundred of the enemy lying dead. At the back the greatest damage must have been caused to the enemy, as the hill sloped down towards the building or temporary fort. The walls consisted of bags of corn meal flour and boxes of tinned beef, biscuits etc. So our fears with regard to breakfast were set at rest. I took a stroll round, when I learnt from 2 of the 24th all about the attack which had commenced the previous afternoon and only finally ceased on our being seen from the top of the hill at sunrise advancing along the road. The men bared their shoulders and I saw that they were black and blue and swollen, caused by the recoil or kicking of their Martinis, proving to what extent they had been firing. In fact they told me that towards daylight they were unable to place the rifle to the shoulder, but held it out pointing to the front and firing. They had during the night to change shoulder constantly, which caused both being in this state. I heard that a friend of mine had been shot, and that his body was with other dead laid out in the cattle kraal. I proceeded thither but found a sentry placed over these bodies numbering five. They were covered with straw. His orders were to keep everybody off. I failed to ascertain who they might have been. I now sought the house, but perceived no change there, with the exception that it was minus thatch which had been pulled off. The outhouses I saw were burnt down. Of course I was told the story of the attack on these, and the gallant rescue from the fire. This was told me by a corporal of ours we had left behind on account of his having a severely blistered foot. He was a young foreigner who afterwards received the Victoria Cross from Sir Garnet now Lord Wolsey on the market square in Maritzburg. Leaving this I walked to the front again, and to my astonishment perceived a Kethla, or ringed native, hanging to the crossbeam that had been erected some days previously for the butchers. It appeared he had been found under suspicious circumstances in the neighbourhood, and so met his end in rather a summary manner.

Orders were out for the burying of all dead, the Contingent and the 24th to provide the fatigue parties. And it was arranged that the first mentioned should dig the holes, on account of their prejudice against touching the dead, and that the 24th should place them therein. And so the dead were buried at Rorke's Drift, occupying some two to three hours; we digging large holes in various places and the 24th with the assistance of reins, placing the bodies therein. I believe there must have been a number of dead taken away by the enemy on their retiring across the river. I may mention here that at various times for a period of six weeks, bodies were found in the caves and among the stones on this mountain, and two months afterwards two brother officers and myself discovered in a cave near the summit three bodies, which were quite hard and sound. These had been wounded and managed to crawl thus far to die …

Lieutenant Archibald B. Milne, Royal Navy

Report of Proceedings of 21st, 22nd, 23rd & 24th Jany. 1879 [National Archives, London, ADM1/6486]

… Then was seen the gallant defence made by the small garrison of 80 men. The dead Zulus were lying about in scores close up to the parapet. Firing was still going on at wounded men trying to escape. For a long time the garrison held the hospital but at last found they had too much ground to defend for so small a number, and the enemy kept creeping up in the bushes in the garden, and coming upon them in rushes. So at last they were obliged to leave it. The sick defended it for an hour longer when at last the enemy managed to burn it with all its inmates.

The officers who so gallantly defended this store were Lt. Bromhead 2/24th and Lieut. Chard, RE.

As soon as our column had had some food, they were immediately set to work to improve the defences. The parapet was heightened and continued along to the edge of the hospital, the thatching of the store was taken off, and all the trees round about cut down. The guns were brought inside, three were mounted pointing towards the river, and the fourth towards the right of the krantz and the direction in which the enemy came the previous night …

'No. 12' of 'Notes on the Report of Proceedings', accompanying the official report by Milne [National Archives, London, ADM1/6486]

12/.

"At Rorkes Drift, one of the prisoners taken gave these undermentioned names as the Regiments who attacked at Isandhlwana …

… Undi Regt. – Kraals Toulwan, Inhlohonhlo, Inhluyegwe – Strength 8000 – (Cetywayos own Regt.) …

Attacking force at Rorkes Drift consisted of from 4 to 5,000 men of the Undi Regt.

This prisoner also stated that they were obliged to fight, should they not do so they would be killed by Cetywayo

The Undi Regt. consists entirely of Ringtops or married men about 35 years of age.

A private of the 2/24th took from one of the prisoners captured at Rorkes Drift some of his own property taken at Isandhlwana the day previous …

Arch. B. Milne
Lieut. R.N.

Extract from a letter written by Milne to Commodore Sullivan, RN, in Durban [National Archives, London, ADM1/6486]

Fort near Rorke's Drift
23rd January 1879

My dear Sir …

… Started again at daylight this morning & reached this place at 7.0. Found that the Hospital had been attacked by 2,000 Zulus last evening at 5 p.m. it was garrisoned by 1 Company 2/24th who held out until the Zulus withdrew at 4 a.m. this morning. They lost 13 killed. Zulus 100 killed. We have lost everything, camp &c. &c. being taken away by the enemy. Be good enough not to make this public until something Official comes out. This is what Crealock thinks best.

Sincerely Yours

Arch. B. Milne.

Charles L.W. Norris-Newman, war correspondent

Extract from an unidentified Natal newspaper, c. January 1879

With Head-quarter Column
The Story Of Isandhlwana
(From the Times War Correspondent.)
Pietermaritzburg, Jan. 26th, 1879

Our surprise and delight may be easily imagined when we heard a good English cheer greet us, and upon getting close up we saw that the place was surrounded by a barricade of mealies in sacks, with the bodies of numerous Zulus lying around. We quickly dismounted and when inside, to our great relief, that the little garrison had received warning in time from fugitives from our late camp, and were able to prepare themselves so that they successfully withstood and repulsed, with severe loss to the enemy, a large body of over 4000 kaffirs, which had attacked them at five on Wednesday evening, and had only retired at daylight that morning …

… The gallant defenders had to relate the whole night's experience to us all, and were then much complimented on their splendid resistance. The small garrison consisted of a little over 130 men, under Lieutenant Broomhead, 2-24th. The following officers were also with him at the time, and gave material assistance: –

Dr. Reynolds, 2-24th, Lieutenant Chard, R.E., Lieutenant Adendorff, 1-3rd Natal Native Contingent, and Messrs. Dunne, Dalton, and Byrne, of the Commissariat department. The Reverend Mr. Smith, was also present throughout the attack.

Several bodies of men who had escaped from the scene of the massacre at Insandhlwana passed by Rorke's Drift, but, although some were strong bodies, they would not, much to their discredit, stay to help the little garrison.

The fire we had seen was that part of the building used as a hospital, which was detached some distance from the house itself, and, therefore, had to be given up. The loss sustained in this night attack is given in my return …

… C.L.N.N.

Captain Henry H. Parr, 1/13th Foot

Extract from a private letter from Henry Parr to Sir Henry Bartle Frere [The Royal Archives, Windsor, RAVIC/033/118, by kind permission of Her Majesty Queen Elizabeth II]

Camp, Rorke's Drift
23.1.79

… The men & officers have behaved admirably working shoulder to shoulder. I finished burying the dead Zulus this morning – natives won't touch dead bodies so our men had to do it & I did not hear a grumble.

To a dead soldier I heard a man say as he was lifting him – "Come on, old comrade, I'm main sorry to put you out of sight, but ye had a soldier's death" …

Extract from *Recollections and Correspondence,* by Major General Henry Hallam Parr, London, 1917

… The Zulu army began to disperse directly after Isandlwana, many returning straight from the field of battle with their booty to their kraals. This contrary to orders, but the severe fighting and the amount of booty which had fallen into their hands had entirely disorganised the Zulu regiments.

The Undi (the royal corps) however, preserved its discipline, and after sullenly and unwillingly retreating from Rorke's Drift, marched straight to Ulundi. The king, according to custom, received them in the grand kraal. He had only as yet received the news that the white man's camp had been taken, and that 'Somtseu's' column had been eaten up. He had not heard of the repulse at Rorke's Drift, nor was he prepared for the terrible gaps made in his regiments. As the men began to file into the enclosure, he saw there had been very different fighting to that he had known in the Swasiland or against the Amatonga.

The Tulwana (the crack regiment of the royal corps, in whose ranks, as already stated, Cetewayo himself had fought in his young days, and to which he still nominally belonged) was the last regiment, and it filed in and saluted. 'Why don't the rest come in?' cried the king impatiently. But the rest of the brave Tulwana could not hear him, for they were lying outside the mealie bags and biscuit-boxes at Rorke's Drift.

We left No. 3 Column on the morning of the 23rd of January, about half-past eight, recrossing the Buffalo River. The crossing this time did not take long. Harness's four guns and wagons, and one mule wagon, which had carried the biscuit, comprised our wheeled vehicles.

By half-past nine, the remains of No. 3 Column had marched up to Rorke's Drift, and were getting their breakfasts round the shattered buildings and temporary parapet, which for twelve hours had sustained so desperate an attack. This over, all hands set to work in putting things to rights; while the Headquarters Staff, the mounted men, and Harness's four guns continued their march to Helpmakaar.

One of the most necessary duties to be undertaken was the burial of the dead and the cleansing of the ground. This had to be taken in hand without a moment's delay, as decomposition comes on quickly under the hot African sun. The superintendence of this work happened to be my duty.

'It's your turn now, comrade, now we've cleared this rubbish out of your way,' said a 24th man to a dead soldier, who was found with two or three Zulus stretched almost upon him. 'I'm main sorry to put you away, mate,' continued he, laying the end of a torn sack gently over the dead man's face, 'but you died well and had a soldier's end.'

Homely words, but what soldier could wish a better requiem?

Trooper Henry T. Simpson, Newcastle Mounted Rifles

Extracts from Henry Simpson's own account which appeared in an unidentified Natal newspaper, c. 1929

"… A few hours' marching brought us to Rorke's Drift, so gallantly defended by Lieutenants Chard and Bromhead with 31 men of the 24th and 21 others. The previous night we have heard the terrific firing, and when we arrived about 9 o'clock in the morning and saw the hospital, where 35 sick men had been billeted, burning furiously, we thought the tragedy of Isandhlwana had been repeated.

"We were formed up in order and given the order to charge; but our feelings of relief can well be imagined when we saw a soldier climb on to the wall of boxes and bags and signal to us. We pulled up. Hundreds and hundreds of natives lay round the laager in heaps. One or two of them had even succeeded in entering the scanty enclosure, but they had been killed immediately.

"I think the firing of the hospital actually helped the defenders, who had been able to see the enemy much better by its glare. Their hands were scorched by their rifles, which had grown red hot with continual firing, and every man was utterly exhausted. Their little bit of laager had undoubtedly saved them from sharing the fate of the 800, and at the same time taught us once and for all that in fighting the Zulu in those days a laager was not only advisable, but absolutely necessary …"

Lieutenant Horace L. Smith-Dorrien, 95th Foot

Extract from *Memories of Forty-Eight Years' Service*, by Horace Smith-Dorrien, London, 1925

… The next day I rode down to Rorke's Drift, some twelve miles, to resume charge of my depot. There was the improvised little fort, built up mostly of mealy-sacks and biscuit-boxes and other stores which had been so gallantly defended by Chard, Bromhead, and their men, and Parson Smith, and all around lay dead Zulus, between three and four hundred; and there was my wagon, some 200 yards away, riddled and looted, and there was the riem gallows I had erected the previous morning. Dead animals and cattle everywhere – and a scene of devastation! To my young mind it appeared impossible that order could ever be restored, but I set to work and next day, whilst sitting in my wagon, I saw two Zulus hanging on my gallows and was accused by the Brigade Major, Clery, (afterwards General Sir Francis Clery), of having given the order. I was exonerated, however, when it was found that it was a case of lynch law performed by incensed men, who were bitter at the loss of their comrades. Other incidents of the same sort occurred in the next few days before law and order were re-established …

1939 Drummer William Sweeney, 2/24th Foot

Oldham Weekly Chronicle, 26 April 1879

… About 3,000 Zulus came on our chaps about three on the same evening. Our boys made a fort of all the bags of corn, and bags of flour, meal, and all sorts of stuff. The enemy came on in rushes times out of number, and our chaps mowed them down as fast as they came up. Several of the Zulus got over the fort, but our chaps on the inside were waiting for them with the bayonet. You would be surprised to see the horrible murders as ever were committed. Those 80 men kept them off from three o'clock in the afternoon on the 22nd, until six a.m. on the 23rd for the loss of 14 men. One of them had a most horrible death. He was assegaied with long knives. His name was Billy Horrigan. He joined the regiment in Cork. Each of the men in the fort that night used 150 rounds of ammunition. The General said if he had 1,000 men like those he would face any 10,000 Zulus …

Trooper Fred Symons, Natal Carbineers

Extract from *The Farmer*, 3 and 10 March 1933, reprinted in *Journal of the AZWRS*, Vol. 4, No. 1. Symons takes up the story as he and the remainder of Lord Chelmsford's column return to Rorke's Drift on the morning of 23 January [Killie Campbell Africana Library, KwaZulu-Natal, South Africa]

… when someone shouted "What's that on the wall?" It's a man waving a flag. There's another, look!. The place is full of them! Are they friends or are they foes? Perhaps they are Zulus & the waving of flags a ruse to get part of our force across the river & then fall upon us. This suspicion was roused by the sight of a large force of natives on the spur of the Biggarsberg beyond the Mission Station where the flag waving was going on …

Rorke's Drift

Pushing on to the Buffalo as fast as possible, Col. Russell ordered the Carbineers to line the bank, dismount and cover the retreat of the Mounted Infantry, if necessary. Fixing the sights of our carbines at eight hundred yards, we stood waiting for the Mounted Infantry to be fired upon, but soon one came back to say, "All right. They're our men" …

… The first corpse that met our gaze was that of a N.N.C. officer who was shot by the 24th for deserting them in the hour of danger. His men fled at the approach of the Zulus but that was no reason for deserting too. Thrice they called him to come back, but he would not. He was a foreigner.

Around the ruins of the hospital lay in heaps the bodies of dead Zulus, some burnt to ashes & a strong smell of roasting flesh pervading the place. A trooper of the Police, who had been in hospital with fever, tried to reach the laager of mealie bags from the burning hospital. A Zulu followed him. The soldiers shouted to the trooper to drop down so that they could shoot the Zulu. He either did not hear or understand & the Zulu stabbed him & was immediately shot himself. In endeavouring to reach the others from the burning building a young soldier was also stabbed from behind.

One patient flung a blanket over himself, smeared his face with ashes, and escaped into the orchard, where he escaped observation and came out safely in the morning.

But the first question we asked was;

"Where are our men, have none escaped?"

The only ones they had spoken to was trooper Fletcher of the Carbineers and R. Hall, the meat contractor …

About the Camp

… Each man was here served out with bread and a rum ration. Then we began to saunter round. Beneath the trees, still fastened by reims to the tree trunk, lay the carcasses of three horses & everywhere lay bodies of Zulus.

The men on the spur of the mountain turned out to be the regiment of N.N.C. deserters who were on their way back to see how the fight had gone. When they saw it was all right, they came down & were brave as ever they were when no enemy was in sight.

The greater part of the day was spent in collecting the dead Zulus, of whom about seven hundred were buried on that and the following day.

The men of the 24th, who defended the place, spoke very highly of the Rev. Geo. Smith, who, they say, carried ammunition round in his hat for the men. One man told me that a private was swearing because he could not get any ammunition and the Rev. George reproved him, saying he should not swear at such a time as this but put his trust in God. Patting his rifle the soldier replied; 'I shall put my faith in this now and God afterwards.'

The palms of their hands were scorched by the heated rifle barrels and over and over again the Zulus would seize the bayonets and try and wrench the rifles away.

Saved from Fire

When the hospital was fired by the Zulus the men at once set to work to pull off the thatch from the dwelling house. A German, or some foreigner, who was with the garrison, saved the building from fire for he saw the Zulu with a lighted bunch of grass on the end of a stick just raising it up to the eaves and promptly shot him. Had that building caught alight it would have been all up with the garrison.

The guns and assegais were collected and thrown into a large hole below the laager and burnt. Most of the guns were loaded (muzzle loaders) and all day long these weapons were discharged in this hole. It is surprising no one got hit.

The men spoke very highly of Chard & another man named, I think, Milne, but I am not sure. Of Bromhead they did not speak well.

Milne, if that was the man's name, ought to get the V.C., if any man deserved it; for when the men were distracted with thirst and parched with the dust from the thatch and smoke, they went to broach a cask of rum, but this man stood upon it and threatened to shoot the first who touched it. He also volunteered to go with a few men and guard the punt, but was not permitted to do so …

Captain William P. Symons, 2/24th Foot

'The Battle of Isandhlwana and the Defence of Rorke's Drift 1879, by Capt. W.P. Symons 2-24th Regiment' [Royal Welsh Regimental Museum, Brecon]. This appears to be Symons' first draft for his account, complete with numerous corrections and alterations, etc. It runs to some forty-four pages, not including additional inserted pages for notes, etc., indicated here by a *. Those sections that he actually crossed out in the original have been, where relevant, included as <u>underlined</u>.

Private

Read by Her Majesty the Queen, the Prince of Wales, the D. of Cambridge, Sir Charles Ellice, Sir A. Alison, the Intelligence Department, &c &c –

The Queen kept this for a fortnight at Osborne in January 1880 and I was <u>order</u> asked by Sir Charles Ellice, then Adjutant General, by, I understood, the desire of Her Majesty, & of H.R.H. D. of Cambridge that the account should not be published until after the death of Lord Chelmsford, & perhaps other persons mentioned.

21st February 1880

An Account of the battle of Isandhlwana and Defence of Rorke's Drift
(Written at Rorke's Drift February, March & April 1879)
… We arrived there, on the Natal side, at 8-30 a.m., without encountering any of the enemy, though two large bodies made their appearance on our left rear, without, however, coming near enough to enable us to fire at them. Fortunately the Pontoons had been left untouched & we crossed easily **i)*.

The Story of the Defence of Rorke's Drift.
One mile from the Buffalo River, on the Natal side, Lieut Gonville Bromhead 2/24th Regt with his Company, letter "B", of that Regiment, had been left to guard Commissariat stores & the lines of communication. The Company numbered 90 men & besides these there were 40 Casuals, 35 of whom were patients in Hospital.

Lieut. Chard Royal Engineers was the senior officer present, & Lieut Bromhead & his Company fought & acted under his able superintendence & orders.

The Post had been desperately attacked by great numbers of Zulus from 4. p.m. on the 22nd until daylight of the 23rd …

… At 3 p.m. on the 22nd January, Lieut Bromhead received the startling news from two fugitives that the General's Camp at Isandhlwana had been taken, & that the Zulus were on the way to attack his post. These men, after giving warning, lost no time in galloping off towards Helpmakaar in continuing their journey & it is fortunate for them that Lt Bromhead was not able afterwards to recognize them. Half an hour afterwards the intelligence was confirmed by a hastily written note received from Captain Gardner 14th Hussars …

… The above warnings gave the Officers at Rorke's Drift a short hour for preparation. It was badly needed, as nothing had been done to prepare the place for defence; the arrangements for so doing having been put off "by order" until the arrival of the expected reliefs of the Royal Engineers & 4th Regt. **ii)*.

The tents of the Company were pitched outside the Farm House or rather houses, as there were two; one, was used by us as a store, the other, as a "Base Hospital," & they were 40 38 yards apart –

At this time Lieut Chard was engaged with the Pontoons down at the river, & receiving like intelligence of the disaster & intended attack from another fugitive from Isandhlwana, moored the Pontoons in the middle of the stream, & made the best of his way back to where Lieut Bromhead & Acting Commissariat Officer Dalton were doing their utmost to render the Post defensible. –

The tents were struck, & the Store House loopholed & occupied. Biscuit boxes & sacks of mealies were piled so as to form a parapet towards the garden on one side, & along the other, facing the Hill, which completely commanded the Houses & Enclosures three wagons were drawn up, & filled up the gaps between them were filled up with more boxes & sacks of grain. These "lines" connected the two Houses & formed what we will call "the Yard". It was a broken & imperfect barricade at the best. On the garden side the parapet was nowhere more than 3 ft. high; towards the hill in places it was raised to 4 & 4½ feet. **iii).*

The advanced guard of the Zulus first appeared about 4-30 p.m. It They came round the South Corner of the Hill in a body 500 to 600 strong, led by a chief riding a grey mare. They halted a moment, & then advanced quietly but quickly, at a run, taking advantage of every bit of cover. It seemed as if they had expected to surprise the Camp Post & capture it with a rush. Our men opened fire at 500 yards. The first man to fall was the mounted chief. He was shot by Private Dunbar, & fell from his horse headlong. Numbers of them fell at once. As soon as the enemy felt the fire, they broke, & the greater part scattered to their left, & occupied the garden & orchard where there was plenty of cover. A few got up to the Houses & lay behind the Field Ovens & Kitchens. Most of these men were soon shot. It was quickly perceived that a very few only of this advanced guard of the enemy had either guns or rifles. In a continuous stream more warriors followed the advanced party, occupied the hill, 400 yards distant & gradually encircled the two houses. Most of the men who had guns rifles were stationed on the hill, & they kept up a rapid fire on the yard.

It caught our men in reverse as they manned the parapet on the garden side, & 5 men were thus shot dead. As the evening set in, the dusky foe enemy crept nearer & nearer. Under cover of the bushes & long grass they were able to get within five a few yards of the Hospital without being seen.

From this point in parties of 15 to 20 they repeatedly attacked the far corner of the Hospital.

They made these attacks in the most deliberate manner. As in their dancing, they stalked out of their concealment, pranced up with a high stepping action, & caring nothing for the slaughter, endeavoured to get over the barricade, and into the end room of the Hospital. Many times, seven or eight at least, Lieutenant Bromhead, collecting a few men together, had to drive them off with a bayonet charge. On being repulsed they would retire to better cover, shout in chorus & strike their shields with their assegais. Our men cheered in response & let them have it. How deliberate & telling was the fire may be gathered from the following incidents.

Private Joseph Williams, a young Welshman of under two years service, had was posted at a small window in the far end of the Hospital to shoot from. Next morning fourteen dead Zulus were found outside his window, & many more down his line of fire. As soon as his ammunition was expended, he & the other men in the room with him defended the door with their bayonets till it was broken & forced open. Poor fellow, he was seized by the arms & hands, dragged out & assegaied, & mutilated before the eyes of his comrades.

Another instance – Private Dunbar, a Canadian by birth, the same man who had shot the Chief on horseback, was posted told off to watch the hill. As the Zulus streamed round the foot from their right, this man of even less service than Williams, got the right distance, & shot eight of them in as many consecutive shots. Lieut Chard was standing by him as he did it.

At last by sheer weight of numbers the enemy burst in the doors of the Hospital & effected an entry. Twenty eight of the patients were got out in time. Most of them were pushed or pulled through a window which opened on the yard. A few escaped by making a bold dash from the Verandah, round & over the parapet. Two or three were caught & assegaied as they attempted this. An artilleryman gunner, a patient, by name Howard, a servant of Colonel Harness, **iv).* ran out of the Hospital, & hid himself in the long grass growing on the bank outside. He covered himself with grass & twigs as well & quickly as he could & remained there all night. He came in unharmed at daylight, although for many hours, the Zulus were constantly around & about him. A small pig was shot dead by his side. **v).*

Sergeant Maxfield of the 2/24th, a fine young soldier was down with fever & delirious. He could not be moved, & was killed in his bed.

The enemy now set fire to the roof of the Hospital. Being thatch it blazed up at once. By its light our men were enabled to see their foes the Zulus better, & many fell before they retreated.

After a pause, commanded and encouraged by an "Induna" or Chief, who from time to time shouted his orders from the hill side, they came on again most pluckily, shouting their war cry "Usutu, Usutu."

The fighting now became desperate, constantly hand to hand along the line of defence. The assailants only used their assegais as stabbing weapons. They seldom threw one. Any of our men showing themselves over the parapet were instantly thrust at. Owing to want of flanking fire, there were places where the Zulus could crouch beneath the barricade in safety. They even seized the men's Bayonets, & tried to wrench them from the muzzles of the rifles. One of the men soldier to whom this happened had just loaded; he pulled the trigger of his Martini, without putting it to his shoulder & blew the plucky fellow to atoms.

At first the hurriedly made & rough lines of defence were constructed to hold a very much larger body of defenders than actually were engaged. A large number of natives & some white men having in the most cowardly manner, at the first whisper of danger, deserted the post & bolted. Lieut Chard with admirable forethought & readiness of resource no sooner grasped the fact than he set men to construct a "retrenchment" or inner line of defence of biscuit boxes, connecting the corner of the store with the parapet on the garden side, & soon after the roof of the Hospital fell in all our men had to take refuge behind this. Had he not done so it is probable that the Zulus, at this period of the attack, would have rushed captured the position. The immediate safety of the little garrison being secured, Lieut Chard, ably assisted by all available hands, constructed inside the inner lines what may be termed a "crow's nest" of mealie sacks. From this commanding position the fire of the defenders was rendered much more effective. Acting Chaplain the Revd. George Smith of Estcourt, Natal; & Assistant Commissary Dunne contributed greatly to the construction & success of these little works.

The enemy now endeavoured to fire the roof of the Storehouse. One fine savage splendid fellow was shot by Corporal Attwood, of the Army Service Corps, as he was holding a lighted brand against the eaves.

And so the fight continued till after midnight, from which time the attack gradually slackened, & the enemy, carrying away as many of their dead & wounded with them as possible, according to their custom in battle, withdrew. Some days afterwards, 50 large shields covered with blood were found by the river side, marking the spot to which they had carried their dead, & cast them into the river.

The last of them left just before dawn. The numbers composing the attack were estimated at 3,000. Many of the bodies by their shields & other distinctive marks, such as plumes, head rings &c were identified as belonging to one of the King's chief & favourite Regiments, & one which bore a great reputation.

Our loss was thirteen killed & ten wounded; three of the latter died soon after of their wounds. Of the enemy, these had all fallen close round the Post, we buried 376, & after days over 100 more skeletons were found lying here & there in the long grass & bush between Rorke's Drift & the spot where the Zulus recrossed the Buffalo River.

The larger proportion, in fact 5 out of 6, of the bodies found were those of old men, many of them quite wizened, & all spare & thin. Very few could be called fine men, & one or two only approached six feet.

Already I have stated that many of them were heaped up contorted – and many others were being dragged off by a fatigue party, to bury, with a wagon rope attached to the heel of the corpse only –

It bestows us We must now mention the names of those who in this memorable fight defence especially distinguished themselves. It must be understood that it was essentially a soldiers fight. Given all credit to the Officers who used the best judgement under the circumstances, & exhibited prompt action & readiness of resource; given also the confidence with which Lieutenants Chard & Bromhead, young officers both, inspired their men, we repeat that it was a fight at the long odds of one white man to 30 black savages frenzied with success & slaughter. Each individual soldier stuck to his post, did his work & duty grandly.

No 395 Private John Williams, with the Joseph Williams before mentioned, was posted in the end room of the Hospital. They held it for more than an hour, as long as they had a round of ammunition left. As they were unfortunately cut off from the rest of the Company they could get no more ammunition. After Joseph Williams was dragged out of the room, John Williams & two of the Patients were the only ones men left alive. The Zulus left them alone for a while to butcher Joseph Williams. Taking advantage of the lull, these three made a hole in the partition wall with an axe, & getting into the next room joined Private Henry Hook, who still at his post was covering the escape withdrawal of the sick. John Williams & Hook, one working, whilst the other kept the enemy at bay with his bayonet, cut holes through three other partitions, & so working their way from room to room, succeeded in getting all the remainder of the sick out through the window into the yard. Private Hook was the last man to leave the Hospital & then it was all in flames.

In another ward Privates 593 William Jones, & 716 Robert Jones had been placed by Lieut Bromhead. They defended their post to the last, & held the ward until 6 out of the 7 Patients entrusted to their charge had been safely removed. The seventh was Sergeant Maxfield. He was left for a while lying delirious & wounded on his bed. Private Robert Jones giving up his rifle went back to try & carry him out. The room was full of Zulus, & he saw them stabbing the body on the bed. It was entirely owing to the personal pluck & exertions of these four men that the last of the Patients escaped.

Acting Commissariat Officer Dalton, until badly wounded in the shoulder, & Corporal Schiess of the Natal Native Contingent, a Swiss by birth, also wounded, deserve the highest praise for their cheery encouragement of the soldiers, & the good work they performed in the defence. **vi).*

Corporal W. Allan, & Private Hitch, both 2/24th men, must also be mentioned for their courageous work & assistance. It was chiefly due to these two men that communication with the Hospital was kept up at all. Holding at all costs a most dangerous post, at the N.E. corner of the Hospital, raked in reverse by the enemy's fire from the hill, they were both severely wounded, but their determined conduct enabled the Patients to be withdrawn from the Hospital. When incapacitated from firing themselves, they continued, as soon as their wounds had been dressed, to serve out ammunition to their comrades during the night.

It was a gallant defence. The young soldiers backed each other up & fought splendidly. They never wavered for an instant. Most of them Welshmen by birth, by a few months of drill & training, & infusion of "Esprit de Corps", had become the best & pluckiest of "Warwickshire Lads", & gloriously upheld the traditions of the old 24th.

It was of the utmost importance that this place Rorke's Drift should not have been captured by the enemy. Had it fallen, Helpmakaar would probably have gone also, and not only would a probable invasion by a triumphant enemy followed by a great panic have fallen on the Colony of Natal, but the safety of the remainder of Colonel Glyn's Column would have been imperilled.

When Lieut General Lord Chelmsford K.C.B. left Rorke's Drift on the morning of the 24th January 1879 for Pieter-Maritzburg, he desired Lieut Colonel Degacher C.B. commanding the 2/24th Regt. to address the men of his Battalion at the first opportunity as follows – "Not having time myself I wish you to tell them how highly I think of their conduct, it was admirable, no troops could have been steadier or more collected, especially during that trying night of constant alarms, the 22nd. As for Lieut Bromhead & his Company nothing that I can now say can express my admiration of the gallant defence they made".

[*Notes made on separate pages*]

**i*). Major Russell of the 12 Lancers was the 1st & I was the second officer of the column to reach Rorke's Drift Post, and the sight there presented was astounding. Several hundred dead Zulus were lying close round the houses & defences. In some places they were heaped together, 5 or 6 one on top of the other. The limbs of many of the bodies were strangely contorted, almost tied in knots, giving the idea of the Martini Henry bullet at very close range causing severe muscular contractions before death.

The appearance of the defenders, most of them men of my old Company "B", in which I had been a subaltern for nearly 15 years, surpassed my attention. Some after their desperate exertions were hysterical and could not speak. Others overjoyed at their escape & our arrival threw their arms about, waved their caps, & cheered. All were begrimed with powder, & blood, & smoke smuts from the burning hospital.

Lieut Bromhead was cool & collected, & his first thought, when he heard that the remnant of the column was returning, was to issue rations, & get breakfast cooked for us.

Private Michael Minahan, the right hand man of the Company, & a great pal of mine, who knew his drill well, & had often kept me straight on parade, took me off to show me where he had been stationed in a corner of the cattle kraal. He could scarcely speak from excitement, but suddenly catching sight of his bayonet, which was fixed at the time, & seeing it covered with blood, he appeared to remember something, & groping about in the straw a yard or two from where he had been posted uncovered the naked body of a dead Zulu, with a broad bladed assegai still in his hand. He then related, chiefly with signs, that this Zulu must have crept in over the wall of the kraal, & crawling under the straw had suddenly seized him by the leg. My friend Minahan had then, as he said, prodded the straw, & one prod right through the body had got home.

**ii).* Lieut. Bromhead stated to me that on the 10th January, when he with his Company to their intense disappointment were detailed to remain behind & occupy & guard Rorke's Drift commissariat store & base hospital, he twice asked permission to place the post in a state of defence, but sanction was refused him by Lord Chelmsford's Staff. Afterwards when the Column had moved on, he became so persuaded of the risk & danger of inaction, that he made up his mind what to do if occasion should arise & Hence followed on the sudden alarm the promptness & correctness of his preparations, which had the warm approval of Lieut Chard an officer of the Royal Engineers.

**iii).* The hill was 400 yards from the post, & it commanded the houses & enclosures.

**iv).* when it was dark.

**v).* He told me next morning that his greatest fear was that the red stripes on his trousers would be seen.

**vi).* It was told that when the Zulus first endeavoured to rush the Post & were checked, Mr Dalton who had charge of the wagon barricade, stood up on one of the wagons & jeered at the Zulus, daring them to come on; and that when thus standing he had no more ammunition left, he threw his helmet at some of them crouching behind the ovens.

Corporal Schiess, they said, "fought like a little tiger". He could not restrain himself, but more than once dashed over the barricade, bayoneted a Zulu, & got back again.

Lieutenant William Weallens, 2/24th Foot

Extract from the *Uppingham School Magazine,* c. October 1879
[from *The Red Soldier,* by Fred Emery, London, 1977]

… Since I last wrote I have heard some particulars of Lieutenant Bromhead's fight here. You must know that he only had 90 men, and that he was occupying exactly the same extent of ground that 600 or 700 do now, with the exception that it was not nearly so strongly fortified. As he had so few men, he could not afford to fortify any one place very strongly, but there was one building used as a hospital which he determined to defend to the last, as there were about twenty sick men in it. Strange to say, the Zulus made most persistent attacks on this one point, and seemingly not caring how many of their men were killed in the attack. They got possession of one room and, having accomplished this, fired the building. This is what was most dreaded; however, most of the sick were removed in safety. One man, named Williams, did a very plucky thing; he got into a small room by himself, and from the window fired away all the ammunition he had. He then tried to make a bolt for it into the fort, but unfortunately fell in getting out of the window. He got up, however, and tried to join the fort, when he was wounded by an assegai. He was caught by the Zulus and literally cut to pieces, as they were so infuriated at the number of them he had killed. He had only about six yards to run to get into the fort, as the hospital was in the same line of defence. It seems very hard that he should have lost his life after fighting so well.

I only hope Bromhead will be well rewarded for his defence of this place, as there is but little doubt that if the Zulus had beaten him it was their intention to attack our line of march, when we should have been taken at a great disadvantage and in country suitable to them, and with their numbers we might possibly have been cut to pieces …

A former member of the Natal Native Contingent

Natal Witness, 19 January 1929

A Native Eyewitness

An old Zulu, probably eighty years of age, who works in Maritzburg, has a very vivid recollection of the battle [Isandlwana]. A member of the Native Contingent under Captain Russell, he viewed the fight from about half a mile away while he and his compatriots were guarding children …

… They cleared from here and went over to Rorke's Drift. There the soldiers had built walls of sandbags and made holes for their guns to go through. There were still thousands of Zulus, though many of them had been left behind. But the soldiers killed lots of them. They fired at them all through the night. Their guns grew hot in their hands. They were burned and their faces were black with the powder. Next morning early the Zulus ran off leaving many dead bodies on the ground, though the soldiers had not lost so many …

Here the old man concluded his tale. He had opened with a very vigorous and graphic description and then as he told of the dead, calmed impressively almost to a whisper. For a moment he stood, one arm on his chest fingering his chin, staring vacantly into the past. Then "Bayete." He gave the Royal salute. "Se ngi gedile." …

CHAPTER 4

'The action at Rorke's Drift was a splendid affair': Contemporary Accounts

Brevet-Lieutenant Colonel Philip R. Anstruther, 94th Foot

Extract from Anstruther's private diary [National Army Museum, London, Anstruther Papers, Acc. No. 5705/22, 'Letters of P.R. Anstruther from South Africa 1879–80']

April 1879

Isandlwarnar is only 9 miles off for I can see the hill plainly and Rorke's Drift which is held by 6 companies of the 24th is only 9 to there we have the two companies of the 24th that were left after Isandlwarnar and very good fellows they are giving us lots of milk & bread & butter.

There is a parson here who was at Rorke's Drift battle and he behaved very well from all accounts. Chard is the fellow to who most praise is due – as Bromhead's idea was to go into the open to fight and of course they would all have been chewed up in five minutes.

April 27th

By the way apropos Rorke's Drift. I think they made a great deal too much fuss about it in England. Of course it was a fine defence but they were fighting for their lives and could not have done anything else. Moreover the 24th men themselves won the battle. They are a grand lot of fellows.

... The parson Smith says he saw from a hill where he had gone to for a walk near Rorke's Drift, the Kaffers forming up in battalion after Isandlwanar so he went down and only just rejoined Bromhead before the attack commenced at 4.30, and they fought for 13 hours. Smith counted over 400 dead Kaffers – which is satisfactory and shows what patience, perseverance & the Henry Martini can do ...

Major General Edward W. Bray, CB, 2/4th Foot

Evening Standard, London, 16 April 1891

To the Editor of the Standard,

... The defence of Rorke's Drift by Lieutenant Chard, R.E., and Lieutenant Bromhead, 24th Regiment, with a Company of the 24th and some few odd soldiers – in all not more than one hundred and twenty-five men – against four thousand five hundred brave Zulus, was the most splendid feat of arms performed in South Africa.

I saw the entrenchments of Rorke's Drift five days after the fight, and was able to form a judgment of the nature of the determined attack of the Zulus, and the defence made by the Spartan band of the 24th Regiment. The biscuit boxes and mealie bags were then in position, and the remains of the Mission House, and burnt down outhouses. The hurried arrangements made by the young Engineer officer for barriers and barricades showed clearly the nature of the defence and the critical position occupied by so small a body of soldiers, who before this position was finished were attacked by the Zulus, armed with rifles, guns, and assegais, and not "with spears only," as supposed by General Swanston. The attack, and a succession of attempts to carry the position with a rush, lasted from four p.m. to five a.m., and the ground all round was covered with dead Zulus. The small garrison had about one-fifth of their number killed and wounded.

What saved the garrison from total destruction was, that the Zulus set fire after dark to the outhouses, which were used as a hospital, and the bright light caused by the fire enabled the gunners to shoot down the Zulus at close quarters wholesale. Surgeon Major Reynolds, V.C., the medical officer at the fight at Rorke's Drift, only a week ago, in talking over the fight at Rorke's Drift, told me that the bright light enabled the men to fire with terrific effect, and that the enemy obtained no cover in the gardens, which otherwise would have enabled them to get close in without being seen.

I told Lieutenant Bromhead, when he was showing me over the ground, that his brilliant defence of Rorke's Drift would not be eclipsed during the war, and that he was sure to be rewarded with a V.C., and Brevet Majority. I had not at the time heard that the young Engineer officer, Chard, was senior to him, Bromhead being the older man …

… I am, Sir, you obedient servant,

Ed. Will. Bray, Major General.

Folkestone, April 14.

Rev. Dr. James Dalzell, Gordon Memorial Mission Station, Natal.

Hamilton Advertiser, 15 March 1879, from a letter written to his brother

26th January, 1879.

Rorke's drift – the few men left who could escape tried to do so towards Rorke's drift. George Macleroy had got away about three miles. Those who knew the river tried other fords. The Zulus, to the number of 4000 or 5000, followed and crossed the Drift, and burnt Mr Witt's dwelling house. Mrs Witt and children with nurse were with us here, and had been so for about a month. Rev. Mr Witt said to Rev. Mr Smith, chaplain to the forces, "Let us get our horses." "No," said Smith, "now it gets interesting." Witt and Hammer, a friend of his fled, and Smith was killed in a few minutes. At Witt's the original dwelling-house had been fortified, and 95 white men, of whom some were sick, were inside. It was fight or die, it was even, and die apparently. Fight they did, as about 1000 dead, about 100 of whom lay in the verandah, abundantly testify. The Zulus began about 7 p.m., and retired in Zululand about sunrise, 5 o'clock next morning. Our men fired about 18,000 rounds of ammunition, so there was a lot of wild firing too, but we don't know about the wounded. Thirteen were killed. I wrote a letter for one of the 95 on Saturday at Helpmakaar, to his wife at Pietermaritzburg. He was one of the sick, but he forgot all about it when the enemy appeared. It didn't cure him, however, as his shoulder was so sore he thought he must go back to hospital.

Lieutenant Charles E. Commeline, 5th (Field) Company, Royal Engineers

Gloucester Citizen, 22 March 1879, from a letter from Charles Commeline to his father

Helpmakaar, Natal, Jan. 31, 1879

… In fact, the army was saved from utter annihilation by the brilliant defence of the little mission house at Rorke's Drift, at which place Chard of our Company was the senior officer. He had with him Bromhead of the 24th Regiment, and his company of a hundred men and Dr. Russell, when at four o'clock in the afternoon they saw a great force of Zulus coming down on them. These had been detached from the main army as soon as it was seen that our poor fellows were done for; doubtless with the intention of destroying the detachment at the Drift and the pontoons for crossing the river, and thus cutting off the General's retreat. The fighting was most desperate, lasting till four o'clock the next morning, and the Zulus probably lost over 1,000 men, 351 bodies being counted in the enclosure of the house. They were twice repelled at the point of the bayonet, their advance being blocked by the dead bodies of their killed. Our fellows only lost 13, most of whom were sick men lying in a hospital close by, which the Zulus fired just as it was growing dark, thus probably saving the remainder by the sacrifice of these few, as the light from the fire enabled our fellows to use their rifles on the masses of the enemy with terrible effect. One gallant old soldier – (of the 24th probably) – saved them again. He observed a Zulu on the opposite hill light a torch, and rush down to apply it to the thatch of the mission house at a retired corner. The soldier leant out of the window and fired at the man at five yards distance and missed him, but loaded again and shot him through the head, just as the thatch had given signs of taking fire. The Zulu was found afterwards dead, with his torch gone out, but raised to the thatch.

Probably no more desperate and brilliant defence of a post has ever been chronicled among the gallant deeds of British soldiers than the defence of Rorke's Drift. Its consequences must also be most important, as the General was enabled to bring his little force back over the river; and such a disastrous repulse must in some way have restored our prestige in the eyes of the Zulus …

Captain Walter P. Jones, 5th (Field) Company, Royal Engineers

Extracts from two letters by Walter Jones to his friend, Mr Jackson [courtesy of the Royal Engineers Museum, Chatham]

Fort Helpmakaar, 16 March 1879

… Owing to the deaths at Isandhlwana Broomhead the second in command at Rorke's Drift got his company by promotion & he gets a brevet, this makes my Chard, who was in command, quite sure of a brevet, when he gets his company a year hence. Chard is in great luck, he left us at Durban, came up here quickly & comfortably, without all the bother of men sick, wagons sticking &c. He leaves Isandhlwana camp an hour before the disaster, being ordered to look after the ponts over the Tugela at Rorke's Drift. He there becomes a hero, gets a fever & goes away on sick leave to a comfortable & hospitable house near Ladysmith 60 miles off & vegetates there ever since. Not one iota of the work or drudgery does he get …

St Pauls, Zululand, 2nd August 1879.

… Chard got his orders to leave the 5 Compy for good & departed yesterday. He is most amiable fellow & a loss to the mess, but as a company officer he is hopelessly slow & slack. I shall get on much better without him & with Porter as my senior sub. – Chard makes me angry, with such a start as he got, he stuck to the company doing nothing. In his place I should have gone up & asked Lord C. for an appointment, he must have got it &

if not, he could have gone home soon after Rorke's Drift, at the height of his popularity & done splendidly at home. – I advised him, but he placidly smokes his pipe & does nothing. Few men get such opportunities …

Major Arthur F. Pickard, VC, CB, Private Secretary to Queen Victoria

A letter to Sir Evelyn Wood, dated Balmoral Castle, 14 October 1879: [Pietermaritzburg Archives Repository, Pietermaritzburg, South Africa]

… Chard has been here and left this morning. He explained the defence of Rorke's Drift to the Queen, Prince Leopold, the Grand Duke of Hesse, and Princess Beatrice in the Queen's private room, and did it all very clearly and modestly. After dinner he did likewise to us in the billiard room on the table, where store and hospital were books and boxes, and mealie bags and biscuit tins were billiard balls.

I gather from all I hear that Dalton was quite as much (if not more) of the presiding genius there, as himself. He conceived the idea of joining the two buildings with mealie bags, etc., before Chard's arrival on the scene; tho' perhaps Chard would have done so, had he not found it in operation. The inner line, which was their great safeguard, was Chard's own idea, I fancy, and when they were deserted by so many of the defenders (natives, etc.) it was soon found that the first line of defence was too extended.

Bromhead (commanding B Company, 2/24th Regiment) had of course great influence over his own men, and kept them in their places or moved them about, controlled their fire with great judgement. Only one and a half boxes of ammunition was left when morning came, besides what they had in their pouches. Chard made no complaint, but it seemed odd to me that he was not consulted as to the distribution of the Victoria Crosses. He is not a genius and not quick, but a quiet, plodding, dogged sort of fellow who will hold his own in most of the situations in which, as an Engineer officer, his lot may be cast …

Brevet-Major Henry Spalding, 104th Foot, Deputy Assistant Adjutant Quartermaster General

Extract from an official despatch by Major Spalding, 1 March 1879 [National Archives, London, WO32/7710:]

A.M.S.

1. At 2 p.m. on the 22nd Inst., I left Rorkes Drift for Helpmakaar, leaving a second horse at Vermaaks. My intention was to bring up Captain Rainforth's Company 1/24th to protect the ponts. Lieut. Chard R.E. on returning from the camp Isandhlana had observed Zulus on the neighbouring heights. I thought they might make a dash for the ponts during the night.

2. Between Vermaaks & Helpmakaar where I arrived at 3.45 p.m. – I met 2 Companies 1/24th under Major Upcher – on returning from Helpmakaar I met Major Upcher who informed me of the disaster at Isandhlana.

3. We advanced as far as Vermaaks with the troops. I then pushed on to the foot of the Burg accompanied by Mr. Dickson, of the Buffalo border Guard. The road was covered with fugitives, chiefly Basutos and people in civilian clothes, but there were one or two mounted infantry. Several of these I ordered to accompany me but all except 2 slipped away when my back was turned.

My object was to ascertain whether the post at Rorkes Drift still held out. In this case I should have sent word to Major Upcher to advance to endeavour to push myself into it.

4. But every single white fugitive asserted that the mission house was captured; and at about 3 miles from the same, I came across a body of Zulus in extended order across the road. They were 50 yards off, a deep ravine donga was behind them capable of concealing a large force. They threw out flankers as if to surround the party. Mr Dickson agreed with me that they were Zulu, an opinion soon borne out by the 'horns' which they threw out. So we trotted back to the troops some two miles in rear.

5. On reaching the summit of a hill from which the mission house is visible, it was observed to be in flames. This confirmed the statement of the fugitives that the post had been captured. This being the case it was determined to save, if possible, Helpmakaar & its depot of stores.

6. It was growing dusk: the oxen had already had a long trek; the hill had to be re-ascended & the heights were said to be lined with Zulus. I examined them with my glass but could not observe the enemy. There may have been a few detached parties, however, as these were observed by competent witnesses. No attack was made by them: and the column reached Helpmakaar by 9 p.m., when wagon laager was formed around the Commissariat Stores. Colonel Hassard, R.E., met us half-way up the Berg & took over command from me.

7. The following morning a dense fog prevailed. About 9 a.m. a note arrived from Lieut. Chard, R.E., stating that Rorkes Drift still held out & begging for assistance. It was considered imprudent to risk the safety of Helpmakaar by denuding it of its garrison, and probable that Rorkes Drift had already been relieved by the column under the General. It was determined to push down to the Drift some mounted men to gather intelligence. I was in command.

A short distance from Helpmakaar Mr. Fynn was met, who communicated the fact that the General's column had relieved Rorkes Drift. At the top of the Berg I met Lieut.-Colonel Russell, who confirmed the news. At about noon I reached Rorkes Drift and reported myself to the General.

H. S. SPALDING,
Major, D.A.A.G.

The Mail, London, 24 March 1879

Sir, – In *The Times* of to-day a letter appears from your Correspondent at Rorke's Drift, describing the defence by Lieutenants Chard and Bromhead, in which the following passage occurs: –

"The post was under the command of Major Spalding … News having arrived that the enemy were advancing on the post and that they would be there in less than an hour, Major Spalding handed over the command to Lieutenant Chard, R.E., and rode to Helpmakaar to bring up the two companies of infantry from that place."

From this it would be inferred that Major Spalding was in command at Rorke's Drift only, and that he surrendered his command to a subordinate on news arriving of an impending attack. Will you allow me to state that Major Spalding writes by the last mail, – "I left for another part of my command just an hour before intelligence of our disaster arrived." This is consistent with Lieutenant Chard's report, which clearly implies that Major Spalding had left before the news of the defeat reached Rorke's Drift.

I am, Sir, your obedient servant,

J.H.S.

March 22.

APPENDIX I

'There's a lot of people who say they were at Rorke's Drift … But all our names are here': Rolls of Defenders

Natal Mercury, 7 April 1879. A slightly abridged version of this – minus the regimental numbers – was published in several British newspapers, including the *Leeds Mercury*, 11 June 1879. According to the accompanying report, the roll had been brought home by one of the defenders, Private John Waters, 1/24th.

Roll of Officers, Non.-Com. Officers and Men present at the Defence of Rorke's Drift, January 22nd, 1879.

1. Sergt. Maybin, General's Staff.		
2. Bomb. Cantwell, R.A.		
3. Bomb. Lewis, R.A.		
4. Gunner Evans, R.A.		
5. Gunner Howard, R.A.		
6. Lieut. J.R.M. Chard, R.E. (in command)		
7. Private Robson, R.E.		
8. Sergeant Milne, 3rd Buffs		
9. 56 Sergeant Edward Wilson,	1-24th Regt.	
10. 625 Private Edward Nicholls,	"	(killed)
11. 1083 Private Jenkins,	"	

12. 1861 Private W. Horrigan	"		(killed)
13. 568 Private Desmond	"		
14. 372 Private Paton	"		
15. 104 Private Turner	"		
16. 449 Private Waters	"		(wounded)
17. 841 Private Jenkins	"		(killed)
18. 129 Private R. Bekett	"		(wounded) since died
19. 1542 Private R. Roy	"		
20. Lieut. Bromhead, Commanding	B Company	2-24th Regt.	
21. 2459 Colour-Sergt. Frank Bourne	"	"	
22. 81 Sergeant Hy. Gallaghar	"	"	
23. 1387 Sergeant George Smith	"	"	
24. 735 Joseph Windridge	"	"	
25. 1328 Lance-Sergt. Thomas Williams	"	"	(wounded), died Jan. 25th
26. 1240 Corporal William Allen	"	"	(wounded)
27. 582 Corporal John French	"	"	
28. 1112 Corporal John Lyons	"	"	
29. 849 Corporal Alfred Saxty	"	"	
30. 2067 Drummer Patrick Hayes	"	"	
31. 2381 Drummer James Keefe	"	"	
32. 913 Private James Ashton	"	"	
33. 918 Private William Bennett	"	"	
34. 1287 Lance-Corporal Wm. Bessell	"	"	
35. 981 Private Chas. Bromwich	"	"	
36. 1524 Private Joseph Bromwich	"	"	
37. 1184 Private Thomas Buckley	"	"	
38. 2350 Private James Bush	"	"	
39. 1181 Private Wm. Camp	"	"	
40. 1241 Private Thos. Chester	"	"	
41. 755 Private Thos. Clayton	"	"	
42. 801 Private Thos. Cole	"	"	(killed)
43. 1396 Private Thos. Collins	"	"	
44. 1323 Private Timothy Connors	"	"	

45. 2310 Private Anthony Connors	"	"	
46. 1467 Private George Deacon	"	"	
47. 1357 Private Michael Deane	"	"	
48. 1634 Private Wm. Dicks	"	"	
49. 971 Private Thos. Driscoll	"	"	
50. 1421 Private James Dunbar	"	"	
51. 922 Private George Edwards	"	"	
52. 969 Private John Fagan	"	"	(killed)
53. 2429 Private Edward Gee	"	"	
54. 798 Private Jas. Hagan	"	"	
55. 1282 Lance-Corporal Wm. Halley	"	"	
56. 1062 Private John Harris	"	"	
57. 1362 Private Fredk. Hitch	"	"	(wounded)
58. 1373 Private Henry Hooke	"	"	
59. 1061 Private John Jobbins	"	"	
60. 593 Private Wm. Jones	"	"	
61. 716 Private Robt. Jones	"	"	(wounded)
62. 970 Private John Jones	"	"	
63. 1179 Private John Jones	"	"	
64. 1428 Private Evan Jordes	"	"	
65. 2437 Private Peter Judge	"	"	
66. 972 Private Patrick Kears	"	"	
67. 1386 Private Michael Riley	"	"	
68. 1528 Private Hy. Lines	"	"	
69. 1176 Private Thos. Lockhart	"	"	
70. 1409 Private David Lloyd	"	"	
71. 1304 Private Joshua Lodge	"	"	
72. 964 Private Jas. Marshall	"	"	
73. 756 Private Hy. Martin	"	"	
74. 1284 Private Chas. Mason	"	"	
75. 1527 Private Michael Michan	"	"	
76. 968 Private Thos. Moffatt	"	"	
77. 525 Private Frederick Morris	"	"	
78. 1342 Private Augustus Morris	"	"	
79. 1371 Private Thos. Morrison	"	"	

80. 662 Private James Murphy	"	"	
81. 1279 Private William Neville	"	"	
82. 1480 Private William Osborne	"	"	
83. 1186 Private Samuel Pitt	"	"	
84. 1286 Private Thos. Robinson	"	"	
85. 1185 Private E. Savage	"	"	
86. 1618 Private Geo. Sherman	"	"	
87. 777 Private Thos. Stephens	"	"	
88. 1812 Private William Fasker	"	"	(wounded)
89. 889 Private Thos. Taylor	"	"	
90. 973 Private Frederick Taylor	"	"	
91. 1280 Private John Thomas	"	"	
92. 1294 Private John Thompson	"	"	
93. 641 Private Patrick Tobin	"	"	
94. 1281 Private Wm. J. Todd	"	"	
95. 1315 Private Robert Tongue	"	"	
96. 1497 Private John Wall	"	"	
97. 977 Private Alfred Whetton	"	"	
98. 1395 Private John Williams	"	"	
99. 1398 Private Joseph Williams	"	"	(killed)
100. 1187 Private William Wilcox	"	"	
101. 1316 Private Caleb Woods	"	"	
102. Drummer Patrick Mecham,	A Company,	2-24th Regt.	
103. 1441 Private John Lyons	"	"	
104. 2404 Private Arthur Pears	"	"	
105. 1731 Private John Manley	"	"	
106. Private Scanlan	"	"	(killed)
107. Drummer Patrick Galgey,	D Company,	2-24th Regt.	
108. Private Chick	"	"	(killed)
109. Private Adams	"	"	(killed)
110. Private Hayden	"	"	(killed)
111. 82 Lance-Sergt. J. Taylor,	E Company,	2-24th Regt.	
112. 934 Private Williams	"	"	
113. 2453 Private Wm. Cooper,	F Company,	2-24th Regt.	
114. Private Cole	"	"	

115. 623 Sergeant Robert Maxfield G Company 2-24th Regt. (killed)
116. 106 Private Connolly " "
117. Private Partridge " "
118. Private Evans, H Company 2-24th Regt.
119. Corporal Graham, 90th Light Infantry
120. Assistant-Commissary Dunne.
121. Acting Commissary Dalton (wounded)
122. Assistant-Commissary Byrne (killed)
123. Lance-Corporal F. Attwood, Army Service Corps
124. Dr. Reynolds, A.M.D.
125. Pearse, (Doctor's servant)
126. Corporal Miller, Army Hospital Corps
127. Private McMahon, Army Hospital Corps
128. Private Luddington, Army Hospital Corps
129. Rev. Geo. Smith, Chaplain, Vicar of Estcourt
130. Trooper R.S. Green, Natal Mounted Police
131. Trooper Hunter, Natal Mounted Police (killed)
132. Trooper Lugg, Natal Mounted Police
133. Lieutenant Adendorff, Natal Native Contingent
134. Corporal W. Doughty "
135. Corporal J.H. Mayer "
136. Corporal C. Scammell " (wounded)
137. Corporal W. Anderson " (killed)
138. Corporal F. Scheiss " (wounded)
139. Corporal J. Wilson "
140. Daniels, ferryman
141. Private (native Umkungu's tribe) Natal Native Contingent (killed)

Roll of defenders compiled by Major Frank Bourne, 7 July 1910 [Royal Welsh Regimental Museum, Brecon]

[Those names in ***bold italics*** were not included on Bourne's first version of the roll. He wrote in the additional names at a later date. He also ticked all of the names that were included on this second amended version, with the exception of five names – Lance Corporal J. Key, 970 Private J. Jones, Private D. Lewis, Private T. Lynch and Private J. Smith. These names were not removed from the roll and it is not clear why each was left unticked.]

2nd Battalion 24th Regiment

Roll of "B" Company who defended "Rorke's Drift" against the Zulu attack on the night of the 22nd–23rd January, 1879.

Lieutenant Bromhead, Gonville (V.C.)	Mentioned in Dispatches. Awarded the Victoria Cross.
2459 Color-Sergt. Bourne, F.	Mentioned in Dispatches. Awarded the Distinguished Conduct Medal.
735 Sergeant Windridge, J.L.	Mentioned in Dispatches.
81 Sergeant Gallagher, H. L.	
1387 Sergeant Smith, G.	
849 Sergeant Saxty, A.	
1328 Lce. Sergt Williams, T.	Mentioned in Dispatches. Died of Wounds, 23rd Jan., 1879.
82 Corporal Taylor, J.	
1240 Corporal Allan, W.W. (V.C.)	Wounded Severely. Awarded the Victoria Cross.
582 Corporal French, J.	
2350 Corporal Bush, J.	
1282 Lce. Corpl. Halley, J.	
1287 Lce. Corpl. Bissell, W.	
2389 Lce. Corpl Key, J.	
1618 Lce. Corpl. Sherman, G.	
2067 Drummer Hayes, P.	

2381 Drummer Keefe, J.	
912 Private Ashton, J.	
1381 Private Barry, T.	
918 Private Bennett, W.	
2427 Private Bly, J.	
1402 Private Buck, W.	
1184 Private Buckley, T.	
Bromatch	
1220 Private Burke, T.	
2420 Private Caine, P.	
1181 Private Camp, W.H.	
1241 Private Chester, T.	
755 Private Clayton, T.	
801 Private Cole, T.	Killed 22nd January, 1879.
1396 Private Collins, T.	
1323 Private Connors, T.	
2310 Private Connors, H.	
470 Private Davies, G.	
1363 Private Davies, W.H.	
1178 Private Daw, T.	
1467 Private Deacon, G.	
1357 Private Deane, W.	
1697 Private Dicks, W.	
971 Private Driscoll, T.	
1421 Private Dunbar, J.	
922 Private Edwards, G.	
969 Private Fagan, J.	Killed 22nd January, 1879.
Harris	
2429 Private Gee, E.	
1362 Private Hitch, F. (V.C.)	Wounded Severely. Awarded the Victoria Cross.
1373 Private Hook, H. (V.C.)	Mentioned in Dispatches. Awarded the Victoria Cross.
1061 Private Jobbins, J.	
1428 Private Jones, E.	

970 Private Jones, J.
1179 Private Jones, J.
716 Private Jones, R. (V.C.) — Mentioned in Dispatches. Awarded the Victoria Cross.
593 Private Jones, W. (V.C.) — Mentioned in Dispatches. Awarded the Victoria Cross.

Lockhart, T
Lines, H.
2437 Private Judge, P
972 Private Kears, P.
1386 Private Kiley, M.
963 Private Lewis, D.
1409 Private Lloyd, D.
1304 Private Lodge, J.
942 Private Lynch, T.
756 Private Martin, H.
1284 Private Mason, C.
1527 Private Minehan, M.
968 Private Moffatt, T.
525 Private Morris, F.
1342 Private Morris, A.
1371 Private Morrison, T.
Private Murphy, T.
1257 Private Norris, R.
Private Neville
1480 Private Osborne, W.
1399 Private Parry, S.
1286 Private Robinson, T.
1065 Private Ruck, J.
914 Private Shergold, J.
Private Stephens T.
1005 Private Smith, J.
1812 Private Tasker, W.
973 Private Taylor, F.
889 Private Taylor, T.

879 Private Tobin, M.	
1281 Private Tood, W.G.	
1315 Private Tongue, R.	
1497 Private Wall, J.	
977 Private Whitton, A.	
1187 Private Wilcox, W.	
1395 Private Williams, J. (V.C.)	Mentioned in Dispatches. Awarded the Victoria Cross.
1374 Private Williams, J.	
1398 Private Williams, J.	Killed 22nd January, 1879.
1060 Private Williams, T.	
1316 Private Woods	

The following Officers and N.C. Officers were attached to above Company.
1st Battalion, 24th Regiment.

Sgt E Wilson	
Private W. Beckett	Killed – H.
Private W. Harrigan	Killed – H.
Private M. Jenkins	Killed – H.
Private W. Nicholas	Killed – H.
Private J. Williams	Killed – H.
Private Roy	Mentioned in Dispatches.
Private Desmond	
Private Paton	
Private Turner	
Private Waters	

2nd Battalion, 24th Regiment.

Sergeant R. Maxfield	Killed – H.
Private R. Adams	Killed – H.
Private J. Chick	Killed – H.
Private G. Hayden	Killed – H.
Private J. Scanlon	Killed – H.

Royal Artillery.	
Bombardier Lewis	H.
Bombardier Cantwell	
Gunner Evans	
Gunner Howard	
Royal Engineers.	
Lieutenant John R.M. Chard (V.C.),	Mentioned in Dispatches. Awarded the Victoria Cross.
Private Robson	
The Buffs.	
Sergeant Milne	
Commissariat Department.	
Asst. Commissary Dunne,	Mentioned in Dispatches.
Acting Commst. Officer Dalton,	Severely Wounded. Mentioned in Dispatches.
Acting Store-keeper Byrne	Killed. Mentioned in Dispatches.
Corporal Attwood.	Awarded the Distinguished Conduct Medal.
Army Hospital Corps.	
Surgeon Reynolds (V.C.),	Mentioned in Dispatches. Awarded the Victoria Cross.
Corporal Miller	
Private McMahon	Mentioned in Dispatches.
Luddington	
Pearse	
90th Light Inf.	
Corpl. Graham	
Natal Mounted Police.	
Trooper Hunter	Killed – H.

Trooper Green	Killed – H.
Natal Native Contingent.	
Corporal Schiess (V.C.)	Severely Wounded. Mentioned in Dispatches. Awarded the Victoria Cross.
Corporal Mayer	H.
Corporal Scammell	
Lieut. Adendorf	
C. Doughty	
Anderson	
Wilson	

Chaplain's Department.	
Revd. C. Smith,	Acting Chaplain.
Civilian	Mr. Daniels.

Note. – Those N.C. Officers and Men marked with an "H" indicate they were patients in Hospital.

By Special Request, and in order to preserve a record of those who took part in the Defence, this Roll was prepared by Major F. Bourne (late Color-Sergeant "B" Company) from the Regimental Pay List for January, 1879, kindly placed at his disposal by the Public Record Office, Chancery Lane, London.
Beckenham, Kent
4th July, 1910.

A Coy.	***Dmr. T. Meecham***
	Pte J. Lyons
	Pte A. Sears
	Pte J. Manley
D Coy	***Dmr Galgey***
E "	***Pte Williams***
F "	***Pte W. Cooper***
	Pte Cole

G "	***Pte Connolly***
	Pte Partridge
H "	***Pte Evans***

Extract from 'The Record of Service of the 1st Battalion 24th Foot' [Royal Welsh Regimental Museum, Brecon]

At the gallant defence of Rorke's Drift under Lieuts Bromhead & Chard the following men of the 1/24th Regiment were present

Sergeant E Wilson
Private P Desmond
Private Nichols
Private D Horrigan
Private D Jenkins
Private Paton
Private Beckitt
Private W Roy
Private W Waters

Hampshire Advertiser, 4 October 1879

Arrival of Major Chard at Portsmouth.

Major Chard, of the Royal Engineers, one of the heroes of Rorke's Drift, arrived at Portsmouth on Thursday, together with the 1st battalion of the 24th Regiment – about 250 of whom belonged to the battalion at the time of the Isandula disaster, the remainder having subsequently been made up by volunteers …

… One small group, standing alone on the jetty, attracted considerable attention, consisting as it did of five men of the first battalion of the regiment, who, on the morning of the Isandula massacre, were told off to escort some prisoners to the rear, and on their return could get no further than Rorke's Drift. There they remained and took part in the now historic defence. The names of these men are Sergeant Wilson, Lance Corporal Roy, Privates Desmond, Payton, and Jenkins …

Truth, 16 October 1879

A propos of the amount of flogging that went on among the regulars in Zululand, it may not be generally known that two of the men that fought at Rorke's Drift were flogged on the morning before …

APPENDIX II

'Farewell to the 2-24th Regiment': The End of the Anglo-Zulu War

Madras Weekly Mail (India), 16 July 1879

Camp Life in Zululand

The following is an extract from a letter from one of the officers of the 24th Regiment, dated Rorke's Drift, 10th April.

"... The rains are nearly over now, and our little fort is more habitable – at one time we were drowned nightly, and it was very rough on the men sleeping in the open, and never a change. None of us have ever slept out of our clothes since the 22nd January, and we are prepared day and night for an attack, which we long for. We are encased in a 'laager' made of stone walls eight feet high, and outside further protected by all sorts of obstacles, wire entanglements, pit-falls, broken glass, small mines, pointed stakes, and assegai heads. The other night we had a false alarm; in two minutes every one was up and ready, and there was one man to every 18 inches of wall. I have built myself a little cubby house out of old boxes, and roofed it with two zinc sheets. I like the greater privacy of the apartment."

Times of Natal (South Africa), 23 April 1879

Rorke's Drift.

Having just returned from a short visit to the celebrated but out-of-the-way corner of the world, Rorke's Drift, I venture to think a letter from me may interest some of your numerous readers. I found the 2nd bat. 24th regt.

thoroughly "at home" there, after their sojourn of thirteen weeks. The officers and men look fit and ready for any amount of hard work, and as they turn out for fatigues in their red nightcaps and blue "jumpers" they give a busy and picturesque look to the laager and its surroundings. They are daily waiting for and expecting an order to move to Dundee, to join General Newdigate's column. Should they be kept at Rorke's Drift they tell me their hearts would break, and certainly most will agree with me that there is no regiment in the country more deserving of being sent to the front. In fact, after all they have done for the General Commanding, I don't see how he can keep them back. For many weeks past, assisted by the men of Major Bengough's Native Contingent, they have been engaged on the new fort, "Melville," so called after the late lieutenant and adjutant of the 1-24th regiment. It is now completed, and is an oblong fort, flanked with towers, a broad ditch surrounding the walls, built partly of masonry and partly of dry wall. An obstacle of six rows of aloes round and outside the ditch completes a position which, manned by 300 Europeans, could not be taken by thousands of Zulus.

Lieut. Porter, R.E., a most affable young officer, has had the entire responsibility of construction, and a more difficult ground to work could not have been chosen. It is composed of huge boulders, heaped together in wild confusion, evidently the result of ice action in the glacial age, reminding one forcibly of the morraines to be found at the foot of modern glaciers, upon which the hardest steel instruments fail to have any effect. The fort commands the ponts and drift, and in the distance, eight miles away, the Isandhlwana height shows in bold relief, a constant reminder of the late heart-sickening disaster.

Amongst my rambles I climbed to the top of the Ascarberg; 680 feet above Rorke's Drift, and had an opportunity of examining the country over which the Zulus passed from Isandhlwana to Rorke's Drift. The wagons are still scattered about the former place as they were left on the 22nd January last. I took with me the description given by that first class imposter and romancer Mr. de Witt to the home papers. He states that the distance between the two places is three miles, and that he could see the place where the camp was pitched, and that he saw the battle and heard the firing from the rifles. The facts are that from the highest point of the Ascarberg to Isandhlwana is in a bee line not less than seven miles, that no part of the camping ground is visible, and that he could not have seen the firing, all for the reason that the hill and ridge hide the camp and battle field. As for his having heard musketry fire at that distance; well, all I can say is, it speaks well for the length of his ears. Verb. sap. I fancy he will get a very hearty reception should he ever return to the colony.

Another place that I visited and found of great interest was the cemetery. It is situated at the back of the old laager, and is surrounded by a wall and ditch. The graves, 25 in number, are neatly and regularly laid out side by side, and rose trees and blue gums just planted will, in due time, bloom over and shade the resting-place of these heroes. In the centre is an obelisk, ten feet high, of white granite, standing on a square pedestal, and the names of the men of the 24th regiment who are there buried and the regimental badge are engraved on the sides.

At night everyone sleeps inside the fort, and you may be sure that I felt very secure, as no less than 28 sentries watch from the walls, and besides these, four non-commissioned officers and one officer keep watch throughout the night, being relieved every two hours. The officer in command also, Colonel Degacher, C.B., is ever nervously anxious for the safety of his little garrison, and frequently goes round during the night.

I noticed that all the soldiers of the 24th regiment had pieces of bullock hide neatly fastened round the barrels of their rifles to prevent their hands being burnt by rapid firing. It is laced round the wood-work, and has a hole cut out for the back-sight. I give this as a useful hint for their *confrères*. It is not unsightly, and does not interfere with the firer's aim.

Natal Mercury, 13 May 1879

A Visit to Rorke's Drift

A private correspondent writes; – "I was at Rorke's Drift yesterday on duty; I started early, before daylight, and got there about half-past nine. It is very similar to the picture that appeared in the Illustrated News. The hill at the back is not so large, and the trees are cut down now. A high loopholed wall has been built all round it; the hospital has disappeared, a portion of the walls being built into the fort. I spent an hour looking over the place in company with a very intelligent non-commissioned officer – one of the defenders. He showed me the place where he shot the Zulu that was trying to light the thatch with a bundle of burning grass on the end of an assegai. The walls of the building are about 12ft high, which accounts for the difficulty they had in setting it on fire. The front of the building has a verandah, and it was in front of this where the celebrated barricade of mealie bags was, and the Zulus never got properly over it. It was very interesting walking round and seeing things. There is a neat graveyard, with a monument of cut free stone built on the spot where the men that fell are buried. It all looks very peaceful and quiet now, and it is hard to realise what once took place. A new fort has been built close to the drift. It is a very fine piece of work, and will be a permanency. Fort Melville it is called. It commands a fine view of the Isandhlwana Hill. I felt strongly tempted to ride and see the latter place. It looks about eight miles, but is rough country. By the road it is 12 miles.

Western Morning News, 23 July 1879

A correspondent of the *Cape Argus* throws a new light on the Rorke's Drift episode, which, while it increases the credit due to the defenders of that post, appears to tell against the present system of enlistment. Speaking of his passing from Dundee to Helpmakaar, he says; –

"At Helpmakaar another road diverges to the historical ford near which B company of her Majesty's 2-24th Regiment made so stubborn a defence after the fatal day of Isandhlwana. Between Dundee and Helpmakaar, while riding down on Saturday last, I chanced to fall in with B company, then on its way from Rorke's Drift to Landman's, the gallant Bromhead being in command. The meeting was disappointing. If the rest of the battalion is in a plight like this distinguished company, Lord Chelmsford has at least some excuse for retaining it in Natal. Surgeon-Major Reynolds, who loves his regiment far too well to deprive it willingly of any chance of active service, is said to have reported the men unfit to march; and, again, supposing B company to be a fair criterion by which to judge of the remainder, I venture to think the surgeon-major (I wish he might be written down V.C.) could come to another conclusion. On the day preceding that upon which I fell in with B company it had marched from Rorke's Drift to Helpmakaar, not more than fourteen miles, and was then proceeding to Helpmakaar in the direction of Dundee. The afternoon was as bright and cool as an autumn day at home; the roads were as level as a bowling-green, and in splendid condition for marching; and yet B company straggled over at the very least six miles of road. Less than half the company were in the ranks, and they were completely "pumped," and terribly footsore. For six miles in the rear of the Major straggled on singly, or by two and threes, the remainder of the men. A dozen or so had given in, and were lying stretched out by the roadside. All were very pathetic in their inquiries as to the distance of the next halting place, and all seemed very much ashamed of their deplorable condition. Effective as B company proved behind improvised breastworks, it is indisputably unfitted, temporarily, at all events, for the work of chasing the agile Zulu wherever he may lead."

Natal Colonist (South Africa), 15 January 1880

Farewell to the 2-24th Regiment.

The invitation of the Mayor and Council to the burgesses to join them in bidding the Heroes of Rorke's Drift 'Farewell' was heartily – we may say eagerly – responded to, and gay bunting floating from many a front in West Street, as well as from the Post Office flag-staff, (which was indeed 'dressed' from the ground to the truck), and from all the flag-staffs in town, showed that preparations were not slack to do honor to the occasion. The streets, too, were lively with groups in holiday attire, who, as noon drew near turned their steps towards Market Square.

At five minutes to twelve the train punctually arrived at the West End Station, every truck filled with men belonging to the gallant 2-24th, who as they came in sight were greeted with cheers by the spectators, who had assembled to welcome them on arrival. The train having halted, the men quickly leaped out of the trucks and formed up outside the station, and the march to the Market Square began, headed by the drum and the fife band, immediately behind them came Company B, the Rorke's Drift Heroes, the other companies following.

The march was continued down West Street, the footpaths lined with spectators, and every door and window or other 'coign of vantage,' occupied. Waving of hats and handkerchiefs, and frequent cheers greeted them as they advanced, and not a few accompanied them on foot and on horseback to the rendezvous on the Market Square. On reaching that spot, there was found to be already quite a large concourse of people, and by the side of the large marquee, gaily decorated with flags, a large number of benches were placed for the accommodation of ladies, of whom there was present a goodly gathering, 'raining bright influence.' A platform had been erected in front of the marquee, and as the 24th men filed in upon the parade ground in front of it, preceded by the drum and fife band and the staff of the colors surmounted by the Royal Crown and Lion, with the ragged case, but bare of the colors, lost at Isandhlwana – cheer after cheer greeted them.

Having taken up their position in front, the Mayor and the members of the Town Council, the Town Clerk, and a few leading burgesses ascended the platform, and Lieutenant Colonel Dunbar dismounting from his splendid charger, gave the order to advance close to the platform, that the men might the better hear the address about to be read.

The scene was a very lively and interesting one. In the space in front of the platform were mustered 341, all told, of the 2nd Battalion of the 24th Regiment, under the command of Brevet Lieutenant-Colonel and Major W. M. Dunbar, and in this number were included fifty-three of the gallant defenders of Rorke's Drift, chief amongst whom was Major Gonville Bromhead, wearing, nearly hidden by his sash, the Victoria Cross, the reward of his gallantry at Rorke's Drift.

The other officers present were Lieutenants Logan, Smyly, Birch and Hare, Lieut. and Adjutant C.V. Trower and Paymaster J. Mahony. Twenty-two sergeants, eighteen corporals, sixteen drummers, and 336 privates, completed the strength of the detachment of the 2-24th on the ground …

… The Rorke's Drift heroes were then called forward, and each presented with an envelope containing a handsomely printed copy of the Address. The following is the list, and as each V.C. man came forward he was deservedly greeted with three cheers, Major Bromhead in particular, being the object of the greatest interest and being cheered lustily again and again throughout the day.

2ND BATTALION 24TH REGIMENT.

Nominal roll of officers, non-commissioned officers, and men of the above battalion who took part in the defence of Rorke's Drift Post on the 22nd January, 1879, and who are now serving with the battalion.

Brevet-Major Gonville Bromhead, V.C., Color-Sergeant Bourne, Sergeants Henry Gallagher, George Smith, James Taylor, Alfred Saxty, Drummers Patrick Hayes, James Keefe, Patrick Galgey, Patrick Meehan, Privates William Bessell, James Bromwich, Thomas Buckley, James Bush, William Camp, Thomas Chester, Thomas Collins, Robert Cole, Timothy Connors, Anthony Connors, William Cooper, Michael Deane, Williams Dicks, Thomas Driscoll, James Dunbar, Geo. Edwards, Frederick Evans, Edward Gee, Jas. Hogan, William Halley, John Harris, John Jobbins, Robert Jones V.C., John Jones, John Jones, Evan Jones, Peter Judge, Michael Kiley, Henry Lines, Thomas Lockhart, David Lloyd, Joshua Lodge, James Marshall, Henry Martin, Charles Mason, Michael Minihan, Thomas Moffat, Frederick Morris, Augustus Morris, Thomas Morrison, Jas. Murphy, William Neville, William Osborne, Samuel Pitt, Thos. Robinson, George Sherman, Thomas Stephens, William Tasker, Thomas Taylor, John Thomas, John Thompson, Patrick Tobin, William J. Todd, Robert Tongue, John Wall, Alfred Whetton, John Williams, V.C., William Wilcox, Caleb Woods, John Momley, George Partridge, Arthur Sears, and Jos. Windridge.

(Signed) W. M. Dunbar,
Brevet-Lieut.-Colonel and Major,
Commanding 2-24th Regt.

In addition to those present, there were a number who had already left the colony, and to these, enumerated below, Major Bromhead, V.C., undertook to convey the copies of the Address which had been prepared for them.

2nd Battalion 24th Regiment.

Nominal roll of men of the above battalion who took part in the defence of Rorke's Drift, but who have since proceeded to England, &c., to be addressed to 25, Bridge Depot, Brecon, South Wales.

Pinetown, Natal,
January, 1880.

Corporals William Allen, V.C., and John Lyons, invalided to England; Private James Ashton, on colonial leave, Pietermaritzburg; Private Charles Bromwich, transferred to 91st Highlanders; Private Frederick Hitch, V.C., invalided to England; Private John French, Capetown; Private Henry Hooke, V.C., Gibraltar; Privates William Jones, V.C., Patrick Kears, Edward Savage, John Lyons, John Canolly, invalided to England.

Notes

1 Official casualty returns from War Office, compiled by J.S. Rothwell, *Narrative of Field Operations Connected with the Zulu War of 1879*, London, 1881 (reprinted 1907 and 1989).

2 Private family letter reproduced in I. Castle and I. Knight, *Fearful Hard Times: The Siege and Relief of Eshowe*, London, 1994.

3 John Maxwell, *Reminiscences of the Zulu War*, Cape Town, 1979.

4 'The Adventures in Zululand of a Leek Man', *Leek Times*, 26 October 1879.

5 Maxwell, *Reminiscences of the Zulu War.*

6 Handwritten account of the defence of Rorke's Drift by Capt. & Bvt. Major J.R.M. Chard, V.C., R.E., dated 21 February 1880. Royal Archives, Windsor. See Vol. 1, 11i, p. 82.

7 Hook's account of Rorke's Drift, edited and transcribed by Mr Walter Wood, *Royal Magazine*, February 1905. See Vol. 1, 31h, p. 201.

8 H.C. Lugg, *A Natal Family Looks Back*, South Africa, 1970.

9 Chard's handwritten account of the Defence of Rorke's Drift, 21 February 1880. See Vol. 1, 11i, p. 81.

10 'Statement made by natives regarding the action of the 22nd January at the Sandhlwana Hill', compiled by W. Drummond. National Archives, London, WO32/7711. 'Umtoyolo' was described as 'A Zulu well known to Mr. Longcast, Interpreter to the Lt. General'.

11 Lt. A. Milne, 'Report of Proceedings of 21st, 22nd, 23rd & 24th Jany. 1879'. National Archives, London, ADM1/6486.

12 'Some days afterwards, 50 large shields covered with blood were found by the river side, marking the spot to which they had carried their dead, & cast them into the river': 'The Battle of Isandhlwana and the Defence

of Rorke's Drift 1879, by Capt. W.P. Symons 2-24th Regiment'. Royal Welsh Regimental Museum, Brecon.

13 *Free Press of Monmouthshire*, 18 April 1913. See Vol 1, 21a, p. 142.

14 Maxwell, *Reminiscences of the Zulu War*.

15 Horace Smith-Dorrien, *Memories of Forty Eight Years' Service*, London, 1925.

16 *Western Morning News*, 25 July 1879. See extract 57b.

17 An account by Frank Bourne, *Sunday Express*, 22 January 1938. See Vol. 1, 6g, p. 45 (Private James Ashton's real name was Anthony McHale).

18 A. Greaves and B. Best (eds), *The Curling Letters of the Zulu War: There Was Awful Slaughter*, Barnsley, 2001.

19 Bernhard Kraft, letter to Missionary Heinrich Schuetze, 3 March 1879, Kraft family papers. courtesy of Ron Lock.

20 Smith-Dorrien, *Memories of Forty Eight Years' Service*.

21 *The Sketch*, 25 July 1906.

22 Henry H. Parr, *A Sketch of the Kafir and Zulu Wars*, London, 1880.

23 Col. G. Hamilton-Browne, *A Lost Legionary in South Africa*, London, 1879.

24 '… the Zulu dead who were buried in two long shallow trenches', account by Mr Barker, A.S.C., *Cape and Natal News*, 24 May 1879.

25 From Clarke's own reminiscences entitled, 'My Career in South Africa', Killie Campbell Africana Library, KwaZulu-Natal, South Africa.

26 Entry for 28 and 29 January 1879, Orders Book No. 1, Rorke's Drift. Royal Welsh Regimental Museum, Brecon, Acc. No. 0248.

27 K. Burge and G. Burge, *War, Fred and Jack: The Zulu War Diaries of Fred Symons*, n.p., 2017.

28 'Bishop Colenso and the Zulus', *Colonies and India*, 5 May 1882.

29 Frances E. Colenso, *History of the Zulu War and its Origin*, London, 1880.

30 *The Sketch*, 25 July 1906.

31 H.P. Holt, *The Mounted Police of Natal*, London, 1913.

32 Hamilton Browne, *A Lost Legionary in South Africa*.

33 Ibid.

34 D. Child (ed.), *The Zulu War Journal of Colonel Henry Harford, C.B.*, Pietermaritzburg, 1978.

35 *The Graphic*, 29 March 1879.

36 Greaves and Best (eds), *Curling Letters of the Zulu War*.

37 *Clonmel Chronicle*, 8 March 1879.

38 G. Reynolds, *A Civil Surgeon Serving with the British Army in the Anglo-Zulu War*, Australia, 2002.

39 'An Interesting Letter from an Ashby Volunteer', *Burton Chronicle*, 1 May 1879.

40 Lugg, *A Natal Family Looks Back*.

Bibliography

Official Records

South Africa

Brenthurst Library, Johannesburg

Killie Campbell Africana Library, Campbell Collections, University of KwaZulu-Natal, Durban

Local History Museum, Durban

Natal Museum, Pietermaritzburg

National Archives Repository, Pretoria

Pietermaritzburg Archives Repository, Pietermaritzburg

Western Cape Provincial Archives and Records Service, Cape Town

United Kingdom

NATIONAL ARCHIVES, LONDON

ADM1/6486: Admiralty Correspondence and Papers. In-letters and papers 1870–1879: Lieutenant Milne, RN to Commodore Sullivan, RN

WO32 Series: War Office Correspondence: Reports and Diary of Operations from South Africa, 1877–78–79

WO97 Series: Soldiers' Service and Discharge Papers, 1855–1913

WO98/4: The Register of the Victoria Cross, 1864–1900

WO103/13: Queen's Submission Book for the Distinguished Conduct Medal

WO138/3: Confidential Report on the Services of Surgeon Lt. Colonel J.H. Reynolds, V.C., Army Medical Staff

ROYAL ARCHIVES, WINDSOR CASTLE, BERKSHIRE: BY KIND PERMISSION OF HER MAJESTY QUEEN ELIZABETH II

Handwritten account of the defence of Rorke's Drift by Capt. & Bvt. Major J.R.M. Chard, V.C., R.E., dated 21 February 1880

Newspapers and Periodicals

Australia

Rockhampton Evening News; *Sydney Daily Telegraph*

India

Bangalore Spectator; *Englishman's Overland Mail*; *Madras Weekly Mail*

Ireland

Clonmel Chronicle; *Irish Times*; *Roscommon and Leitrim Gazette*

Singapore

Mid-day Herald

South Africa

Cape Argus; *Cape Times*; *Natal Colonist*; *Natal Mercury*; *Natal Witness*; *Times of Natal*

Switzerland

Le Bien Republic

United Kingdom

Army and Navy Gazette; *Beeston Gazette and Echo*; *Birkenhead and Cheshire Advertiser*; *Brecon County Times*; *Bristol Mercury and Daily Post*; *Bristol Times*; *Cape and Natal News*, *Cardiff Evening Express*; *Carmarthen Journal*, *Croydon Chronicle*; *Daily Mail*; *Daily Telegraph and Courier*; *Derbyshire Times*; *Dundee Courier*; *Dundee Weekly News*; *The Era*; *Free Press of Monmouthshire*; *Gloucester Citizen*; *The Graphic*; *Hampshire Advertiser*; *Haslingden Gazette*; *Herefordshire Times*; *Leek Times*, *Lincoln, Rutland and Stamford Mercury*; *London Evening Standard*; *Manchester Evening Chronicle*; *Manchester Evening News*; *Manchester Weekly Post*; *Merthyr Express*; *Montgomery*

County Times and Shropshire and Mid-Wales Advertiser; *Nairnshire Telegraph*; *Somerset County Gazette*; *Nottingham Daily Express*; *Oldham Weekly Chronicle*; *Pontypool Free Press*; *Radnor Express*; *The Sketch*; *South Wales Argus*; *South Wales Daily News*; *South Wales Daily Telegram*; *Surrey Advertiser and County Times*; *Truth*; *Western Daily Mercury*; *Western Mail*; *Western Morning News*; *Western Times*; *Woolwich Gazette and Kentish Advertiser*

Contemporary Journals, Magazines and Miscellaneous Publications

General

Chums; *The Farmer*; *The Listener*; *Macmillan's Magazine*; *The Mission Field: A Monthly Record of the Proceedings of the Society for the Propagation of the Gospel, 1871–1881*; *The Month: Catholic Review*; *Punch*; *Royal Magazine*; *Strand Magazine*; *V.C. Magazine*; *Windsor Magazine*

Medical

The Lancet; *Medical Press and Circular*; *British Medical Journal*

Military

Army Medical Department Annual Reports; *Army Medical Services Magazine*; *Journal of the Army Medical Corps*; *Army Service Corps Journal*; *Royal Engineers Journal*; *South Wales Borderers Regimental Journal*

Published Sources

Ashwood, R., *For Queen and Country: The Zulu War Diary of Lt. Wilfred Heaton 24th Regiment of Foot*, Darlington, 2005.

Awdry, E. (ed.), *The Gospel Missionary for 1891*, London, 1891.

Baynham-Jones, A.R., and Stevenson, L., *Rorke's Drift By Those Who Were There*, Brighton, 2003

Bennett, I.H.W., *Eyewitness in Zululand*, London, 1989.

Blair Brown, D., *Surgical Experiences in the Zulu and Transvaal Wars*, London, 1882.

Burge, K., and Burge, G., *War, Fred and Jack: The Zulu War Diaries of Fred Symons*, n.p., 2017.

Castle, I., and Knight, I., *Fearful Hard Times: The Siege and Relief of Eshowe*, London, 1994.

Child, D. (ed.), *The Zulu War Journal of Col. H. Harford*, Pietermaritzburg, 1978.

Colenso, F.E., *History of the Zulu War and its Origin*, London, 1880.

Emery, F., *The Red Soldier*, London, 1977.

Gordon-Roe, E., *The Bronze Cross*, London, 1945.

Greaves, A., and Best, B. (eds), *The Curling Letters of the Zulu War: There Was Awful Slaughter*, Barnsley, 2001

Hallam Parr, Sir H., *A Sketch of the Kafir and Zulu Wars*, London, 1880.

——, *Recollections and Correspondence*, London, 1917.

Hamilton Browne, G., *A Lost Legionary in South Africa*, London, 1879.

Holme, N., *The Silver Wreath: Being the 24th Regiment at Isandlwana and Rorke's Drift, 1879*, London, 1979.

——, *The Noble 24th*, London, 1999.

Holt, H.P., *The Mounted Police of Natal*, London, 1913.

Johnson, B.C., *Rorke's Drift and the British Museum: The Life of Henry Hook V.C.*, London, 1986.

Knight, I. (ed.), *There Will Be an Awful Row at Home About This*, Shoreham by Sea, 1987.

——, *By the Orders of the Great White Queen*, London, 1992.

——, *Zulu: The Battles of Isandlwana and Rorke's Drift*, London, 1992.

——, *Nothing Remains But to Fight*, London, 1993.

——, *The Anatomy of the Zulu Army*, London, 1995.

——, *Rorke's Drift 1879*, London, 1996.

——, *Zulu Rising*, London, 2010.

Laband, J., *Fight Us in the Open*, Pietermaritzburg, 1991.

——, *Kingdom in Crisis*, Pietermaritzburg, 1992.

Laband, J., and Matthews, J., *Isandlwana*, Pietermaritzburg, 1991.

Lane, R. *The Quiet Sergeant, Henry Edward Gallagher: A Rorke's Drift Man*, London, 2003.

Lloyd, W.G., *John Williams, V.C.*, Cwmbran, 1993.

Lock, R., and Quantrill, P. (compliers), *The Red Book: Natal Press Reports, Anglo Zulu War 1879*, Pinetown, 2000.

—— (compilers), *The 1879 Zulu War through the Eyes of the* Illustrated London News, Durban, 2003.

Lugg, H.C., *A Natal Family Looks Back*, Durban, 1970.

Lummis, W.C., *Padre George Smith of Rorke's Drift*, Norwich, 1978.

Maxwell, J., *Reminiscences of the Zulu War*, Cape Town, 1979.

Mitford, B., *Through the Zulu Country: Its Battlefields and Its People*, London, 1883.

Norris-Newman, C.L., *In Zululand with the British throughout the War of 1879*, London, 1880 (reprinted 1988).

Parry, D.H., *The V.C.: Its Heroes and Their Valour*, London, 1913.

Paton, G., Glennie, F., and Symons, W.P., *Historical Records of the 24th Regiment*, London, 1892.

Preston, A. (ed.), *The South African Journal of Sir Garnet Wolseley, 1879–80*, London, 1973.

Reynolds, G., *A Civil Surgeon Serving with the British Army in the Anglo-Zulu War*, Australia, 2002.

Smith-Dorrien, H., *Memories of Forty Eight Years' Service*, London, 1925.

Stevenson, L., 'The Noble Sapper on the Box – Charles Robson R.E.', *Royal Engineers Journal*, August 1995.

——, *The Rorke's Drift Doctor, James Henry Reynolds, V.C., and the Defence of Rorke's Drift*, Brighton, 2001.

Thornton, N., *Rorke's Drift: A New Perspective*, London, 2016.

Vijn, C., *Cetshwayo's Dutchman, Being the Private Journal of a White Trader in Zululand during the British Invasion*, London, 1880.

War Office, Rothwell, J.S. (compiler), *Narrative of Field Operations Connected with the Zulu War of 1879*, London, 1881 (reprinted 1907 and 1989).

Wheatley, K., *Legacy: Heroes of Rorke's Drift*, Eccles, 2005–10.

Whitton, F.E., *Rorke's Drift*, unknown, 1979 (reprinted from *Blackwood's Magazine*).

Index

Entries in **bold** signify the main entry/account for an individual.